Environmental Movements, State and Civil Society

Environmental Movements, State and Civil Society

ISWAR CHANDRA NAIK

RAWAT PUBLICATIONS
Jaipur • New Delhi • Bangalore • Guwahati • Kolkata

ISBN 978-81-316-0767-1

Published by
Prem Rawat for **Rawat Publications**
Satyam Apts, Sector 3, Jawahar Nagar, Jaipur 302 004 (India)
Phone: 0141 265 1748 / 7006 Fax: 0141 265 1748
E-mail: info@rawatbooks.com
Website: www.rawatbooks.com

New Delhi Office
4858/24, Ansari Road, Daryaganj, New Delhi 110 002
Phone: 011 2326 3290

Also at *Bangalore, Guwahati* and *Kolkata*

Typeset by Rawat Computers, Jaipur
Printed at Nice Printing Press, New Delhi

Dedicated to
my loving son
Aarush

Contents

Foreword 9

Acknowledgements 13

Abbreviations 17

1 Introduction 21

2 Environmental Movements at a Glance: Theoretical Approaches 43

3 Background of Environmental Movements in Odisha 80

4 Profile of Kashipur 125

5 Livelihood and Environmental Movement in Kashipur 145

6 Environmental Movement, State and Civil Society in Kashipur 178

7 Conclusion 232

Appendix 241

Bibliography 245

Index 260

Foreword

I am immensely pleased to write a foreword in this book *Environmental Movements, State and Civil Society* by Dr Iswar Chandra Naik. It is all the more heartening that a book is being brought out on this juncture. The basic thrust behind choosing the book is that in spite of enormous gains of the developments in the post-Independence period deep disparities are continuing in society that are only widening with the transitory times. The state and its machinery have increasingly failed to deliver their promise, thus resulting in strong people's movements. The policy of development has resulted in development of the few and impoverishment of the many. Our institutions are not capable enough to cater to the needs of the people at large. Many a times, the state's functioning is not in consonance with the aspirations of civil society. The developmental model adopted by independent India has often witnessed conflicts over the livelihood and the environment. These mechanisms of development claims are not merely to grab a greater share of the livelihood and the environment but also involve different ways of using nature. The unplanned development and industrialisation have promoted not only problems of livelihood and environmental case but also fuelled the environmental movements. The livelihood based environmental movements have grown in frequency and intensity and involved people from all sections of society. They revolve around issues over forests, land, water, and fisheries, and have generated a new movement, i.e. struggling for the rights to livelihoods and the dignity of life. These movements have added a new dimension to Indian democracy, governing systems and civil society.

The paradigm of development is pursued to achieve progress and modernisation. This paradigm reflects the aspirations of dominant social and economic groups and serves their interests but has negative effects on the poor in general and the marginalised communities in particular. The model of economic growth relies heavily on the exploitation of existing natural resources through large dams, mines-based industries, infrastructural and manufacturing projects. These projects require huge areas of land which is acquired by the government. This causes displacement, landlessness, loss of livelihood, loss of dignity of life, loss of culture and impoverishment. It involves reverse transfer of assets from the poor and the marginalised groups to the corporate and industrialists, exacerbates inequity and further widens the gap between the poor and the rich.

Environmental movements in India have become a major issue in recent decades because in the name of national development the poor people are deprived of their livelihood. So it results in the impoverishment and marginalisation of a large number of families, most of them from the already powerless communities. In such a situation the book draws our attention to environmental movements against establishment of industries in Odisha and raises before us the questions as to what kind of development people need in India and what are the major challenges before the Indian government. As such we ought to be very clear as to what are the issues, impediments and the responses of the state governments towards people's resistance. It is also of utmost importance to understand as to how the State is tackling the issues. We need better understanding of the issues of people's movements against industrialization which are directly related to the issues of inclusion of the project-affected people in the developmental process wherein the direct focus has to be on the empowerment of the marginalised. All development is meaningless without empowering the marginalised and creating a more equitable and all inclusive society. These development plans and models are causing deprivation to millions of poor people in the countryside, people who depend on these resources for their livelihood. People affected by industrialisation are mostly tribals, dalits and landless peasants, women and poor. Environmental movement is preeminent among the new social movements because it is related with the matter of livelihood security and sustainability. The burgeoning marketisation and commodification of mining and forest areas has virtually jeopardised the tribal culture, identity, forest rights and ultimately the livelihood and security of the forest-dwelling masses.

I am confident that the deliberations, discussions and the outcome of this book are more important for those who are fighting for their rights. I convey my heartiest greetings to Dr Naik and wish a grand success in life.

Anand Kumar
President
Indian Sociological Society, New Delhi

Acknowledgements

One can hardly conceive a more ambitious undertaking than to represent in a few hundred pages nothing less than a history of deprivation, displacement and struggle, all in the name of national development. A journey is easier when you travel together. Interdependence is certainly more valuable than independence. This book is the result of five years of my Ph.D. work whereby I have been accompanied and supported by many people. I now have the opportunity to express my gratitude to all of them.

The first person I would like to thank is my supervisor Prof. Anand Kumar, who gave impetus to my ideas and equipped me with the knowledge and skill to carry out this doctoral work successfully. In spite of his exceptionally untiring responsibility he has gone through my chapters and made valuable suggestions. His never-ending support and benevolent care made me overcome the anxiety and come upto this stage. I am extremely grateful to him. He could not even realise how much I have learned from him. Besides being an excellent supervisor, Prof. Kumar was a good friend to me.

My sincere gratitude also goes to all faculty members of CSSS, especially Chairperson Prof. Susan Viswanathan, Prof. Eshanul Haq, Prof. Maitriyee Chaudhary, Dr V. Sujatha, Dr Nilika Mehrotra, Prof. Nandu Ram, Prof. Tiplut Nongbri, Prof. Avijit Pathak, Prof. Dipankar Gupta, Prof. S.S. Jodhka, Prof. Vivek Kumar and Dr G. Srinivas. Their ideals and concepts have a remarkable influence on my academic career.

During this work I have collaborated with many friends for whom I have great regard, and I wish to extend my warmest thanks to all those who have helped me with my work. All my friends and classmates gave me the feeling of being at home at University and extended their support at the time of need. I want to thank Dr Rama bhai, Dr Rajkumar, Dr Sartik, Dr Biren bhai, Tila Kumar, Anjan, Pravati, Sunil, Jagarnnath, Natabar, Luna, Manoj, Sarbeswar, Smruti, Saroj, Puspita, Jharana, Sukhdeep, Sudeep, Baijyanti, Minakhi, Jyoti, Sushree, Priyadarshani, Krushna, Munna, Bully, Sarat, Sankar, Dr Kapila, Dr Niranjan, Dinesh, Amesh, Tusar, Sankar Bagh, Pooja, Siddharth, Pradeep, Ashish Kumar, Asish Das, Kiran, Gadadhar, Manash, Prasant, Gopal, Saroj, Rajat, Shiba, Hemant, Madhu, Bijay, Viswa and others.

I am also grateful to the CSSS at JNU for providing me with an excellent work environment during the past years and non-teaching staff Mrs Suman Sharma, Mr Negi, Mr Bharat Kumar, Mr Rajveer Singh and Mr Bhupender for their cheerful assistance.

I would also like to thank former Prime Minister Dr Manmohan Singh, UPA Chairperson Smt Sonia Gandhi, Ministry of Social Justice and Empowerment and University Grant Commission (UGC) Chairman Prof. Sukhadeo Thorat for the Rajiv Gandhi National Fellowship (RGNF); the financial support not only enabled material well-being but also enhanced the social value of the research.

I would like to say a big ‘thank you’ to all the people especially the residents of Kucheipadar village, Maikanch, DP colony and leaders of the movement namely Bhagaban Majhi, Sumani Jhodia, Mukta Jhodia, Makaranda Muduli, Krushna Saunta, Laxman Majhi, Medha Patkar and Praful Samantara who agreed to be interviewed by me for this work in some form or the other. I am grateful to NGO Agragamee. I would also like to extend my thanks to Susant Singh, Tahasildar of Kashipur who provided me necessary information for the book. The constructive part of the whole was that it made me feel responsible to participate in seminars and discussion forums. These discussions helped me a lot.

I am very grateful to my Bapa late Daitari Naik, Maa and my elder brother Mr Jogendra Pr. Naik for their love and patience during my study period. Without their encouragement and understanding it would have been impossible for me to finish this work. My special gratitude to my brothers Brahmananda, Bada nana, Ani nana, Narendra nana, Purusottam nana, Kshirendra nana, Laxman, Giridhar, Manindra; nephews: Pramod, Bebe, Puchi, Raja, Popoo, Buchu, Ramesh, Jhuda, Deepoo, Kerlia; nieces: Chandramaa, Runi, Rebati, Pramodini, Jhuni, Sabesh, Bhuri; my sisters-in-law: Smt Nabanita and Ramadula; my sisters: Smt Joshwanti and Hemabanti and their families; and Kaka and his family for their loving support.

I am grateful to my father-in-law, mother-in-law, Dr Naresh bhai, Dr Sandhya Rani Behera, Subha bhai, Bada nani, Subhasini nani, Naba, Tiki, Khushi, Mahesh, Kai Naik, Purtibash, Susanta, Lalu, Bihari, Himesh and Poonam for their support.

Lastly, not in the list, I would take the opportunity of thanking my wife Minati who helped me in moral, physical and intellectual support to finish this work. Without her support, it would have been impossible to complete this work.

Finally, I would like to thank Rawat Publications, particularly, Sachin Ji, Pranit Ji and their team for taking the responsibility to publish this book.

Though help flows from various quarters, still some errors and omissions are unavoidable.

18 May 2015
Katikhaman **Iswar Chandra Naik**

Abbreviations

AAY	Antyodaya Anna Yojana
APL	Above Poverty Line
AWC	Angan Wadi Centre
BALCO	Bharat Aluminum Company
BCFMC	Balugaon Central Fishermen Marketing Cooperative Society
BDO	Block Development Officer
BJD	Biju Janata Dal
BJP	Bhartiya Janta Party
BPD	Business Partner for Development
BPL	Below Poverty Line
CAFL	Chilika Aquatic Farm Limited
CBA	Chilika Bachao Andolan
CMM	Chilika Matsyajibi Mahasangha
CPI (ML)	Communist Party of India (Marxist Lenin)
CPI	Communist Party of India
CRPF	Central Reserved Police Force
CSE	Centre of Science and Environment
DRDA	District Rural Development Agency
DWCRA	Development of Women and Children in Rural Area
EAS	Employment Assurance Scheme

EIA	Environment Impact Assessment
FDI	Foreign Direct Investment
FFW	Food for Work
FIR	First Information Report
GASS	Ganatantrik Adhikar Suraksha Sangathan
GEM	Grassroots Environmental Movements
GP	Gram Panchayat
GPC	Gandhamardan Protectional Committee
GPEO	Gram Panchayat Extension Officer
GSYP	Gandhamardan Surakshya Yuva Parisad
HAL	Hindustan Aeronautics Limited
IAS	Indian Administrative Service
IAY	Indira Awaas Yojana
IDCO	Industrial Development Corporation
IFAD	International Fund for Agricultural Development
INC	Indian National Congress
INDAL	Indian Aluminium Company Limited
IPS	Indian Police Service
IRDP	Integrated Rural Development Programme
IRPF	Industrial Reserved Police Force
ISFP	Integrated Shrimp Farm Project
JGSY	Jawahar Gram Samridhi Yojana
JRY	Jawahar Rojgar Yojana
KBK	Kalahandi, Bolangir, Koraput
KGPS	Khepanastra Ghati Protirodh Samiti
KYS	Krantadarshi Yuva Sangha
MFP	Minor Forest Produce
MLA	Member of Legislative Assembly
MNC	Multinational Company

MOU	Memorandum of Understanding
NALCO	National Alumina Company
NCMP	National Common Minimum Programme
NFWP	National Food for Work Programme
NGO	Non-Governmental Organisation
NHRC	National Human Rights Commission
NREGA	National Rural Employment Guarantee Act
NREGS	National Rural Employment Guarantee Scheme
NSM	New Social Movement
NSS	National Service Scheme
NSS	National Sample Survey
NTFP	Non-Timber Forest Products
NTR	National Test Range
OBC	Other Backward Caste
OIC	Office In-Charge
OKM	Odisha Krushak Mahasanga
OMC	Odisha Mining Corporation Limited
OSFCFL	Odisha State Fishermen Cooperative Federation Limited
PDS	Public Distribution Systems
PESA	Panchayat Extension to Scheduled Areas Act
PHC	Public Health Centre
PIA	Project Implementing Agency
PMGSY	Pradhan Mantri Gram Sadak Yojna
POSCO	Pohang Steel Company
PPSS	POSCO Pratirodh Sangram Samiti
PRF	Proposed Reserve Forest
PRI	Panchayat Raj Institutions
PSSP	Prakutika Sampada Surakshya Parisad
PUDR	People's Union for Democratic Rights

SC	Scheduled Caste
SEZ	Special Economic Zone
SFDA	Small Farmer Development Agencies
SGRY	Sampoorna Grameen Rozgar Yojana
SGSY	Swarnajayanti Gram Swarozagar Yojana
SHG	Self-Help Groups
SIIL	Sterlite Industries (India) Limited
SP	Superintendent of Police
ST	Scheduled Tribe
TISCO	Tata Iron and Steel Company
TPDS	Targeted Public Distribution Systems
TRYSEM	Training of Rural Youth for Self-Employment
UAIL	Utka Alumina International Limited
URDS	Utkal Rural Development Society
VAL	Vedanta Alumina Limited
VAW	Village Agriculture Worker
VLC	Village Level Committees
VEC	Village Education Committee
VLL	Village Labour Leader

1

Introduction

The political transformation, which occurred in post-colonial countries, had never been truly translated into the societal sphere, though the anti-colonial struggle gave a tremendous impetus to nation building. The state and its apparatus have increasingly failed to deliver their promise, thus resulting in strong people's movements. The policy of development has resulted in development of the few and impoverishment of the many. Our institutions are not capable enough to cater to the needs of the people at large. Many a times, the state's functioning is not in consonance with the aspirations of civil society. It has created a significant actor, which has emerged in this sector in the post-colonials: the new social movements.

'New social movements' (NSMs) are the emancipatory movements that have emerged in the post-war West, which then percolated to the rest of the world. These movements represent a wide range of collectives that fall outside the institutionalised and organised groups of the society. They mobilise large masses and, organise movements that cut across previous alliances and, in the process, create social space for political action. Under the rubric of the new social movements are placed the women's, the students', the peace and the environmental movements. In Indian context, the sociologists and the political scientists including Ramachandra Guha (1989), Gail Omvedt (1993), Baviskar (1995), Rajendra Singh (2001), Ghanshyam Shah (2002), Poona Wignaraja (1993), Manoranjan Mohanty (1998), T.K. Oommen (1990) etc. have contributed through analysing the women's, environmental, farmer, and dalit (ex-untouchables) movements as the NSMs.

The developmental model adopted by independent India has often witnessed conflicts over the livelihood and the environment. These mechanisms of development claims are not merely to grab a greater share of the livelihood and the environment but also involve different ways of using nature. The unplanned development and industrialisation have promoted not only problems of livelihood and environmental case but also fuelled the livelihood and the environmental movements. The livelihood based environmental movements have grown in frequency and intensity and involved people from all strata. They revolve around issues over forests, land, water, and fisheries, and have generated a new movement i.e. struggling for the rights to livelihoods and the dignity of life. These movements have added a new dimension to Indian democracy, governing systems and civil society.

In recent years, the environmental movements (EMs) have successfully asserted people's right to manage their resources and brought a significant change in the existing policy programme to facilitate such local management. In case of these movements, trans-national networks of organisations have emerged with initiatives that have their roots in local issues and with local, regional or national bases of popular support (Lele and Quadir, 2002: 22).

The pattern of development, adopted by the State is generally depleting our stock of soil, water and plant resources at a terrifying rate. These development plans and models are causing deprivation to millions of poor people in the countryside people who depend on these resources for their livelihood. People affected because of unstructured industrialisation plan are mostly tribals and landless peasants, women and poor. It is a question of survival and livelihood and not of enhancing the quality of life (Guha, 1989: 14).

The struggle against loss of livelihood and environmental degradation has increasingly come to be understood as a part of the democratic struggle for nation building and a new model of development. Efforts to promote livelihoods and environmental rights have brought together numerous segments of the social movements, who have sought to ensure access to essential natural resources such as land, water, air and forest products in adequate amounts and with sufficient quality to guarantee peaceful living. The use of natural resources is needed for the specific socio-cultural groups such as tribals, dalits, fishermen and other indigenous people.

The concern for the present day environmental problems in most of the developing countries like India is of relatively recent origin. Even the recent awareness and concern for environmental protest movement at the grassroots level is due to efforts made by individuals and NGOs. Some of the contemporary movements, however, acquired the status of ecological or environmental movements in retrospect as these movements have widened their focus from basic survival needs to ecological concerns (Sethi, 1993; Gadgil and Guha, 1994). In general these movements are often grouped under tribal or peasant movements (Shah, 1990) and also under new social movements (Omvedt, 1993; Wignaraja, 1993). The reason being that ecological aspects are linked with the problems associated with peasants and tribals whose survival and livelihoods are dependent upon the status of natural resources.

Environmental protest movements in India, therefore, are not necessarily for the 'green' or 'clean' earth as in the West, but for the very survival of the local poor (Rao, 1994). Even among these ecological movements, only a few can claim success in achieving some of their objectives. The success of the movement is often linked with its popularity rather than the importance of the issue.

Though the local people's participation is vital for the success of any grassroots level movements in India, this aspect, however, is given due importance in the case of a few micro level movements where livelihood and sustainable development are the main objectives. And the results or achievements of these movements are exemplary. It is likely that the type of environmental issues addressed by contemporary movements might be different but the livelihood initiative comes entirely from the people concerned. Besides, the sustenance of the movements depends on people's participation although their popularity may come from leadership and external support like NGOs, academicians, researchers etc.

Statement of the Problem

The purpose of the present research is to study about tribal struggle at Kashipur in Rayagada District of Odisha against mining industry and their major concern about the land, water and forests (*Jal, Jamin, Jangal*) and all the natural resources of the locality, which is the only source of their livelihoods. The research seeks to examine the nature of tribal dependence on minor forest products and to what extent the people are losing their basic rights to traditional livelihood due to the process of industrialisation and 'development'.

Objectives of the Study

Major objectives of the study are as follows:

- To find out the reason for people's opposition to the establishment of alumina plants in Kashipur.
- To explore changes taking place in socio-economic and cultural aspect of Kashipur people due to the industrial establishment.
- To evaluate the role of Agragamee and the other NGOs in mobilising tribals of Kashipur against the aluminium plants.
- To evaluate the role of people's agitation against the environmental degradation caused by alumina plants.
- To analyse the role of women in environmental protest movement in Kashipur.
- To analyse the response of the state government and the bureaucracy towards the people's movement.

Hypotheses

Major hypotheses are as follows:

- The present process of developmental model is in violation of human rights because the tribals and dalits in Kashipur not only lose their rights to the minor forest productions but also the right to their home, land and livelihood.
- The establishment of aluminium companies has created major negative socio-economic changes among the tribal people of Kashipur.
- The government and the bureaucracy have failed to understand the core issues and they have not responded positively to the people's demand.
- The existing NGOs have played a major role in mobilising tribals against the aluminium plants.

Review of Literature

Sumi Krishna's *Environment Politics: People's Lives and Developmental Choice* (1996) narrates that in the relatively short period of two to three decades since the emergence of environmentalism as an organised movement in contemporary India, environmental advocacy has matured from protesting against environmental damage to questioning the very character and course of development. The work is a gender sensitive enquiry into the issues like why environmentalism has not yet had a greater impact on people's lives or developmental policy in India. Sumi Krishna does not restate well-known arguments against conventional development, but provides instead an introspective analysis of the environmental movements and debate. She challenges several ideological assumptions relating to environmental issues and questions the effectiveness of environmentalism in dealing with complex problems such as population growth, technological choices and conflicts over the use of resources. The role that tradition, caste, women and local communities play in environmental issues are dispassionately analysed. She argues that environmentalism should be directed towards a broader agenda aimed at progressive changes in the structure of society. She emphasises that people's live and their interaction with the environment will change over time. She also argues that environment should extend the range of choices for the poor, not diminish them.

S. Bhatt in his work *Environmental Protection and Sustainable Development* (2004) has focused on the emerging field of research in sustainable development and environment protection. He emphasises new ideas in law and science for sustainable development that mankind is exploring for life on this planet. Bhatt also mentions problems in the issues like accruing the administrative working of the ministry of environment and forest, the working of environment protection act 1986 in India, combining law and science in environment management, the world charter of nature 1982, the present state of environment in India and recent works for sustainable development in India. It really highlights the issues of environmental protection, people's rights and sustainable development.

Michael Redclift and Graham Woodgate's *The International Handbook of Environmental Sociology* (1997) is a major interdisciplinary reference work on the developing field of environmental sociology. They bring together the work of more than 30 scholars from some 10 countries and range of sociological traditions. The environmental sociology is still very much in its infancy. Nevertheless, it does provide the reader with some background in the origins and development of the field, a flavour of the variety of way in which sociologists engage with the environment and some examples of the analyses that may result from these different approaches. As a result, it demonstrates not only the sociological interest in global environment issues, but also the global importance of environmental issues in general.

First, we need to understand that how the development paradigm exploits and deprives the tribal. The edited book, *Tribal and Indigenous Peoples of India: Prospects,* in which Behura (2002) analyses the status of the tribal communities of Odisha shows this. Forest plays an important role in the life of tribal people. The life and the culture of the tribal people are closely related with the forest. Minor forest produces constitute about 15–50 per cent of the income of several tribal communities. Behura also argues that in Odisha, the tribal people's social structure, economy, political organisation and religion are all tuned to the practice of shifting cultivation. The tribal people wielded their traditional rights over the lands they occupied and freely practised shifting cultivation on forest-clad hill slopes.

He also analyses that industrialisation and mining operations in Odisha have led to uprooting of tribal villages, and the industrial nomads have become displaced. They have lost their home, land and immovable assets. However, as a result of their exposure to urban culture the level of their aspiration in most cases has escalated, although they have no ability to fulfill their mounting aspirations.

Prakash Gole's *Nature Conservation and Sustainable Development in India* (2001) highlights that the current economic beliefs and prescriptions along with technological models will have to change if sustainable development is to be the goal. Education will have to emphasise on conservation and restoration of natural resources and not their exploitation and destruction. Scarce resources such as land and water cannot be conserved and equitably distributed through greater storages and fertilisation. It is only through understanding of the ecology of streams and rivers, protecting various habitats and theme by enhancing the quantity and quality of these resources that the good can be achieved. The wetlands development will go a long way in protecting biodiversity. Biodiversity conservatism in critical habitats like sea coasts, hills and mountains as well as protected areas should get the highest priority if sustainable development is to become a reality.

In Vineeta Hoon's *Living on the Move: Bhotiyas of the Kumaon Himalayas* (Livelihood and environment 4) (1996), the title of the book, *Living on the Move* aptly subsumes the Bhotiya way of life. The Bhotiyas, who are the subject of this book, constitute a small tribe inhabiting the upper reaches of the Garhwal and Kumaon Himalayas in Uttar Pradesh. They inhabit a very rugged and inhospitable region of this mountainous terrain where life is tough and labourious. The Bhotiyas have adapted themselves to this environment which is conspicuously reflected in their culture and economy. Overall Bhotiya economy is characterised by three modes: barter trade; sheep and goat husbandry entailing transhumance and nomadism; and crop cultivation during summer time. Trade and animal husbandry being more important occupations, a sedentary lifestyle was not for the Bhotiyas. The present book is an outcome of the author's doctoral dissertation. Her study is based on extensive and prolonged fieldwork. The main aim of the study was to understand the response of the Bhotiyas who still practise transhumance and nomadism, which in her opinion are marginal environment that they inhabit.

The book is organised in ten chapters and opens with an ethnographic, ethno-historical profile of the Bhotiyas. The author clearly specifies her aim in undertaking this study which is mainly to observe the condition of nomadic people under the pressure of development and forces of modernisation. The author has described the transhumant Bhotiyas in a very exhaustive and analytical manner. This is an excellent analytical-empirical study of contemporary Bhotiya society.

Amita Baviskar's *In the Belly of the River: Tribal Conflicts over Development in the Narmada Valley* (1995), which grew out of a Cornell University doctoral dissertation, critically examines various efforts to mobilise the tribals of the Narmada valley following the agitation opposing the damming of the river. The author herself lived for a period in the tribal village of Anjanvara and participated in agitations against the dam and for tribal rights over the forest. Amita Baviskar seeks to highlight the fact that the

Narmada Bachao Andolan (NBA) is not really a movement of the tribal people questioning the dominant model of development, as claimed by its leaders. In her view, rich patidar farmers committed to energy-intensive 'Green Revolution' agriculture are a 'dominant presence' providing material support to the agitation, for it is they who suffer the most through submergence caused by the dam. And the relationship of the tribals with their environment is based on strategies for survival, and is not necessarily consistent with a 'conservationist ethic'. Baviskar's account of the Khedut Mazdoor Chetna Sangathan (KMCS - Peasants and Workers Consciousness Union) illustrates the problems faced by a small isolated group with meagre resources trying to confront the Forest Department over the tribals' right to forest land. The problem is not only one of security of tenure, but of a fragile, low-productivity economy facing rapid devastation of its natural resource base. It is truly ironic how a book written by an author with overt sympathies towards the NBA has ended up being used by proponents of the dam in denigrating the Andolan. There is no doubt that few tribals in India today are living in harmony with nature, this relationship having been inexorably fractured over time. The NBA is trying to make the voice of the tribals heard by a nation which has no time for these marginalised people. And in focusing on the plight of the Narmada valley as a whole (while underplaying the class aspect), the NBA is no different from most nationalist movements in the struggle against colonialism. Indeed, the Narmada agitation is best seen as an example of the many movements in contemporary India espousing the cause of backward and neglected regions, where the tribals are, indeed, fighting for their very survival. It is, of course, true that the NBA is now faced with the enormous challenge of transforming itself from a purely oppositional agitation to a movement for the articulation and implementation of a new people-centred agenda of decentralised, sustainable development of the tribal hinterlands of India. This task grows in urgency in the present context of liberalisation, given that the state may abdicate its role in the development of these forsaken regions. The experience of the KMCS described by the author underscores the need for grassroots organisations to make the state accountable towards the people of these areas. They must be careful not to let their opposition to the state coalesce with that of devotees of the market. Today, in the remote and backward regions of India, the state watched over by grassroots NGOs and panchayats, must be forced to do what the market forces cannot do and the private sector will not do. In the introductory chapter of this book the author beautifully interlaces episodes from the field to argue about her own case for 'particular observation'.

Ramachandra Guha *Environmentalism: A Global History* (2000) is a wonderfully told story of the history of the emergence and evolution of environmental ideas over the past century and a half. Guha uses the writings of poets, activists, academics of various callings, and politicians of various hues of red and green, to trace the roots of and courses taken by various strands of environmental thinking. One is introduced, then, not only to key ideas about the environment, and their thematic and geographic trajectories, but also to a whole slew of personalities, some better known than others as commentators of the environment.

Guha identifies two waves of environmentalism. The first, initiated during the middle of the 19th century, was in response to the pollution generated by the industrial revolution, and to the massive deforestation that was taking place in the colonies around the world. The second environmental wave traced by Guha has its origins in the 1960s, ignited by Rachel Carson's passionately written *Silent Spring,* which takes its title from the disappearance of the bird that traditionally heralded the arrival of spring – the robin, victim of the huge increase in pesticide use all over the United States. If the first was in many ways an intellectual response to observed environmental phenomena, the second wave saw a transformation of these ideas into social movements, including groundswell of protest that forced governments in various parts of the world to adopt some or the other element of a variety of environmental agendas.

Through both the first and the second waves of environmentalism, Guha suggests that three distinct strands of thought can be traced. The first, 'Back to these lands', a call to society to return to a simpler, less consumerist lifestyle; the second, 'Scientific conservation', insistently focused on the abilities of science and centralised state control to sustainably manage the use of natural resources; and the third, the 'Wilderness idea', focused on the setting aside of areas within which wild flora and fauna could flourish, and within which humans could enjoy the aesthetic beauty of nature, undisturbed by permanent human habitation.

Guha pointed repeatedly to the continuity of ideas across these two waves of environmentalism, suggesting that if the environmental movement of today is a child of the 1960s, them 'it is also perhaps a grandchild of the 1860s'. Each of the three themes just mentioned appears in both waves. If William Wordsworth, Ruskin Bond and Edward Carpenter were part of the first wave of environmentalism, and key proponents of a simpler lifestyle in the middle of the l9th century, then Arne Naess, a close student of Gandhi, has been one of its most vocal champions in the latter half of the 20th century. Similarly, if American, British and German foresters were at the forefront of scientific conservation between the 1860s and 1920s, then, more recently, North American and European environmentalists have worked closely with government agencies to use science and centralised control to force industry to reduce pollution. And if colonial hunters in India and Africa insisted on the setting aside of areas free of native population, within which they could hunt and spend their time in leisure, their counterparts exist today within myriad conservation agencies around the world, all calling for the setting aside of wilderness areas free of any form of permanent human habitation, within which leisure activities are permitted and encouraged.

Moving on from a discussion of ideas, Guha takes us through various environmental movements of the past few decades, his lively pen taking us from the activism on the American west coast, through rural England, to the Amazon and the killing of rubber-tapper cum activist Chico Mendez and the Chipko movement in the Himalayas, India. A lengthy essay on the rise and consolidation of the Greens as a force in German politics makes for fascinating reading. Through this discussion, he makes the key point that the ability of environmental protest to flourish as a movement is largely linked to the nature of the political space within which such protest is articulated. Within the USSR between the 1930s and the 1980s, within Socialist China today, and within the Nigerian dictatorship, any questioning of development from an environmental perspective has been ruthlessly eliminated. Environmental reform is most critically linked to political reform, as can be seen from the fact that those parts of the world most committed to political freedom, the West in general, have also managed to put in place environmental legislation that is the envy of environmentalists in most other parts of the world. Guha stresses the fact that the presence of structural inequities with regard to the ability to access natural resources has invariably been at the core of protests within the Third World. While industry has had carte-blanche access to timber, water and other natural resources, and the unquestioned right to pollute these resources, it is the poor, who depend on such resources for their livelihoods, who are both blamed for their destruction and forced to bear the brunt of the environmental damage resulting from industrial expansion. Most environmental protest in the South has its origins in the fight against such inequality. It is a fight for resources and for livelihoods, rather than a fight on behalf of the creatures of the plant and animal kingdoms.

Although Guha does not explicitly make the point, there are interesting parallels and differences with regard to the predominant character of environmental movements in the First and Third Worlds. Comparable with movements that highlight issues of environmental justice in the Third World, is the ongoing fight in the American north-west, where wildlife lovers have called for a ban on further logging within old growth forests. Lumberjacks and others threatened with losing their jobs in the timber industry have coined the bumber sticker 'Are you an environmentalist, or do you work for a living', nicely capturing a hostility expressed by many poor communities all over the world. On the whole, however, the wilderness lobby in most parts of the Third World tends to be small, largely confined to a small, largely apolitical, and therefore ineffective, urban middle class, in stark contrast to a large, often politically motivated middle class in the western world. This is a brief book, and one that covers a great deal of intellectual and activist terrain – both temporal and geographic. Even so, Guha has written a compelling and highly readable history of environmentalism.

Roger Jeffery and Nandini Sundar (eds) *A New Moral Economy for India's Forests: Discourses of Community and Participation* (1999) describes how the global rediscovery in the 1980s of participatory approaches to more effective development and resource management has inspired many different initiatives, and a vast amount of academic and grey literature. In India, past development failures, social movements and donor pressure have provided the impetus for policy initiatives towards new forms of institutionalised community participation. Joint Forest Management (JFM), now more than a decade old, is among the most prominent of these initiatives. It has been perceived by development practitioners, governments and donors as an unprecedented success story, the model for managing all kinds of natural resources with local involvement.

Much of the literature on community participation valorises a view of communities in which classes, castes and genders blend seamlessly into wholes. In refreshing contrast, editors Roger Jeffery and Nandini Sundar have a more complex and nuanced approach. Introducing the concept of a 'moral economy' the norms and obligations that govern economic practices within a community, they suggest that new moral norms may be discerned in the forest management initiatives of the 1980s that makes space for local participation. Their wide ranging introduction touches upon many of the current issues in the debate; also the selection of contributions seeks to unravel the conceptualisation and practice of community participation, and the working of JFM on the ground.

Each of the contributors offers critical insights that contradict many prevalent approaches, both popular and scholarly. Sumit Guha's analysis of the historical management of forest resources in central western India shows that community demarcated use of resources is the result of modern colonial fiat rather than socio-biological adaptation. Sivaramakrishnan's account of the acquisition of central control over zamindari forests in Midnapore, West Bengal, from the 1930s to the 1960s, points to the context and process by which different social classes and ethnic groups emerge as a community.

Arun Agrawal vigorously undermines the ghost of the traditional community, arguing that community should not be seen simply as quick solution to long-standing social problems; instead, there is need for reflexive analysis of the reasons for the turn to community at this historical time.

Moving to the much abused word 'participation' with its whiff of paternalism, Amita Baviskar contrasts official rhetoric and the actual practice of eco-development in the Great

Himalayan National Park of Himachal Pradesh. Unlike JFM, in which sharing authority and responsibilities is structured into the agreement, eco-development has been unable to generate a working consensus between the forest department and villagers. Savyasaachi's ethnographic account of the forest dwelling Kuiunka of Phulbani district of Odisha reveals the wide gap between the people's cognition of their living space, and indeed its creation, through shifting cultivation and the forest department's view of the destructive character of such cultivation. This lack of dialogue can be aggravated even by efforts to institutionalise people's participation, as Vasavada Mishra and Bates show in their case study of the working of village level committees in Dewas district of Madhya Pradesh and Sambhalpur of Odisha. They raise an important issue: why are structures being established that are parallel to panchayats? A multiplicity of committees may not broaden the base of leadership in a village.

The balanced review of the Western Ghats Forestry and Environment Project during the 1990s by N.C. Saxena and Madhu Sarin concentrates on Uttara Kannada district in northern Karnataka. Their research team found that the philosophy of joint forest planning and management was widely accepted by all levels of the state forest department, and that there was significant change in their earlier adversarial relationship with the village level committees. Nevertheless, there are institutional and policy constraints which limit the effectiveness of the project in empowering the people and in ensuring the sustainability of such forest conservation efforts. Also dealing with Uttara Kannada, Mariette Correa points out that when the village is treated as the unit of intervention, the participation of women and disadvantaged groups is likely to remain superficial. The project does not even attempt to address gender related issues within the household and the village. Catherine Locke elaborates on this, arguing that currently there is no adequate conceptual or operational basis for gender policy and planning in JFM. She suggests that institutionalising women's bargaining strength within JFM would require that forest professionals collaborate with social scientists and community development practitioners to understand gendered roles and relationships. A similar point is made by Bhaskar Vira regarding the interface between the community and the bureaucracy. He suggests a framework to incorporate field-based research on communities into the forest management process and the participatory agenda.

The second edition of John Hannigan's *Environmental Sociology* (2006) offers an insightful examination of some of the contemporary debates in the field. In his preface to the book, Hannigan comments on the extensive development of environmental sociology as a field of enquiry since the publication of the first edition. The maturation of the area is reflected in the many revisions and additions included in this new edition. Hannigan has dropped the original subtitle *A Social Constructionist Perspective* in his acknowledgment of the progression of the debates around realism and constructionism in environmental sociology, particularly the more recent attempts at synthesis. The additions and revisions within the text are numerous and combine with the previous analysis to create a lively, reflective and even handed discussion of environmental concerns and debates.

The book begins with an examination of the historical tendency within sociology to exclude the environment as a topic for study. Here, he provides an extended discussion of Marx, Weber and Durkheim, identifying the utility within their works for better understanding of environmental deliberations. This constitutes a brief but fascinating overview of contemporary attempts to utilise classical social theory to extract ecological insights. Other major additions include an extended appraisal of Beck's 'risk society' thesis and Mol and Spaargaren's version of 'ecological modernisation theory', as well as a critical review of contemporary perspectives that have attempted to transcend the nature/culture divide.

Hannigan provides a succinct outline of both Beck's and Mol and Spaargaren's work. In his subsequent discussion of the recent developments in the constructionist realist debate, Hannigan offers a considered critique of theorists, such as Irwin in his work on co-constructionism and Latour and Callon in their contributions to Actor Network Theory. The most thought provoking part of this discussion appears in his recognition of the 'long-standing tension in environmental sociology between the role of the sociological analyst and that of the environmental activist' (p. 24). If one denotes environmental concerns as socially constructed, one risks demoting ecological problems as a political concern. On the other hand, to imply the reality that environmental issues run against the wealth of sociological analysis, demonstrates the construction of environmental risk.

The most significant revisions to this second edition can be found in Hannigan's discussion of environmental discourse and in his offering of a new perspective, labelled 'the emergence approach to sociology'. In his examination of environmental discourse he provides an excellent insight into the utility and difficulty encountered in the use of discourse analysis in environmental sociology. The discussion flows smoothly from his prior exploration of the constructionist realist debate. This is assisted through his acknowledgment of the close identification of discourse analysis with social constructionism. He continues in his examination of discourse detailing the significance of power in relation to environmental discourses. Through these two chapters on discourse, Hannigan formulates an astute analysis of the significance of discourse as it features in environmental studies.

In other chapters Hannigan provides commentary on a range of areas of pertinence in environmental studies, such as risk, the media and the complex role of science. In the final chapter 'Toward an Emergence Model of Environment and Society', Hannigan posits his own notion of how the environmental field might be conceptualised. 'Emergence', Hannigan writes, 'denotes process, flow, adaptation and learning' (p. 138). From this broad definition of the term he proceeds to provide an outline of 'emergence' as it features in various areas, such as complexity theory, the sociology of disasters and the sociology of environmental flows. This dealt with; he turns to drawing these strands together to formulate 'an emergence model of nature, environment and society' (p. 148).

In this endeavour, he provides an interesting introduction to the possibilities that the notion of 'emergence' might hold for environmental studies but does not expound this in any great detail; this task is left for future development. Thus, this chapter acts as an interesting introduction to the notion of applying 'emergence' in addressing some of the stickier problems in environmental sociology such as the bridging of the nature/society divide but is not elucidated in great enough detail to allow assessment of whether this approach can achieve such aims or not.

Ghanshyam Shah (ed.), *Social Movements and the State Readings in Indian Government and Politics,* vol. 4 (2002). Comprises of sixteen pre-published articles brought out as part of a series on 'Readings in Indian Government and Politics' by Sage Publications. It revolves around the conceptualisation and theoretical debates on social movements, including the Indian state.

Ghanshyam Shah's introduction deals with definitional, conceptual and typological problems, including the relations between social movements and the state. The organisation of the book makes it easy to read. What makes it difficult, however, is when one is forced to treat the issues of communalism/fascism as part of social movements.

A.G. Frank sets the tone on different forms of social movements at the global level, which is rightly critiqued by Dhanagare and J. John. Frank's famous 'Nine Theses' centre on the following: these social movements differ in dimension, reach and goals, but they all carry social power, are cyclical in nature, and tend to disappear when conditions change. The social bases of social movements differ in each continent, although most are largely concerned with autonomy rather than state power. These social movements are defensive and 'appear as agents and reinterpret delinking from contemporary capitalism and transition to socialism' (p. 33); they are involved in multiple relations including social coalitions and in the long run, would become irrelevant. Some of the formulations, however, cannot be transplanted to understand the social movements developing in India. The most important problem in the 'Nine Theses' is the silence on 'political power', including the 'cultural specificities of the movement'.

Rajni Kothari's argument linking the state and masses is one of the best pieces in the anthology. He unveils the relationship between the changing nature of the state from welfare to a corporate state, and the betrayal of the 'cause of masses' in the process. At the same time, he is optimistic that the ambiguity of the state would create spaces for the masses on two counts: one, negotiation on various issues through the mediation of social movements; and two, the strengthening of civil society vise versa the state. However, the question will remain as to how the state will behave when the civil society/social movements contest its legitimacy through different modes.

D.N. Dhanagare and Sumanta Banerjee deal with the leftwing Telangana and Naxalite movements. If the former Telangana movement emerged as a reaction to the feudal state of Hyderabad, the Naxalite movement emerged out of the contradictions within the left movement. There are reasons why these movements came to an end, and rather than disunity and wrong class alliances, it was more the issue of internal ideological differences that caused the withdrawal of the movement. On the other hand the Naxalite movement spread to other parts of India. This does not mean the absence of different shades or heterogeneity in the left movement. It is in this context that the 'dilemma' of the left movement needs to be located. These dilemmas centred on the issues of strategies, tactics and class alliances, assessing the Indian political situation and analysing the class contradictions. At the same time one cannot negate the fact of transplantation of Marxist ideas mechanistically, without studying the 'culture of social practices', that cost the movement dearly. In the process one can argue that 'Marxism was never localised properly'; it remained an alien concept in the context of the varied social relations or practices in India.

Three articles concentrate on such social movements as farmer's movements (Dipankar Gupta in UP and Maharashtra), organised labour and militant unions in Mumbai (Salim Lakha) and the tribal solidarity movement (Surjit Sinha). These movements belonged to different phases, different ideological currents and historical settings, but the book has treated all of them as post-colonial movements. At the same time one has to ask the question as to how to perceive these social movements; are they 'new' or 'old'? The inclusion of this particular debate would have given a new dimension to the volume.

Gail Omvedt ventures into the issues of the dalit movement in the post-Ambedkar period, taking the Dalit Panther Movement and the Republican Party as reference points. Despite revolutionary rhetoric, they failed to 'forward the kind of total transformation that Baba Saheb had envisaged' (p. 303). There were many reasons for this, such as ideological dilemmas and the problem of *jati* identity politics. Nonetheless, in the present context, the dilemma has sharpened with capitalism and globalisation increasingly threatening their identity on the one hand, and the New Hindutva appropriating its politics to its own advantage. There are four more articles with varied interests. The women's movement by Lakshmi

Lingam, whose main thrust is to establish a 'common platform for moving towards common agenda of understanding for future' (p. 331). Ghanshyam Shah, in his analysis of two movements, tries to understand the politics of agitation within the larger politics of the state. Amalendu Guha enters into the binary opposition of nationalism and chauvinism, while Ramachandra Guha provides a good historical narrative of the philosophy and agents of environmental movements in India. The most debatable article in this anthology is by Peter van der Veer. His article on 'Hindu Liberation Movement' has all the potential to be trapped in the New Hindutva ideology. This can be seen in the way he constructs his arguments: 'It seems reasonable to suggest that the very location of a mosque on Ram's birth site has always been humiliating' (p. 419). However, there is a danger in assigning the tag of social movement to a communal or fascist agenda.

Ghanshyam Shah explores a wide range of problems and issues in specific areas of Indian polities and locates them within wider debates on politics, society, economy and culture in this series. He focuses on the interface of social forces, political institutions and processes in an attempt to understand the Indian politics.

A variety of approaches have been deployed by social scientists in general and political-sociologists in particular to understand (a) the relationship between state and society, (b) democracy and development, (c) state and classes controlling its power, (d) formulation of public policy, and (e) its implementation between different segments and regions, religions, castes, languages and cultures. The review of issues of theoretical and substantive importance both within institutional structure and outside can illuminate the complex interplay of socio-political forces and political processes and dynamics of social formation and political transformation in modern India. In general above literature has been used as the base of this study. It has been complemented by intimate understanding of the Kashipur movement from close quarters for last several years by the researcher.

Area of the Study

Kashipur block is coming under of the Tribal Schedule areas of Odisha. This block was earlier in Kalahandi district, which was merged with Koraput district in 1962 (District Gazetteers, 1966). After the reorganisation of districts of Odisha in 1992, it became a part of Rayagada district. There are 412 revenue villages and 109 hamlets divided into twenty Gram Panchayats (GPs). Kashipur block came under the jurisdiction of Rayagada district on 2 October 1992. Total geographical area of Kashipur is 1,505. 90 sq kms, and the total population is 1,21,044 (Census, 2001). Out of the total population 61 per cent belong to the Scheduled Tribes, 20 per cent to Scheduled Castes and the rest to the other castes.

Kashipur is covered with rich natural resources i.e. forest resources, which is one of the major source of livelihoods for the tribal people. This region is the house of rich mineral resources particularly Bauxite. Kashipur has been one of the centres of national attention since last one decade. The rich mineral resources attracted multinational companies (MNCs) to establish factory and extract Bauxite from this region. The result reflected in negative impact on the livelihoods of the tribal. With the approval of Government of Odisha, three companies have set up their industries at different places in the Kashipur block. Main reason is that, the rich deposit of Bauxite mines attracted many private industries, including corporate and multinational companies to establish Alumina Plants. The first Alumina Plant construction was started at Doraguda village which is very close to Kucheipadar village – Utkal Alumina International Limited (UAIL). Sunger is the second village, about 20 kms away from Kashipur block headquarter where the L & T Company has decided to establish another Alumina Plant. There is a third village Kansariguda, about 10 kms away from Tikiri Police Station, where the Aditya Birla Company has decided to set up its Alumina Plant.

There has been people's agitation against the establishment of all these Alumina plants. There has been strong people's protest against all these companies since last one decade in Kashipur block of Rayagada district, Odisha. The epicentre of the Kashipur Environmental Movements (KEMs) is Kucheipadar village which is about 12 kms away from Tikiri Police Station.

'Prakrutika Sampad Surakshya Parishad' (PSSP) which was established on 14 February 1996 is a people organisation constituted to carry out all agitation programmes in order to protect the interest of the local area people and the local communities (PSSP, 1996). As a result a number of men and women have been arrested by police and imprisoned in Rayagada jail. There had been another agitation by the people on 16

December 2000 in Kashipur against the alumina project and factories resulting in confrontation between people and the representative of the MNCs. It is reported that the MNCs have also used the local political representative and some of the criminal elements to disturb the movement. This led to police intervention and firing in which three agitators were killed. Since then, the movement is on, but there has not been any evaluation of this study. Therefore, I want to study this movement, which, will be retrospective analysis of an environmental protest movement against the establishments of Alumina plants and for the people's right for livelihoods.

Scope of the Study

Odisha has a long tradition of powerful peoples' movement in the post-independence period. For example, (1) the Chillika Bachao Andolan in the Puri, Khorda and Ganjam district, (2) the Baliapal Movement in Balasore district, (3) the movement in Gandhamardan Hills in Sambalpur district in 1980s and 90s, (4) Kalinganagar people's agitation in Jajpur district, (5) anti-POSCO movement in Jagatsinghpur district, (6) anti-Vedanta movement in Kalahandi district, and (7) the peoples' protest movement in Kashipur block of Rayagada district are few of them. In this study, the researcher has chosen the Kashipur protest movement a famous environmental movement for an in-depth analysis from the livelihood perspective. The movement is chosen with the assumption that the nature of discourse they generate, issues they highlight and the actors which participate in them, are representatives of the protest movement in particular and environmental movements in India in general.

Structure of the Book

First chapter is introductory which contains statement of the problem, the objectives and hypothesis, review of literature and about the area of study. The second chapter is titled 'Environmental Movements at a Glance: Theoretical Approaches'. This chapter discusses the theoretical explanations about origin and development of social movement and new social movement. To comprehend the social movement in a more lucid manner, this chapter delineates the different approaches: Marxist approach, structural-functional approach, Johnson's value consensus approach, Smelser's strain theory and Eisentadt's modernisation theory.

Unlike social movement, the new social movement is overarching and non-class in nature. Nevertheless, environmental movement is preeminent among the new social movements because it is related with the matter of livelihood security and sustainability. The burgeoning marketisation and commodification of mining and forest areas has virtually jeopardised the tribal culture, identity, forest rights and ultimately the livelihood and security of the forest dwelling masses.

The third chapter is titled 'Background of Environmental Protest Movements in Odisha'. This chapter provides us with a picture of the nature and emergence of social movements in Odisha. A common thread which covers each of these movements is that these are protest movements which revolved around livelihood rights and use, often projected against government or the industrial capitalists. Many of the protest movements have been undertaken by the tribes of Odisha having the core idea of livelihood and right to use natural resources which they have been using for their survival since time immemorial. The emergence of such movements really make it more clear that nationalist project of development is antithetical to tribal development project. In the process of undertaking development projects the government is in a way marginalising the already marginalised section of our society. The analysis of movements in Odisha also make it clear as to how people's agency or mass participation can bring change in society, which is obvious from the movements like Baliapal, Chillika Bachao Andolan, Gandhamardan movement, Kalinganagar protest, anti-POSCO movement and anti-Vedanta movement.

The fourth chapter deals with poverty in Odisha particularly the KBK districts including Rayagada. In this chapter information is given about social composition, literacy rate, languages and religions, festivals, livelihood in Kashipur, the market, Rajiv Gandhi and the new era of development, the PDS in Kashipur Block and other related aspects of social things of Kashipur block.

The fifth chapter is titled 'Livelihood and Protest Movement in Kashipur' which is based on fieldwork of livelihood and protest movement in Kashipur of Odisha. This chapter provides details to social composition, natural resource, livelihood movement, sources of livelihood, livelihood systems of tribal, role of forest produce in rural livelihood, food gathering, hunting, forest, medicine and health, cultural significance of Baphalimali mountain, forest and fuel, food pattern in Kashipur, wage labourer and government programmes, impact on tribals, multiple displacements and related problems in Kashipur block.

The sixth chapter is titled 'People's Movement in Kashipur Block' which is based on fieldwork on livelihood and environmental movements in Kashipur of Odisha. This chapter provides details to underline that the people of that locality are much more concerned about the livelihood issues than the environmental one. This chapter also highlights various truth of the people's movement regarding the origin and development, major difficulties, the leadership of the movement, the local way of mass mobilisation, supporters of the movement and participation of people and women, and response of the state administration and police repression.

Method of Study

The present study is descriptive and analytical in nature. It is based upon a combination of qualitative and quantitative data.

The interview schedule methods have been used to collect the primary data. In this context, attempt has been made to take the response of the people through an interview schedule, which has been completed by focused group discussions. Interviewing key informants like politicians, activists and representatives of NGOs was also done. We have collected information with the help of purposive sampling. The whole process has been carried out in the local dialect. The primary data collected from the field was substantiated with the help of information from the secondary source. It includes the basic literature on the subject such as, books, research journals, newspapers, gazetteers and pamphlets.

It has used snow ball research methods. The sample size of the study is 160 respondents. Based on the sample, the researcher carried out interview in 20 villages from Kashipur block. Apart from individual interviews, focus group discussions were also place. Primary sources were included in the study discussions with local leaders, news reports, and government officers (Tahsil Officers). Mostly it used participatory research with field notes.

2

Environmental Movements at a Glance

Theoretical Approaches

This chapter seeks to discuss various theoretical perspectives on environmental protest movements. The chapter also highlights an argument on the definitional aspect of social movement by bringing out a clear demarcation between the old and new social movement. As focus of the thesis is to understand new social movement in general and environmental movement in particular, thrust of this chapter will be on environmental movement as a new social movement along with its origin and development in the Indian society.

Social Movement: Origin and Development

The term 'Social Movement' lacks a precise and universal definition among the scholars of all discipline, even scholars belonging to the same discipline. Like so many other terms such as democracy, masses, popular, equality, the term movement is often used differently by different social activists, political leaders and scholars. Many of them use the term 'movement' interchangeably with organisation or union. Some use it to mean a historical trend or tendency such as renaissance, analytic movement, empiricist movement etc. (Shah, 2002: 18–22).

Social scientists have shown increasing interest in the study of social movements and their linkages with social changes. Social movements are becoming a matter of increasing concern for general public administrators and are looked at with concern by policy makers. Some scholars are of the view that social movements belong to the area of process and have connection with the social structure (social institution, social relationships, values and norms) and social change. It is however not necessary that only social movements lead to social change, social change can take place independently of social movement (Mukherji, 1977). Social movement as an instrument of social change differs from imitative or emulative process of social change. The latter centres around acquiescence, request, obedience and loyalty and seeks to bring about change without endangering the law and order situation. But the former focuses on protest, conflict, challenge and revolts.

In the nineteenth century the political leaders and authors who used the term were concerned with the emancipation of the exploited classes and the creation of a new society by changing property relations. Thus during this period of time, the concept of social movement had a specific meaning in the European continent. This identification of social movement lasted until the second decade of the nineteenth century which attracted few people belonging to labour class with limited goals of eliminating bourgeoisie institutions. Today this narrow meaning of social movement is no longer reasonable. Now it refers to a mass movement aiming at comprehensive and fundamental changes in the social structure and social order. It differs from classical sense of the social movement which implied creation by an entirely new social-economic and political order especially concerning the institute of property and distribution of power (Heberle, 1968).

In the 1960s and 1970s, European and American societies witnessed the emergence of large-scale movements around issues which were basically humanistic. The goals and values of these movements were essentially universalistic in nature (Singh, 2001: 96). The social transformation from 'modern' to 'post-modern' reflected in a similar way in the transformations in the social movements which changed from the 'old' form of 'classical' and 'new classical' movements to 'new social movements'. A large number of scholars, such as (Oommen, 1972, 1990, 2004), (Gupta, 1979, 1980), (Singh, 2001), (Guha, 1982), (Shah, 2002, 2004), (Rao, 1978), (Omvedt, 1993) and others have made serious attempts to discuss, elaborate and highlight some of the elements of the contemporary 'new social movements'. Even if we look at the past records of Indian society, a wide range of social movements have taken place including tribal movements, dalit movements, women movement, Bhoodan movement, Naxalbari movement, working class movement, peasant movement, Jharkhand movement, Tebhaga movement, Telengana movement and Other Backward Class movements. However, it is important to note that the environmental movement and human rights movements are characteristically very different from other social movements. What is worth remembering here is that their action, strategy and mode of mobilisation are 'global' in nature and the issues concerned cut across the boundary of nation and society.

Historically the term 'social movement' gained currency, particularly in European language in the early nineteenth century. Since the early 1950s various scholars have attempted to provide definitions and the theoretical-conceptual tools of social movement as a social phenomenon. The idea of social movement suggests bringing about social transformations, distribution of resources, protecting the global environment for sustainable development and struggle for justice. Therefore, the objective, ideology, leadership and organisations are important components of the social movement analysis. It provides direction for evolving strategy and programmes and keeps the participants together so as to develop their feeling of 'we-ness' and collective identity (Shah, 2002: 17).

From the Marxist approach, they are mainly interested in bringing about revolutionary changes in society. According to them social movements are situated in the economic structure of the society, i.e. antagonistic relations between the 'haves' and the 'haves not'. It is a class based social movement, in which the oppressed class is engaged to bring about revolutionary social changes by overthrowing the dominant class in power (Shah, 2002: 19–21), or social movement is carried out as a united effort on the part of the deprived social categories to bring about social change (Oommen, 2004: 180). He has also stated that social movement is a weapon of the weak against the strong whether viewed globally or within the confines of state-society (Oommen, 2004: 184).

Rajani Kothari argues that democracy in India has become a playground of growing corruption, criminalisation, repression and intimidation of the large portion of people. Furthermore, role of the state in social transformation has been undermined. So people have started asserting their right through various struggles. The mass mobilisation at the grassroots level is both necessary and desirable (Shah, 2002: 26). Thus social movement also includes organised struggle to overthrow not only the established government and regime but also the socio-economic and political structure which sustains it. It also aims at replacing the structure by an alternative social order. However, the movement will neither have the potentialities to root out the existing system completely nor will they succumb to the traditional structure entirely. So social movements provide the stage for the confluence between old and the new values and structures (Oommen, 1977: 16; Shah, 2002: 27). According to Oommen, the characteristics of social movements are charismatic, ideological and organisational.

Social movements are classified on the basis of issues around which participations get mobilised. Some of the movements are known as environmental, civil rights, linguistic, nationalists, human rights etc. Other sociologists classified social movements on the basis of the participants such as peasant, Tribal, students, women, dalit etc. In many cases the participants and issues go together. These social movements have participants from all the strata or from a number of strata. In the issues of ecology, for instance, preservation of forests is raised by Chipko Movements. In the tribal movements the issues of the land right and forest are prominent as these are associated with the livelihood of the tribals (Shah, 2002: 27).

Social Movement in the Indian Context

Studies on social movements have been very popular particularly from the mid-1960s in India. However, no precise definition has been accepted by the Indian scholars of different disciplines or even scholars belonging to a particular discipline.

Ghanshyam Shah (1990: 16) has identified that some studies use the term movement interchangeably with 'organisation' or 'union'. Some use it to signify a historical trend or tendency. Some political leaders and social reformers call their activities 'movements' even if their organisation has a very small following, may be less than a dozen members. Just issuing press statements on public issues is said to be launching of a movement. Obviously, the term movement is used in a very loose sense by different sets of people.

In a simple sense, social movement may be said to signify a collectivity of human beings on the move in a socio-political sense. It represents a collective endeavour which would obviously involve certain goals, means and the process to achieve the goals. While talking about social movements, M.S.A. Rao (1978) refers to the issues of its genesis, ideology, organisation, leadership, structure, internal dynamics, and social consequences. In his view, 'a social movement is an organised attempt on the part of a section of society to bring about either partial or total change in society through collective mobilisation based on an ideology' (Rao, 1978: 2).

A broad definition of the concept is offered by Paul Wilkinson.

> A social movement is a deliberate collective endeavour to promote change in any direction and by any means, not excluding violence, illegality, revolution or withdrawal into 'utopian' community ... . A social movement must evince a minimal degree of organisation, though this may range from a loose, informal or partial level of organisation to the highly institutionalised and bureaucratised movement and the corporate group ... . A social movement's commitment to change and the raison d'être of its organisation are founded upon the conscious volition, normative commitment to the movement's aims or beliefs, and active participation on the part of the followers or members (cited in Shah, 1990: 16–17).

Social movements involve collective action which may be both legal or institutional and illegal or non-institutional. There are actions which follow the path of acquiescence for change in situation. According to Johnson, the action which is legally permitted and 'widely accepted as binding in society or part of society' (cited by Shah, 1990: 18) at a given time is institutionalised action. These types of actions include e.g. petitioning and fighting legal battles in courts. Shah talks about several forms of non-institutionalised collective action which include protest, agitation, strike, satyagraha, hartal, gherao, riot etc. He does not think that agitation or protests are social movements in strict sense of the term. However, he notes that more often 'a social movement develops in course of time, and it begins with protest or agitation which may not have the 'organisation' or 'ideology' for change' (Shah, 1990: 19). Shah treats agitation, protest, strike etc. as 'movements' or more as a part of a social movement of a particular stratum of society (ibid.).

Shah categorises movements as reform, revolt, rebellion and revolution in connection with changes in the socio-political system (Shah, 1990: 96). Reform movement does not involve challenging the existing system *per se*. It is geared to changes in the relations between the parts of the system for making it more efficient, responsive and workable. In contrast, a revolt challenges the existing authority with the objective of overthrowing the ruling regime. A rebellion involves an 'attack on existing authority without any intention of seizing state power'. But in case of a revolution, a section or sections of society launch 'an organised struggle to overthrow not only the established government and regime but also the socio-economic structure which sustains it, and replace the structure by an alternative social order' (Shah, 1990: 26–27).

Partha Mukherjee (1977) classifies movements based on the criterion of quality of change it intends to bring about or the kind of change that has been effected. According to him the nature of movements could be 'accumulative', 'alternative', and 'transformative'. If social mobilisation demands changes 'within' the system, the changes that are likely to happen would be accumulative. If the social mobilisation is aimed at creating new structures which would qualitatively affect the entire system, then the change, in case attained, will be alternative. But in transformative movements social mobilisation seeks to replace one structure and substitute it by another. Rao (1978: xiv) calls the accumulative movements as quasi-movements, and the other two as social movements in full sense. Rao himself talks about three types of social movements on the basis of the consequence of a movement. He says that there are movements which aim at bringing about 'reform' in some area of life or the other, involving new relationships, activities, norms and values. In contrast, 'transformative' movements are oriented towards effecting changes in power relations i.e. the super-ordinate and subordinate relationships. There are also movements which aim at 'revolutionary' changes in all domains of life and in all basic values (Rao, 1978: 3).

As there are different types of social movements they could be put into two categories, one referring to changes 'within' the system, and the other implying changes 'of' the system. The reformist and alternative/transformative movements fall in the first category and the revolutionary movements in the second category. This is in terms of their ideological orientations and consequences. Reformist movements would refer to changes of 'minor' nature within the system. Transformative movements would involve 'major' changes within the system. And replacement of one system by another would be the trait of revolutionary movements.

This general typology of social movements could be applied to understand the nature of changes which have taken place in the past and are presently occurring in the area of natural resource protection in general and livelihood security of the poor in particular. There are different stakeholders of the natural resources like land, water and forest. These include different sections of the society such as different castes, classes, communities, gender etc. and the state itself. Historically, there have been changes in the access, control, ownership and management of natural resources by different stakeholders. Traditionally, the natural resources have been considered as 'commons' characterised by collective/community/local control, ownership and management. But the state has gained hegemonic/dominant position in the area of natural resources especially water, land and forest. There has been the trend of privatisation of the commons. As a result, various social movements have emerged relating to protection of natural resources and livelihood of the poor, including the dignity of life in different periods of history in India.

In the early 19th century social movement was in vogue among social scientist and social activist. The social movement goes through three phases (Singh, 2001). The first phase of social movement started before the Independence of India that is the classical social movement. The second phase of social movement started after the independence of India and continued up to the 70s. This phase has also been known as the neo-classical social movement. The third phase of the social movement started from mid-sixty and is continuing even today as the 'New Social Movement' (Shah, 2002). On the basis of socio-economic issues, the classification of social movements can be done as peasant movement, tribal movement, dalit movement, other backward class movement, working class movement, student movement and middle class movement. But human right movement and environmental movement are new phases within the new social movement. The emergence of 'New Social Movements' in India, forms, styles and issues of their mobilisation, mass participation across the caste and class justified the 'newness' of these movements. In contemporary Indian society, the emergence of a sizeable aggressive and conscious people about the right claims and share of the resources of the nation and the growing awareness of the people to collectively fight against the state's monopoly over them, have newly shaped the movements (Singh, 2001: 192).

Indian sociology and social anthropology has so far studied the elements of continuity and change in the social structure and social process. In order to provide a theoretical perspective to the presentation of social movement as general and environmental movement in particular, social change and transformation of society can generally be seen as responses 'to a set of key challenges to the evolution of this society' (Singh, 1993: 11). Social conflict refers to people's behaviour in relation to others which, opposition, strike and struggle and such social values as power, property, prestige and honour at the cost of the other, state between classes, castes, religions etc. type of conflict that lead to relatively organised conflict, collective actions, protest especially social movement. In the recent year social movement has attracted the attention of sociologist and social anthropologist in India. 'Social movement is to be an organised effort on the part of a section of the population, involving collective mobilisation based on ideology to bring about changes (either partial or total) in the social system' (Rao, 1979: xvi). This is an orientation to bring change, either partial or total, in the existing system of relationship, values and norms, although there are efforts which are oriented towards resisting change and maintaining the status quo (Rao Reprint, 2002: 02).

The transformation of the concept of social movement goes from the traditionally class bound concept of the 'Old' or classical to the non-class, 'New' or contemporary movements (Rao, 2002:

87, 89). Rajendra Singh has divided the theoretical tradition of social movements into classical, neo-classical and contemporary or new social movement. The classical social movement studies mostly the collective behaviour before 1950s. The neo-classical social movements or 'Old' social movement engulfs the movements from 1950s to 1970s. The neo-classical studies represent the contributions of both western and Indian sociologist. The new social movements are propounded by scholars from Europe and America. Social movement studies are new to India in general and to Indian sociology and social anthropology in particular. However, historian and political scientists have for long been engaged in the study of organised protests and collective actions. When movement studies entered the Indian social science scene, the research gained momentum for two reasons. First being a virgin terrain, a large number of scholars were eager to seize it and by the mid-1970s social movements became a fashionable area of research. Second, movement studies gained currency in India in the context of the massive, long and protracted anti-colonial struggle (Oommen, 1990). Understandably, an overwhelming majority of movement studies are analysis of the anti-imperialist struggle and the mobilisation associated with it. Record relating to such movements invariably relate to the articulations and activities of the movement of elite and its opponents.

Social movements are one of the major forms of collective behaviour. In the last four decades the studies of social movement have attracted the attention of a large number of sociologists, political scientists and social anthropologists in India. Question is that why do people join the various types of social movements? It shows that something is wrong with some people. Yes, it is true that when something goes wrong with the society or some section of communities then people try to change it through collective protest. The classical definition that, 'social movements are collective enterprises to establish a new order of life', captures what is central in any conception of social movement, group behaviour directed in concerted way to bring about social change (Blumer, 1969). It is 'an effort by a large number of people to solve collectively a problem they feel, they have in common'.

Defining Social Movement

The definition emphasises the part played by the social movement in the development of social change. It has an ideological component i.e. a set of ideas which are specific discontent, prescribe solutions and justify change. A much comprehensive definition states that 'a social movement occurs when a fairly large number of or an otherwise identifiable segment of population deliberately bind together for collective action in order to alter, reconstitute, reinterpret, restore, protect, supplant or create some portions of their culture or social order to better their life chances by redistributing the power of control in a society' (Singh, 1972). This movement may continue over a length of time through repeated collective actions. McLaughlin gives representative definitions of social movements; 'collective enterprises to establish a new order of life' has been considered a classic definition. Among other definitions are 'group venture extending beyond a logical community or a single event and involving a systematic effect to inaugurate changes in the right, behaviour and social relationships and a collectivity which acts with some continuity to promote or resist changes in a society or a group of which it is part' (McLaughlin, 1969). Pal Wilkinson gives a working concept of social movement. Social movements are clearly different from historical movements, tendencies or trends. It is important to note however that such tendencies or trends and the influence of the unconscious or irrational factors in human behaviour may be of crucial importance in illuminating the problems of interpreting and explaining social movement.

A social movement must evidence a minimal degree of organisation. Though this may range from a loose, informal or partial level of organisation to the highly institutionalised and bureaucratised movement and the corporate group (Paul, 1971). Indeed much of the literature of the social movements has been concerned with natural histories, models or theories of movement and its development. Such models have attempted to stimulate changes in movement structure and organisation ranging from states of initial social unrest and excitement and the emergence of a charismatic leadership to a revolutionary movement's seizure of power.

A social movement's commitment to change and the basis of organisation are founded upon the conscious volition, normative commitment to the movement's aims or beliefs and active participation on the part of the followers or members. This particular characterisation of social movement in terms of volition and normative commitment is endorsed by something approaching a consensus among leading scholars in this field. It is the conscious volition of individuals, acting collectively that brings about the embodiment of ideologies in social movements (Paul, 1971).

Conceptualising Social Movements

Over the years sociology and social anthropology of social movements have been involved with some key conceptual problems. Some recurring areas are:

- Definition and classification involves, to begin with, identification of the core features of a movement. These have been said to include, for instance, sustained collective mobilisation, orientation towards partial or total change or counter attempts to maintain status quo. Classification of social movements has most often been conceptualised around the consequences of a movement such as reform, transformation, revolution. However, the locus of a movement provides another criterion of classification. On this account movements may be classified into linguistic, religious, sectarian, caste etc.
- There has been emergence of theories, questioning the structural conditions under which movements have taken place. Some of the better known theories in this region have been those of relative deprivation, strain and revitalisation. While Merton developed relative deprivation in relation to reference group theory to analyse social mobility, conflict theorists contributed to the understanding that dissatisfaction with the status quo is not determined by absolute conditions. Gurr (1971) introduced several classifications in the concept of relative deprivation. According to him relative deprivation implied a discrepancy between expectations and perceived capabilities involving economic conditions, political power and social status. The structural conditions of relative deprivation provide the necessary conditions or the generation of a movement.
- Strain theory propounded by Smelser (1962) treats structural strain as the underlying factor leading to collective mobilisation. Strain is considered as the impairment of relations among parts of a system leading to malfunctioning of the system. Revitalisation theorists like Wallace posit on

the other hand that social movements develop out of a deliberate organised and conscious effort of members of a society to construct a more satisfying culture. Ideology or the strong value base that sustains the solidarity of participants by way of non-material rewards is a relatively recent addition to social movement theorization. It is considered to be an important marker of a social movement.

- Collective mobilisation is a crucial component in the study of social movement; it is not only related to ideology but to the nature of leadership and organisation. Collective mobilisation becomes spontaneous if the leadership is charismatic. But there are social movements which are characterised by collective leadership with a division of labour among different types of elites. While business elites support the movement financially, the political elite take the charge of leadership. The intellectual elite are drafted to formulate the ideology and spread the message. Collective mobilisation becomes diversified depending upon the talents of the participants of the movement. Any social movement tends to develop an event structure over a period of time. A past event influences the choice of strategy in the events to be followed. A set of event centred around an issue constitutes a phase and the course of a movement consists of several phases. And it is necessary to identify these events and phases to analyse the particular course of the movement.
- Social scientists have shown increasing interest in the study of social movements and their linkages with social change. Social movements are becoming a matter of increasing concern for general public administrators and are looked at with concern by policy makers; social change can take place independently of social movement (Mukherji, 1977).

Components of Movements

Objective, ideology, programmes, leadership and organisation are important components of social movements. They are interdependent and influence each other. The objectives of the movement change from narrow, particular local issues to broad aims for social transformation (Shah, 2001).

Sometimes a movement which begins with broad objectives may in the process get narrowed down to one or two particular issues. Ideology also undergoes change. It provides direction for evolving strategies and programmes and also keeps the participants together by developing feeling of we-ness. The various strategies and programmes are evolved to mobilise the people. They sustain the movement for a long period. Leadership which initiates or emerges in the course of the growth of the movement plays a crucial role in articulating the ideology and objectives, evolving strategies and programmes and maintaining the spirit of the participants. Neither of these components are apriority and static. They evolve; they get changed in the course of the movement. They are in a rudimentary form in some movements and well developed in others. Though all these components are found in all type of movements or 'insurgencies', including the so called 'spontaneous' rebellions, their forms differ from unstructured to well organised (Guha, 1983).

Social movement has to be distinguished from the collective behaviour that usually takes the form of crowd behaviour, mob action, riot and panic. The phenomenon of collective behaviour may range from responses to the disaster, the disorderly street mob or radical social upheaval to the peaceful shift in the orientations of individuals and small groups. Whenever any custom which is conventionally and officially accepted fails to take account of or runs counter to deeply felt sentiments or common perception of reality, people create a current of agitation by their actions. The collective behaviour is a problem solving activity rather than structural, social action. The phenomenon of collective behaviour very often remains confined to a particular society though it might give rise to a chain of reactions at another place. But it is not as widespread as social movement. It is the behaviour of the participants that is never determined by prior expectations with the position they occupy in stable social structure. So collective behaviour is ubiquitous which causes tentative disruptions but introduces certain modifications in the social structure.

The collective behaviour occurs sometimes in complete isolation or sometimes it is part of an offshoot of a wider social movement. A social movement is very often preceded by collective behaviour against the established social order. The experiences in collective behaviour can be related to a conversion process, since it may produce new image (ideological commitment) or new groupings out of which social movement grows. Collective actions which follow the path of acquiescence for social mobility and change in status are not treated as 'social movement'. The action which is legally permitted and widely accepted as binding in society or part of society at a given point of time is institutionalised action. Such actions include petitioning, voting in elections, and fighting legal battles in court of law. Sometimes these methods are accompanied by other collective actions and used as tactics. Such mobilisation though can be treated as a social movement; the anthology is largely confined to the direct actions of a group of people (Shah, 2001). Non-institutionalised collective action takes several forms such as protest, agitation, strike, satyagraha, hartal, gherao, and riot. Agitations, protests, strikes, and riots are often but not always part of a social movement of a particular structure of society. Some collective actions are often labelled by authorities as riots but they are more often than not a part of ongoing movements.

In terms of the criterion of leadership there are millenarian, messianic and chiliastic social movements. In a post-industrialised and globalised society traditional groups and institutions have lost control over loyalties and behaviour of the individuals. The weakening of primary group attachment and the impersonal character of large scale organisation alienate men from the source. Such alienated people are easily mobilised around charismatic qualities and symbolic goals (Gusfield, 1971). The term millenarian is now used not in its specific and limited historical sense but typologically to characterise religious movements which emphasise immanent, total, ultimate world and collective salvation.

The social movement strives to bring about entirely new socio-economic and political order. To justify their aims, social movements develop an elaborate and a consistent set of ideas which its members must accept uncritically. It is a foundation of group cohesion and solidarity. Founders of modern socialism Karl Marx, Engels as well as conservative advocate of social reform Lonez Von Sten deserve a credit for having demonstrated that ideology is linked with social situation of certain classes expressing the socio-political interests or needs of these classes; and if they are not linked in this way to the actual social situation of certain classes expressing the socio-political interests then the idea will remain without practical effect (Rudolf, 1960). Ideology codifies and recognises beliefs, myths and outlooks and directs responses to specific social situation. It is not only a framework of consciousness but also a source of legitimising actions. The formulation of ideology is an important aspect of any social movement. It provides the source of legitimisation of new values, norms, institutions and relationships envisaged by the leaders. It provides the basis of interest articles and for establishing new identities. Social movement therefore must develop sooner or later a comprehensive ideology and theory which should be convincing to the movement of participants. Such an ideology, therefore attempts 'to justify their aims, typically resort to abstract principles concerning the nature of man, his destination and his natural rights in combination with a critique of the existing economic, political and cultural institutions. The ideas of liberty and equality are common to all of the social movements and sometimes it is combination with the idea of national unity and independence' (Mukherji, 1977). It is this ideology that gives directionality to change by specifying the proximate and ultimate goals. The arrangement of such goals in temporal priority enables the formulation of long term strategies, programmes and tactics. Social movement ideology is usually formulated by the leadership and often in abstract terms but it is a necessary input which provides the requisite passion to the rank and file which finally culminates into collective actions. And this ideological vision of the leadership needs to be translated into problem oriented, issue centred programmes taking into account the existential conditions of the specific social category which is sought to be mobilised into collective actions. The success of a movement largely depends on the perception by participants of the organic links between the ideology and programmes of the movement (Oommen, 1982).

Typology of Social Movement

The literature on social movements abounds with typologies or classification which is made in terms of various criteria which range from being purely descriptive in nature to those which have been deduced from a body of theory. The locus of the movements is a criterion of social movements. On this count social movement may be classified into linguistic, religious, secular, sectarian, caste, peasant, workers, tribal, ethnic, feministic etc. Scale and spatial spread is also a criterion in terms of which it may be classified into national, regional and local social movement (Singh, 1988).

The most important criterion of the classification is that of consequences of the social movement and its orientation to the crusting culture and society. On this basis the movement may be reactionary, conservative, reversionary or reformative, transformative, revolutionary, nativity and revivalist (Shah, 2001). When social movements' advance aims at bringing back the 'good old days' they are called revival. Movements have also been classified on the basis of structural changes, reformist, transformative and revolutionary (Rao, 1948). Reform movements bring about partial changes in the value system; transformative movements aim at effecting middle level structural changes; and the objective of revolutionary movements is to bring about radical changes in the totality of social and cultural systems. These movements also vary in terms of conflicts embedded in them. Conflict is the least in reform movement; it acquires a sharper focus in transformative movements; and in the case of revolutionary movements conflict is based on the Marxist ideology of class struggle. Movements have also been classified on the quality of change like accumulative, alternative and transformative (Mukherji, 1977). While accumulative changes are intra-systemic, alternative and transformative are systemic changes. Alternative change is geared to create new structures while transforming change seeks to replace the existing structure and substituting it by another Mukherji (1977) distinguished between the natures of change they pursue. Thus 'any collective mobilisation for action directed explicitly towards an alternation or transformation of the structure of a system, or against an explicit threat to an alteration or transformation of a system, can be understood as a social movement. Collective mobilisations aimed at changes within a system are quasi-movements. Conflict over specific issues which mobilise support of 'existing groups' through legitimate institutional structures and are able to pressure the system describe the behaviour of quasi movements. Collective mobilisation aimed at wide ranging and far reaching changes in the major institutional system is a revolutionary movement'. A revolutionary movement may encompass a variety of social movements and quasi-movements. A social movement likewise may give rise to a variety of quasi movements and quasi-movements may have a variety of manifestations. Each of these developments gives rise to the emergence of three distinct types of movements: charismatic, ideological and organisational. Such a typology doesn't insist that the movements are necessarily oriented to change. They may not only lead to system stability but in fact pursue it as a goal. It recognises that even if all movements are change oriented from the point of departure of the system state, some of the movements may be stability oriented from the perspective of the point of distinction.

Apart from these attempts to evolve general typologies of movements there have been a few efforts to categorise movements among one or other social collectivities like tribes, peasants, caste etc. Social movements are also classified on the basis of issues around which participants get mobilised. In terms of the space, structure and agency, a movement has the probability of becoming local or regional. The regional movements emerge and grow out of the specific conditions of a region. Regional movements are more or less confined to a definite area and emerge due to the local conditions (Puri, et al., 2000).

Approaches About Social Movement

Theoretical perspectives on social movement have approached the issues of social mobilisation and collective action from different entry points. Various strands of thought related to social movements are to be found in the Marxist approach, Neo-Marxist approaches, structural functional approach, political Process approach and resource mobilisation approach. Under various conceptual categories such as 'social mobilisation', 'collective action', 'community solidarity', 'collective behaviour' etc. notwithstanding the conceptual disagreements implicit in various approaches there lies at the bottom, a common thread running through these in terms of a commonly shared understanding of interests among the participants and the large socio-economic forces operating at the macro level (mainly emphasised by modernisation theorist under the conceptual construct, 'social change'). Among various theoretical perspectives there is a kind of consensus that social movements are manifestations of collective aspiration to social change. There are disagreements as to how a social movement is best defined and what might distinguish it from a political party or pressure group, whether it is to be seen in terms of an attempt to transform cultural patterns or merely as another actor in institutional politics. Social movements can be distinguished from other collective actions in that they have mass mobilisation and collective action as prime sources of social sanction and power (Scott, 1990).

At the heart of collective mobilisation are the interest of social groups which get mobilised and their positions in the societal alliance influencing the allocation of values. In this perspective social movement can be seen as a collective attempt to advance or defend common goals through collective action and mass mobilisation. Most social theorists agree that social movements as a mover of collective action involves a social relationship which got manifested in classical workers movements, students, civil rights movements and of late New Social Movements of post industrial age.

According to Marxist approach the causes of social movement are located in the economic structure of society and the antagonistic interests between the propertied and labour classes are inherent in a class based society which generates contradictions. The former used the coercive power of the state including religion, education and mass media to impose their ideology on society and control the exploited classes. The latter resist, protest and occasionally revolt or launch organised and collective action against the dominance of the propertied classes. Their effort is to bring about revolutionary political change by overthrowing the dominant classes in power. According to Marxist scholars members of the same class have common consciousness regarding their position in society and the common interests they share. This facilitates their collective action against the ruling classes and state, demanding a qualitative shift in the present state of affairs. Revolutionary would be an extreme mode to bring in this change (Chaterjee, 1985). There is a great deal of variation amongst the non-Marxist scholars, in their approach towards analysing social movements. The ideological positions regarding a need for social and political change and the role of movements therein differ. It is argued by some scholars that the mass movements are the product of mass societies which are extremist and anti-democratic.

Structural functional approach views change in terms of structural differentiation, reintegration and adaptation. According to this sequential model of change, a movement may appear in any one of the stage. Emergence of specialised and autonomous units, elaboration of division of labour and intensification of role specialisation relieve consideration, stresses and strain in the system which renders one or another social category socially deprived which in turn may inspire movements. But these movements are viewed as temporary aberrations, pathological, indicative of transient anomies, movements that are incapable of effecting long term and on-going processes of change because specialisation permits maximum control over the environment by assuming more effective roles and creating more efficient units. Whereas the Marxist traditions characterised the quest for social change, by means of collective action as a positive and unavoidable feature, the structural functional approach would consider any such collective mobilisation as pathological, undesirable, disequilbrating and harmful for the societal well being. If the Marxist tradition aimed at superseding the existing social arrangement, the concern of structural functional approach was to maintain status quo by means of preserving the equilibrium of existing arrangement of social organisation. In a functional system, conflict and change are values no more desired and rather are deviants. Collective behaviour outside the domain of conventional modes of participation thus came to be treated as a challenge to the established order. Structural functional tradition sought to replace conflict as the essential feature of social life with an alternative model based on 'consensus' and such an explanation of collective action and popular mobilisation based on 'consensus' or equilibrium model or social organisation was extended by various social scientists. Coming to their individual arguments Korn Hauser (1959) postulated a mass society comprising of 'atomised individuals' consequent upon rapid social changes. Such atomised individuals in modern societies, devoid of all primordial societal bonds, uprooted from the traditional social organisation are according to him, most prone to participate in current spate of protests and social mobilisations.

Neil Smelser (1962) observed in the strains theory that the strain on any part of the whole system results in malfunction of the existing relationship among its various parts. He uses the term deprivation to describe ambiguity in the allocation of economic resources as well as resources of power and status. The cause of deprivation leads to revolutionary activities. There are also structural strains apart from deprivation leading to social movements. He counts six necessary conditions for the development – structural conduciveness, structural strains, growth of a generalised belief, precipitating events, mobilisation of participants for action, and social control mechanism. He visualises social movements as inherently irrational and weak rather than as articulating new vision for future.

Eisentadt (1966) seeks to explain the phenomenon of social movements as a consequence of structural strains in the social system brought about by the process of modernisation. For him modernisation is both the cause and consequence of social change. Modernisation undermines traditional sources of political authority and creates new bases of political association and new political institutions. The process of modernisation creates a gap between the degree of mobilisation and the capacity of political institutions to absorb the demands of new mobilised groups (Deutsch, 1961). Links of the phenomenon of social mobilisation is to be the issues of political development. Like other modernisation theorists he also visualizes social mobilisation as a process in which major clusters of old social, economic and psychological commitments get eroded or broken down and people become available for new patterns of socialisation and behaviour. This theorisation also postulates the uprooting or breaking away of old settings, habits and commitments followed by the induction of mobilised persons into some relatively stable patterns of group membership, organisations and commitment. For him social mobilisation coming in the wake of modernisation would broaden the politically relevant state of the population. Thus, these scholars are in favour of excluding the masses from day to day participation in politics which hampers the efficient functioning of the government.

The Indian scholars who approved of the agitations against foreign rule for independence did not approve of them in the post-independence period, particularly in the 1950s and 1960s. They condemned them outright as dangerous and dysfunctional for civilised society. Though some others don't favour revolutionary change in the political and economic structure, they advocate political change which is confined to change in government and political institutions.

Social psychological theorists on the other hand have explained the social mobilisations not through the structural stresses and strains but by the means of subjectively felt conditions of relative deprivation arising out of a distinct shortfall between the growing expectations of various social groups and its fulfilment. This approach in a way reversed the Marxian tradition that increasing misery and poverty will eventually create objective conditions for a revolutionary outburst. Socio-psychological approach gives precedence to the subjective feelings and perception of the participating individuals over structural, objective and historical logic preferred by Marxian tradition. T. Gurr (1971) claims that relative deprivation is the basic condition or civil strife of any kind. For him deprivation is primarily psychological, therefore, he doesn't deal with the socio-economic structure. The psychological dimension of the participants is important but not sufficient. He operationalised relative deprivation as the perceived discrepancy between men's value expectations and value capabilities. This approach considers relative deprivation as the causal factor behind various kinds of protests and mobilisation with varied degrees of intensity ranging from small scale mobilisation to the revolutionary mode.

The decade of sixties can be taken as a watershed in theorisation on social movements. In the large scale social mobilisation during the decade from the students' movements, Black Civil Rights Movements, Peace Movements, anti-war demonstration etc. made social science practitioners realise that their conceptual tools were inadequate to deal with this transformed reality. This was the decade when the western social scientists had predicted an end to the ideological conflicts and more pluralist and pragmatic consensus to emerge. All theoretical reflections weren't equipped enough to grapple with this newly found enthusiasm towards popular protest and mobilisation. Neither Marxists with their concern to define the precondition of revolution by examining the structural contradictions of the capitalist system nor the American structural functionalism with its focus on integrative mechanisms of institutional collective behaviour could explain adequately these mobilisations, protests and social movements. The events of sixties resulted in a more specific and direct theorisation. A more direct effort was made by the social science theorists to understand and explain this newly found social reality which was contrary to earlier effort that addressed the issue rather historically treating the social system as a single unified, homogenous and absolute whole.

Theoretical paradigms which were developed in the wake of the development of sixties are Resource Mobilisation Approach, Political Process Approach and Identity Oriented Approach. Resource mobilisation approach on collective action goes into the organisational dynamics of social movements by focusing on various kinds of mobilising structures, networks and organisations through which groups seek to organise themselves into social movement (Zald and Carthy, 1996). It sought to focus on mobilisation processes and on the formal organisational manifestation of these processes. Thus, social movements came to be characterised in terms of opportunities, strategies, moves of organisation, sophisticated organisational forms, competition with groups, and authorities having opposing interests. Social mobilisation phenomenon in resource mobilisation approach was seen as based on strategic instrumental reasoning, cost benefit calculation and rationally determined interests.

Another theoretical paradigm on social mobilisation which ascribes supreme importance to organisational dynamics of social movements is political dynamics of social movements. This political process approach places the pattern of social mobilisation within the large political context of a society and seeks to explain the phenomenon of protest in a cross cultural comparative perspective on the basis of degree of acceptability of the culture of protest by the political regime of the day. Unlike modernisation theorists who portrayed the phenomenon of social movements as an indirect consequence of social change, these scholars linked it up to the changing face of power equation in the wake of modernisation or social change process. Thus, the argument of political process theorists goes against the classical theories of collective action such as theory of mass society, relative deprivation which stress on direct links between social change and social movement. Political opportunity structure implies those signals to socio-political actors which encourage them to use their internal resources to form social movements. The idea implicit behind this theorisation was to explain the vacations in the degrees and patterns of social mobilisation in different national political contexts. In a way the political process approach was also an effort to establish a causal link between the institutionalised, political and social movements. Change in the institutional structure or informal power relations of given national political system is treated as an important factor influencing social mobilisation. Underlying conviction of this approach is that social mobilisation and collective behaviour are shaped by the broader set of political constraints and opportunities unique to the national context in which they are embedded.

Identity oriented approach focuses on substantive objective of social mobilisation and not merely on organisation. The key question is how social movements produce new historic identities for society. What is important in this approach is its emphasis on the normative character of movements and their capacity to effect cultural change like the invention of new norms, institutions and social practices in their struggle to redefine social identity. This concern with the norms and identity over organisation and the pragmatic context led many scholars to ignore the elements of calculation and self interest that are focus of resource mobilisation approach. Social movement for them is organised collective behaviour of a class actor against his class adversary for the social control of historicity in a concrete community. Social movement is perceived as an action directed towards predetermined ends. Social movements are not generated spontaneously and rather are results of the structure in which group action moves, providing at the same time identity to the group. In this context new social movements are conceived as potential bearers of new social interests in a new historical era termed as 'Post Industrial' society. Social movements are characterised as principle agents of social transformation generating cultural space. These new social movements are a specific type of social mobilisation in response to new types of challenges peculiar to modern day societies. Scholars of new social movements agreed that conflict among the industrial class is of decreasing relevance and that representation of movements as largely homogenous products is no longer feasible. However, there were differences in emphasis of the relations to the possibility of identifying the new central conflict which would characterise the model of the emerging society defined as post-industrial, technocratic or programmed. Alain Touraine (1971), an influential exponent of this approach holds that social movements are the central forces fighting one against the other to control the production of society by itself and the action of classes for the shaping of historicity. In the industrial society the ruling class and popular class oppose each other as they did in the agrarian and the merchantile societies and as they will do in the programme society where new social classes will replace capitalists and the working class as the central actors of the conflict. In 1980s this approach was emphasised by Clause in whose view movements develop a fundamental, meta-political critique of the social order and of representative democracy, challenging institutional assumptions. Among the principal innovations of the new movements, in contrast with workers' movements is a critical ideology in relation to modernism and progress; decentralised and participatory organisational structure, defense of interpersonal solidarity against the great bureaucracies. New social movements are characterised by an open fluid organisation, an inclusive and non-ideological participation and greater attention to social and economic transformation.

Another contribution to the definition of the characteristics of new movements has been made by Alberto Melucci (1989), who asserts that the new social movements try to oppose the instruction of the state and the market into social life, reclaiming the individuals' identity and the right to determine his or her private affective life. New social movements don't limit themselves to seeking material gain but challenge the diffused notion of politics and of society themselves.

Thus the new social movements today are what must mobilise people in pursuit of common concerns. Far more than classical worker's movements, these social movements motivate and mobilise hundreds of millions of people in all parts of the world mostly outside established political and social institutions that people find inadequate to their needs (Porta and Mario, 1991). This popular movement is manifest in identity seeking and responsive mobilisation or social movement with little or no membership ties. The ecological/green movement and the peace movements can be termed new. They respond to social needs which have been more recently generated by world development.

Despite variations in the analytic plane in which these approaches have tried to examine single social reality (collective action), there seems a unifying theme in all these theoretical traditions as these all presume 'social movement' as a consequence as well as cause of a social process namely social change. While neo-Marxist tradition highlighted the super-structure based relationship and the dynamic relationship between the relations and forces of production bringing in its wake a social change which would define the mass mobilisation for socialist revolution; structural functional tradition on the other hand highlighted the societal change due to modernisation bringing certain structural deficiencies giving rise to mass mobilisation. Modern approaches on the other hand illuminated different aspects of mass mobilisation vs. organisational culture, psychological and political aspects. If resource mobilisation approach confines itself to the issue of organisation and institutions (instrumental aspects of social mobilisation), the political process approach on the other hand focuses on the political context of social movements. Identity approach brought back the entire debate to the realm of perceptions, traditions and commonality of experiences. It goes into the cultural bedrock of collective behaviour and brings to the fore the issue of collective i.e. group identity. Thus identity as a perceived boundary of social categories viz. women, students, ethnic group, etc. acts as a conduct for channelising motivational sentiments into a mobilisation fact.

In a way all these approaches with their shortcomings have tried to explain the phenomenon in totality and none can claim absolute position in explaining it fully. At the same time these various approaches have brought out the importance of one component or the other of this reality.

A social movement, like an organ takes birth, develops functions and then dies. Some movements die an immature death for they failed in their move for social change. Some movements are simply started and then gradually accommodated in the existing power structure. Some movements again grow and successfully achieve their defined goals. In a nut shell, a social movement is a tight-knit collective action going through various phases. They rise, consolidate and eventually succeed, fail or change. Mauss (1975) suggested that social movements typically pass through a series of various stages. These stages are:

- *Incipiency:* It is the first stage which begins when a large number of people become frustrated about a problem and do not perceive any solution to it through existing institutions.
- *Coalescence:* At this stage groups begin to form around leaders to promote policies and to promulgate programmes. A dominant group or coalition of groups emerges that is able to establish itself in a position of leadership. It's goals become the goals of many and its actions command wide participation.
- *Institutionalisation:* It is the stage when social movements reach the peak of their strength and influence. It becomes firmly established in the formal, rational organisations that have the power to affect lasting changes in the social order.
- *Fragmentation:* It is quite possible that having achieved their goals, social movements undergo fragmentation and gradually begin to fade. Their organisational structures are longer seen as necessary because the changes they sought to bring about have been institutionalised or the changes they sought to block have been prevented.
- *Demise:* Eventually many social movements experience demise or cease to exist. The organisation they created and the institutions they introduced may well survive, however they are no longer set apart from the mainstream of the society. Transformed from social movements into institution, they leave behind well-entrenched organisations that guarantee their members the goals they sought.

What most characterised social movement is that they do their own thing in their own way. The most important thing is that social movements have to offer both to their participants/members and to others in their world their own participatory self-transforming trial and error approach and adaptability.

New Social Movement

In the contemporary social science literature, the term 'new social movement' is in vogue. It is largely West Europe-centric, derived from some of those movements there in the 60s and 70s. These movements are generally related to the issues of the post-modern society. They are not raising primarily economic issues and are not concerned with state power but these movements are basically concerned with protecting and enlarging the autonomy of civil society. These movements are not class based. They raise the issue of humanity cutting across the interests of all classes. In that sense new social movements are social and not political (Shah, 2002: 19). The new social movements are socio-cultural movements. Collectively is a major component part in NSMs. They have no formal organisational structure, hierarchy and command and are not driven by any particular ideology. These movements are based on identities and develop around specific 'issues'. The new social movement is primarily against the state.

Ramachandra Guha (1991), Gail Omvedt (1993), Poona Wignaraja and Fuentes and Frank (2002) are some of the theorists who have emphasised the relevance of new social movement from a developing countries' perspective. According to Fuentes and Frank, these new social movements are popular social movements and expressions of people's struggle against exploitation and oppression and for survival and identity in a complex dependent society. In such societies these movements are attempts at and instruments of democratic self-empowerment of people, and are organised independently from the state. Its institutions and political parties are a reflection of people's search for alternatives (Frank and Fuentes, 2002; Shah, 2002: 46). New social movements are revolutionary in aspirations and anti systemic in their impact. They are oriented as single issue efforts to bring about change. These are 'social movements' in the sense of having a broad overall organisational structure and ideology aiming at social change. They have a new ideology which is characterised by the use of non-Marxist concepts of exploitation and oppression appropriation by the state from peasants through the market and a corresponding rejection of class, class politics and ideology together with the vanguard role of the urban working class and political parties. These are movements of socio-economic categories such as exploited by traditional working (Omvedt, 1993: xv–xvi).

The emergence of the new social movements or micro-struggles or people's movement is understood and explained in various ways in the background of the failure of the established socio-political institutions to deliver and decline of other social movements. People are looked upon as powerful, autonomous expressions of popular dissent. These movements are seen as more flexible and open in nature, which makes it possible for them to address multi-dimensional injustice. The loose organisational network of the people's movement contributes to their positive potential. Thus, these movements are seen as helpful in the further democratisation of the polity and that is enriching the agenda of social transformation (Deshpande, 2004: 379–409).

New Social Movement in India

The new social movements are 'new' themselves. They are 'new' because these movements were either ignored as exploited by traditional Marxism (women, dalits, shudras and tribals) or were exploited in ways related to the new processes of contemporary capitalism (peasants forced to produce for capital through market exploitation managed by the state, peasants and forest dwellers (tribal) victimised by environmental degradation).

What makes the new social movements 'new' is not simply because they represent social groups/sections or are oppressed and exploited in new ways by the processes of world capital system, but because they are verging towards a new or alternative path of development (Omvedt, 1998: 238). They are challenging the states' indicators of growth and asserting liveability, sustainability and equality as new parameters of development. This new discourse of development has important implications for the development paradigm in the knowledge society. The state claims for the new social movements express a sustained critique of the ideology of development (Paraguli, 2001: 258–285). The post-industrial society produces a condition for people to rise up its defense of human rights for the question of social justice. New social movements emerge only on specific issues, as for instance the big mobilisation for peace, protection of environment, protection of human rights etc.

In the 1960s and 1970s European and American societies witnessed the emergence of this new social movement around issues which were basically humanist, cultural and non-materialistic in nature. The goals and values of these movements were essentially universalistic (Singh, 2001: 96). The seventies also saw a number of grassroots, micro-movements in India, such as dalit movements, movements for civil liberties and democratic right, women's movement, environmental movements and various movements of religious and ethnic minorities. The nature of these movements is different from that of the earlier movements. Most of the new social movements are defined by their non-class, non-materialistic focus and emphasis (Singh, 2001: 101). Societies moved from the industrial societies to post-industrial society, modern society to post-modern society and it has led to the change in the nature of social movement i.e. from old to new social movement. The emergence of new social movements in India deals with the form and styles of their mobilisation, the type of claims they stake, and the issues they have come to respond to including the justification of their 'newness' in the contemporary setting of the Indian society. That it relates to the emerging 'representation' of Indian society has come to be characterised by the emergence of an aggressive and restless consciousness of people about their 'right', their 'claims', and their stake of the resources of the nation on the one hand, and on the other, by the growing awareness of their abilities to collectively contest, compete and even to enter into conflict, and confrontation, against the state of adversary (Singh, 2001: 192–193). The phase of the 'new social movements' is in vogue in the contemporary discourse among social scientists and social activists. They use the term for these movements which is 'new', such as women's movements, environmental movements, identity, peace movements are the result of the issues of the 'post-modern' society (Singh, 2001). These movements are not class based and they do not raise economic issues, nor are they concerned with state power. They raise the issues of humanity cutting across the interests of all classes. In that sense the new social movement is social movement and not political movement (Shah, 2004: 23).

The state and its apparatuses have failed to deliver their promises, these resulting in a strong disenchantment with the system. The policy of development followed by the state resulted in development for the few and impoverishment for many. The state's developments have led to the annihilation of tribal people through displacement and livelihood and tampering with their culture. New social movements therefore, emerged to provide the conceptual critiques of development and modernisation.

The new social movements are non-class and non-materialistic in focus. They radically alter the Marxist paradigm of explaining conflicts and contradiction in terms of class and class conflicts. To Marxian analysis, all forms of struggle are called as class struggles and all forms of human groupings as class groupings. Many contemporary struggles such as anti-racism, disarmament, the feminist movement and environmentalism are not class struggle, nor do they reflect a movement of classes. Their groupings are beyond class. The new social movements are trans-national movements. These movements articulate, project and struggle for human issues and for issues relating to the very condition of human existence. Their conception of conflict and tension are international. For example new social movements seek answer to questions related to peace, disarmament, nuclear pollution, and nuclear war relating to the defense of the planet (the earth), the ecology, environment and human rights. New social movements generally evolve a grassroots politics, grassroots action, that often initiate micro movements of small groups, targeting localised issues with a limited institutional base. These movements are anti-systemic in character. The new social movements are making a bid for direct participation (Omvedt, 223–240).

Ideologically, new social movements are profoundly different from the Marxist perception of ideology as a unifying and totalising element for collective action. New social movements exhibit a multitude of ideas and values. New social movements often involve the emergence of new dimensions of identity. The grievances are based on a set of beliefs, symbols, values and meaning, rather than on the economic grievances that characterise the working class movements. Many contemporary movements are 'acted out' in individual actions rather than through or among mobilised groups. The movements become the focus for the individual definition of him or her and action within the movements is a complex mix of the collective and individual confirmation of identity.

New social movements often involve personal and intimate aspects of human life e.g. what we eat, wear and enjoy. There is disdain on behalf of new social movements for conventional politics. Consequently new social movements maintain elements of autonomy from traditional mass parties. New social movements seem to be segmented, diffused and decentralised. There is a tendency toward considerable local autonomy of local section (Larana, Johnston and Gusfield, 1998: 61).

Environmental Movement

Environmental protest movements are within the fold of 'new social movement' in India. However, strictly speaking environment movements are more organised form of social movements for saving environment and survival of people in it. They are relatively recent in time and space. They emerged as a critique of the dominant development paradigms' popularity. The environmental movement reflects people's struggles and significant protest against the western model of development or modernisation. The victims of this model of development want to wage on organised social activity consciously directed towards sustainable use of natural resources (Seth, 1976: 178–179). Article 21 the right to life includes the right to live with dignity and Article 48A Protection and improvement of environment and safeguarding of forests and wildlife says the Constitution of India.

In 1976 under the leadership of Jayprakash Narayan, the People's Union for Civil Liberties and People's Union for Democratic Right (PUCL and PUDR) come into existence. The PUCL divides civil rights and democratic rights and generally does not take up the latter. The PUDR on the other hand believes that social, economic and political rights cannot be separated and they are needed to support the movements which undertake social and economic issues of the oppressed classes. The PUDR believes that the struggle for civil liberties is part and parcel of the entire struggle of the oppressed for a better life (Shah, 2004: 246).

Environmental Movement in India

The development of 'green politics' or 'eco-greens' or the 'green movement' in Germany and North America in the early 1980s boosted the formation of the 'green network' and the 'green movement' throughout the world, including India. The struggles of the people on the issues of their livelihood and access to forest and other natural resources are coined as environmental movements (Shah, 2004: 250). The centre for science and environment provide valuable material not only on various aspects of the environment but also people's protest and struggles for their life and right to livelihood. The rural communities scratch the earth and depend on rain for growing their own food, gather wood or dung and food for cooking purpose. They build their own huts with bamboo sticks and draw their sustenance from nature. Such people depend on the environment and on their own habitat to meet their material needs. The poor rural as well as the tribal communities are under the pressure of modernisation, technological innovation and development project in the contemporary society. For example industries, dams and mining have been physically displaced. Similarly millions of forest dwellers, tribals, dalits and peasant since independence of India have been thrown out from their habitat regarding them not only powerless but without food and occupation as well.

In India the western developmental model was put into force after India gained independence. The necessity of modern technological innovations and the promotion of development of capital sought to increase the country's capital output, expand the provision of basic needs including education, health facilities, piped water supply, electricity and within a short time develop the economy to match with the west (Banuri, 1990). Environmental protest movements in India directly address the particular problem. The first major environmental protest movement in India in the recent time was the 'Chipko Movement' in the Garhwal Himalayas, which made public conscious about the space of nature in the life of the local people and the disastrous consequences of the efforts to conquer that space. It provides the platform for discussion of the harmful effects of technological intrusion into the environment, which in the process tramples over thousands of people whose lives revolve around the environment. Several different movements in other parts of the country followed by 'Chipko Movement', 'Narmada Bachao Andolan' etc. have entered the environmental debate in the public space in India. National and international attention was directed to these movements and the discussion of concern for protecting the environment for future sustenance of human life and those immediately affected by it gained form and shape.

The environmental movements are both new and different in terms of their participations, methods of interventions, issues raised by them, their impacts in the term of redress policy shifts, consciousness and the discourse they provide, which makes them significant in social mobilisation in the present times (Singh, 2001). The agitations are carried out primarily by these directly affected by the establishment of industries, dams and mines in that localities which include the rural peasant, the forest dweller, tribal and dalit communities, their women folk and son etc. It also includes the unhearing space where voluntary organisations, the media, social activists, professional, civil and human right groups or activists and academician who have created a public space that supports the movements have a functional role. Environmental movement in India attained significance not only as new social movements which focus on ecology but also as the active battlefield where a whole lot of motivated people, backed by supportive allies from different walks of life are rejecting the dominant official developmental paradigm.

Their cause is genuine and crucial for the future of not just those who are active in the struggles but of those as well who live in the protected walls of fancy homes. It is the expansive horizon of the environments which make them interesting subject for study and understanding in sociology and social anthropology. The environmental movements reflect the agony of the Third World countries, which have to face the domination of the west, which in turn shapes the unsuitable politics at home.

Some important studies focusing on the themes of the movements are the Chipko Movement (Guha, 1991) and Naramada Bachao Andolan (NBA) (Baviskar, 1995b). Both the authors, however, do not want their studies to be treated as mainly on environmental movements. But Guha called his study of peasant resistance focusing on the ecological dimension, environmental changes, use of natural resources and social protest. Baviskar (1995b) studies the tribals and their relationship with nature and their conflict over state sponsored 'development' of Madhya Pradesh (Shah, 2004). According to Guha and Gadgil the environmental movement can be defined 'as organised social activity consciously directed towards promoting sustainable use of natural resources, halting environmental degradation or bringing about environmental restoration' (Shah, 2004: 252). So that the main issues are the people-culture, livelihood and nature relationship which is central to environmental movements. In the struggles around the issues of forest resources and their use, the main participants have been the tribals and other peasant communities depending on forest resources, their livelihood, connected with natural resources for their survival.

The origin of modern environmental protest movements in India can be ascribed to the Chipko movement in the central Himalayan region in the early 1970s. Chipko movement was launched to protect the Himalayan forests from destruction. Many struggles were organised to protest against the colonial forest policy during the early decades of 20th century. People's main demand in these protests was that the benefits of the forest, especially the right to fodder, should go to local people (Bahuguna, 1990). These struggles have continued in the post-independent era as the forest policies of independent India are no different from that of the colonial ones. However, the origin of 'Chipko' (*chipak jayenge*, to hug) had taken place during the year 1973. The environmental aspects of development gave rise to numerous conflicts and protests over natural resources and ecological issues. However, despite numerous forest-based movements during the last two decades in India, there are close links between the livelihoods of the local people and the nature of the movement.

The most popular environmental movements in India, which have environmental protection as one of their objectives, relate to major dams. Among them are Tehri Dam, Silent Valley Project and Narmada Bachao Andolan, and the longest struggle among the anti-big dam protests was the opposition to Tehri Dam, being constructed on the river Bhageerathi in the Garhwal region. The Tehri Baandh Virodhi Sangarshan Samithi, committee for the struggle against the Tehri Dam founded by veteran freedom fighter Veerendra Datta Saklani, has been opposing the construction for more than a decade (Gadgil and Guha, 1994).

One of the early and complete successes of environmental movements was the abandonment of the Silent Valley hydroelectric project in Kerala. This movement was organised by the Kerala Sastra Sahitya Parishat (KSSP) in collaboration with wild life conservationists. In this project, however, there was no local people's involvement as there was no displacement of people. The movement was fought primarily on environmental grounds and mostly at the intellectual level. The major concerns of this movement were the adverse environmental impact on Silent Valley, one of the last surviving natural tropical forests in India and protecting a rare breed of monkey, lion-tailed macaque. With the active support from the international organisations like World Wildlife Fund and the International Union for the Conservation of Nature and Natural Resources the movement assumed international importance (Sethi, 1993). Though it gained popularity and coverage, the ultimate success of the movement was attributed to the then Prime Minister Mrs Indira Gandhi's desire to enhance her image among the International Conservation Community (Gadgil and Guha, 1994).

The most popular movement in the environmental history of India is Narmada Bachao Andolan. Though the movement started as early as late 1970s, along with the clearance of the project, it received momentum only during late 1980s. In fact, one of the main leaders of the movement at present like Medha Patkar has been working toward proper rehabilitation programmes for the dam displaced people. Their demands included complete stopping of the dam, resettlement and rehabilitation benefits to the oustees (Wood, 1993). These demands were aptly supported by environmentalists who oppose construction of large dams for ecological reasons. The movement, however, gained wider public attention with mobilisation and organisation of tribals and the joining of the eminent social workers like Baba Amte, Sunderlal Bahuguna and Medha Patkar.

Role of Civil Society in Environmental Movement

Environmental protest movements in India now pose a challenge to the dominant ideology of the meaning and patterns of development. They are not being guided by any particular philosophy. These movements represent a wide spectrum of groups and social activists that cut across specific regions and issues. They mobilised large number of people, organised popular protest and created new socio-political activism.

The beginning of the 1990s witnessed the emergence of many NGOs that have been working with environmental issues. Community organisations have emerged through local initiatives, which in some areas extend social traditions of protecting local rights and environment (Swain, 1997: 829). At present more than 950 Indian NGOs are exclusively devoted to environmental issues

(Peritore, 1993: 807). The environmental movement has been viewed as essentially action by the marginalised poor to protect environmental means of livelihood and substance of environmental resources such as land, water and forests that constitute the material basis of the production.

Therefore, environmental movements in India are not necessarily for the 'green' or 'clean' earth or for saving mankind's heritage and endangered species as in the west, but are related with the very survival of the local poor (Reddy, 1998: 685–695). So the environmental movements have focused on the 'issues of livelihood'. The ecological movements are based on the need to protect nature and the need to strengthen people's collective rights to common resources. The environmental movement in India has essentially emerged as a response to a wide spectrum of struggles and conflicts over the use of natural resources and social justice issues and human rights.

The specific development projects against which sustained movements have been launched by the environmentalist include dams, power projects, industrial plants, and mining. The Silent Valley movement in Kerala has been the harbinger in the environmental uprisings against the large dams in the country (Panda, 2005). The 'Narmada Bachao Andolan' against the multi hydropower project covering central and western part of India and against the Tehri dam in the North are the well-known and relatively recent examples of anti-dam movements. The movements against the dams and power projects are mostly localised agitation.

Regarding mining, the long battle between on the one hand mine owners and state as well as Central government and, on the other hand the local people, stone extractions in Doon Valley was fought in the Supreme Court of India. The Gandhamardhan Protection Youth Council (GPYC) in Odisha is fighting against the Bharatiya Aluminum Company's (BALCO) bauxite mine project in Odisha. The PSSP Kashipur has been protesting against the mining companies (UAIL, L&T and Aditya Birla groups) in Kashipur of Odisha. The environmental movement was against the Missile Test Range at Baliapal, the protest movement against Gopalpur steel plant and the Chilika Bachao Andolan in Odisha. In the Bionashankar region of Maharashtra people have taken up the issue of displacement due to declaration of certain areas as national parks or as world life sanctuaries. The Himachal Bachao Andolan is an example of recent environmental movement related to tourism in India and we have seen that the other parts of country like Kerala, Tamil Nadu etc. are fighting against the grading commercialisation of sharing and prawn cultivation.

Summary of the Chapter

This chapter underlines a theoretical explanation on origin and development of social movement and how social movement transmitted into new social movement. Though the concept of social movement is western in origin, concept and nature, its use is not unvarying in the context of social movement in India. Social movement in India emerged as a crusade against imperialism and colonialism. But in the post-independent India it is understood as a mechanism to nip exploitable nature of the state in the bud.

However, to comprehend the social movement in a more lucid manner, this chapter delineates on different approaches in this regard: Marxist approach, structural-functional approach, Johnson's value consensus approach, Smelser's strain theory, and Eisentadt's modernisation theory.

In addition to the abovementioned explanation, new social movement emerged with broadening the nature, scope and content of social movement. Unlike social movement, new social movement is universal, overarching, non-class, and non-materialistic in nature. Nevertheless, environmental movement is the preeminent of new social movement because it is the matter of livelihood security and sustainability. The burgeoning marketisation and commodification of mining and forest areas has virtually jeopardised the tribal culture, its identity, forest rights and ultimately their livelihood and security.

3

Background of Environmental Movements in Odisha

This chapter seeks to discuss various environmental protest movements in Odisha. The chapter also highlights the situation of the other development projects in Odisha. Since focus of my thesis is on new social movements in general and environmental movement in particular, this chapter will discuss environmental movements in relation to the issues of livelihood in Odisha.

Most of the rural poor people in India depend directly or indirectly on the land, water, forest, other natural resources and environment for their livelihood. Anti-dam and anti-mining movements in India have a long history. Since the last three decades, several anti-dam and anti-mining struggles have posed a major challenge to the Government of India. The first struggle against the construction of a dam was fought in early 1920s by peasants of western Maharashtra. Under the leadership of Senapati Bapat, they opposed the Mulshi dam built by the Tatas (Vora, 2004: 23). After independence, large dams and industries were considered as symbols of India's national development. The human miseries, livelihood and ecological costs were justified in the name of development. Against this background, people's movements have raised several fundamental questions. This debate has raised myriad questions: Development at what cost? Development for whom? Whether this development is for the society as a whole or confined to only a section? How far justifiable this development is, which displaces the people, who are residing at the location since hundreds of years and now they are being compelled to be

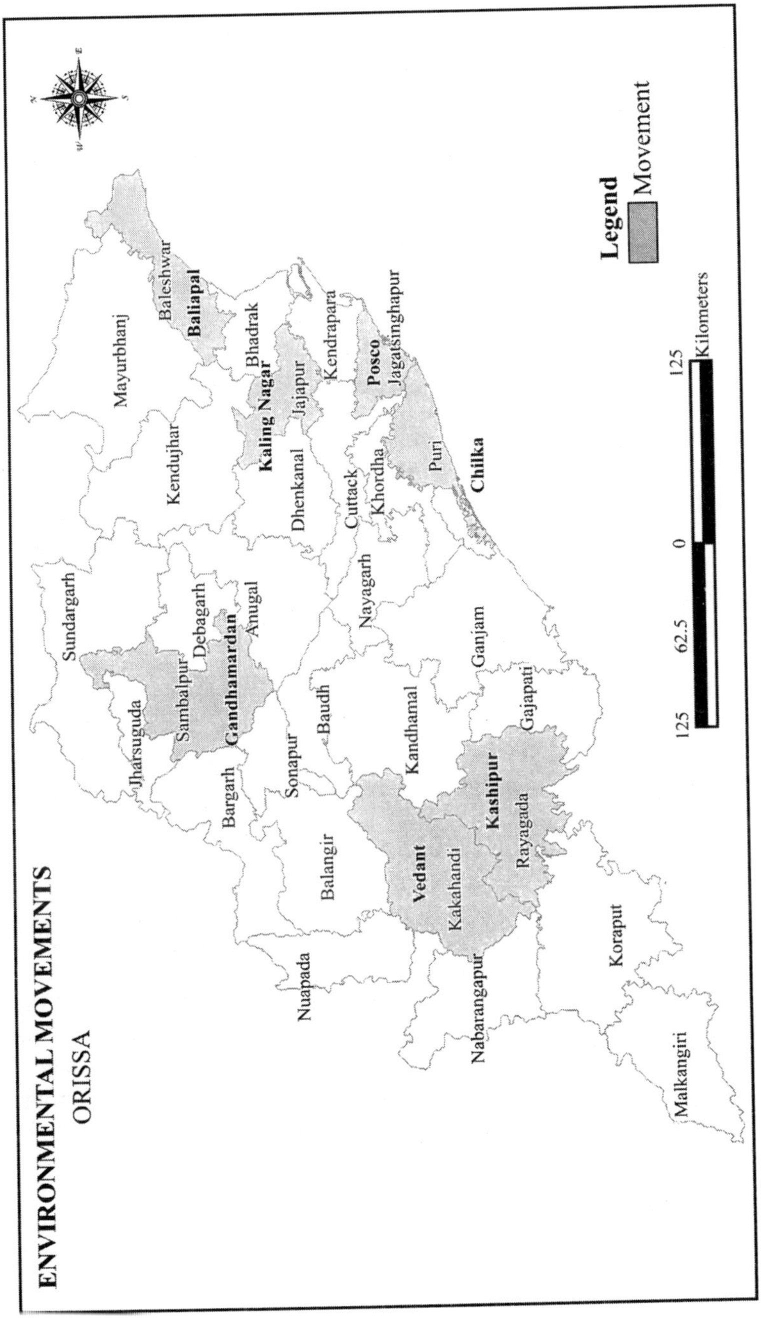
ENVIRONMENTAL MOVEMENTS
ORISSA
Legend
Movement
125
62.5
0
125
Kilometers
Mayurbhanj
Baleshwar
Baliapal
Bhadrak
Kendrapara
Jagatsinghapur
Posco
Kaling Nagar
Jajapur
Kendujhar
Dhenkanal
Cuttack
Khordha
Puri
Chilka
Sundargarh
Debagarh
Anugal
Nayagarh
Ganjam
Gandhamardan
Sambalpur
Jharsuguda
Bargarh
Sonapur
Baudh
Kandhamal
Gajapati
Kashipur
Rayagada
Vedant
Kakahandi
Balangir
Nuapada
Nabarangapur
Koraput
Malkangiri

refugees? What are the responsibilities of the government and civil society towards such ecological refugees? Various large infrastructural projects undertaken throughout the world have been questioned. Struggles against the destruction and devastation caused by large dams and industries have challenged the very basis of state's unquestioned power to take control over people's lives and resources.

Role of the politicians, planners and bureaucrats are crucial in pushing forward such developmental works, particularly, in the field of compensation disbursement to ensure people's right. The indigenous people are largely dependent upon community assets because of their traditional way of life and lack of private property. So compensation is indispensable, even though it is just a pittance for the uprooted. One observation has showed that the time gap between the distribution of compensation and the actual displacement is very high, which may be up to seven to ten years. In the mean time people consumed the amount given as compensation and when actual displacement occurs, they have hardly anything to survive, which further leads to impoverishment and miseries.

Considerable research has focused on conflict as a result of competition for scarce environmental resources and on the characteristics of competing groups (Homer and Thomas, 1995: 587–612). It has been proved beyond doubt that livelihood is the 'missing link between poverty, environmental degradation and conflict' (Richard Matthew, Mark Halle and Jason Switzer, 2002: 17). It has been identified that there are various circumstances under which loss of livelihood security leads to conflict. These circumstances are characterised by inequitable access to natural resources and unsustainable or incompatible use of that leads to scarcity and vulnerability (ibid., 390). It is important to observe the question of security when communities have no rights or only limited rights to the natural resources on which their livelihood depends. The natural resources are often located in these areas where the tribal people live. If development is the real issue behind the displacement of these indigenous people then we need to look at the definition of development. Harris and Todaro (1970: 126–142) says that development means to increase the availability and widen the distribution of basic life sustaining necessities such as food, cloth, shelter, health, and protection. Greater emphasis should be given to the humanistic and cultural values. He goes to the extent of saying that development means to expand the range of economic and social choices available to individuals and nations by freeing them from the forces of ignorance and human misery (Mahapatra, 1996: 4–6). Displacement leads to serious problems including uprooting of social and cultural life, livelihood and personality disorder.

Environmental Movements in Odisha

Odisha is one of the poorest and most backward states of India. During the 10th plan, 66 per cent of its population was below poverty line and only 10 per cent of its cultivable lands were irrigated (*India 2005*: 847). The present day Odisha is a creation of an administrative mechanism by which the coastal districts were integrated with the interior districts like Sambalpur to form a single province in 1936. Later, some other Oriya speaking princely states were added to this province. This state can historically, economically and socially be divided into two broad regions: the coastal regions and the inland districts or non-coastal districts. The former is fertile, agriculturally rich and has a high proportion of upper-caste population of Brahmins, Karans and the peasant caste of Khandayats. The inland districts on the other hand are hilly and forested with a high proportion of tribal and scheduled caste population of more than 42 per cent. Agriculture in Odisha is characterised by large landholdings, low productivity, little to no technological change, and intense fragmentation of land among the peasantry. Successive state governments have shown little imagination for changing the nature of the situation and have practised a standard development policy, that of establishing large multipurpose capital intensive projects which attempt to lessen the state's rich natural resources. All these programmes have given employment to those it has displaced by making them part of the construction industry. Later most of those who are displaced become migrants having been forced to leave the state to seek employment elsewhere. It has been the state policy to set up these development projects in the inland districts where poverty level is relatively high. These modern 'temples' such as dams (Hirakud, Upper Kolab, Machhakund, Balimela, Upper Indravati, and Rengali among others), mines based industries like in Rourkela, companies like NALCO and BALCO, and defense projects such as HAL in Koraput, the Air Force base in Charbatia and the Naval Academy at Chilika, unfortunately did not lead to spin offs of industrial development as expected by those who formulated this policy. Rather, these policies, projects have led to massive displacements, uprooting people from the land, disrupting settled agriculture based pattern of life, and the consequent destruction of environment. However, they have not implemented the rehabilitation programmes properly, so people have been pushed to survival levels. Families and individuals have been forced to migrate.

Table 3.1

Chronology of Movements in Odisha

Name of the movements	*Years*	*Against and issues*
Gandhamardan movement	1982	The Bharat Aluminum Company (BALCO) in the Gandhamardan Hills was being opposed (BALCO Hatao Andolan) by local tribal people whose life, livelihood and survival was directly under threat.
Baliapal movement	1985	The struggle against the establishment of the National Test Range (NTR), India's first missile testing project, an agricultural belt that may turn out to be the most prosperous area in Odisha.
Chilika Bachao Andolan	1990	The Integrated Shrimp Farm Project (ISFP), a joint venture of the Tata Iron and Steel Company (TISCO) and the Government of Odisha, for intensive prawn cultivation and export, posed a direct threat to the livelihood of fishing communities living around the lake.
Kashipur movement	1995-till	UAIL Project will source bauxite through open cast mining from Baphli mali of Kashipur block. The protest movement is, therefore, on the grounds of displacement and encroachment upon their forest, land and livelihood patterns.
Kalinga Nagar movement	2003-till	The major companies such as the Tatas, Visa, Jindal, Mesco and some others have already started their projects. The people complained that they were paid less and were being forced to lose their means of livelihood.
Lanjigarh movement	2004-till	The Vedanta Alumina Limited, a subsidiary of M/S Sterlite Industries (India) Limited is going to mine bauxite deposit from the Niyamgiri hills. The people's organisation was formed to protect the forest, land, water and their livelihood.
POSCO movement	2006-till	The South Korean steel major Pohang Steel Company (POSCO) and government of Odisha's establishment of steel plant and construction of captive port resulted in loss of people's livelihood.

The environmental movements are against this exploitative and the development oriented model in the state of Odisha. There have been powerful people's movements in the last two decades, like the Chilika Bachao Andolan, the Baliapal movement in Balasore district and the movements in Gandhamardan Hills in Sambalpur district. In the recent past, the people's movement against the Gopalpur steel plant, the people's agitation in Kashipur block of Rayagada district against UAIL, people's movement against the Tata steel plant in Kalinga Nagar, the Niyamgiri Surakshya movement against Vedanta and people's protest against POSCO in Jagatsingpur are prominent. Hence it is important in this context to focus on the nature and emergence of such movements, which can provide some important insights for the current topic.

The Baliapal Movement

The struggle against the establishment of the National Test Range (NTR), India's first missile testing project, in the Baliapal and Bhograi blocks of Balasore district in Odisha, popularly known as Baliapal movement, has been a significant movement. This has been termed as an 'environmental movement' since it is concerned with the appropriation of land previously used by the people and now acquired by the missile testing range (D' Monte, 1989: 18). In its search for a site for the NTR the Defense Ministry found this area, richly endowed by nature for agricultural prosperity, as best suited for pitching the project (Ravi, 1988). With the announcement of the decision, the people of the area declared they would die fighting the defence establishments.

The area of the site extends over 2 square kilometers in two blocks, a major part of it being in Baliapal (Patel, 1989: 604). The original proposal envisaged acquisition of 99 villages in Baliapal and 31 villages in Bhograi area, 609 families with a population of but the unofficial figure was one lakh (*Indian Express*, 1988). In May 1986, the second displacing, the government decided to acquire only 68 sq km for the range with an adjacent safety zone of 34 sq km spread over 55 villages. Now officially it was supposed to displace around 50,000 people though the unofficial figure was 70,000 (*Indian Express*, 1988). It is here that an agitation was launched which questioned the government's right to establish and place a project in an agricultural belt that may turn out to be the most prosperous area in Odisha (Ramdas, 1988: 81).

The movement began in December, 1985 with the formation of the Uttara Balasore Khepanastra Ghati Protirodh Samiti (KGPS), which did not allow the government to evict people from the site of the National Testing Range (NTR). For some time people of nearly 100 villages in Baliapal – Bhograi area, under the leadership of the KGPS, fought a running battle with the government. They refused to give their homes and farms, which the defense ministry wanted for setting up of the rupees 1,600 (Ravi, 1988) crore National Testing Range (*Patriot*, 1988).

Mobilisation Cutting Across All Sections

It was an agitation that was able to mobilise all inhabitants of the area, cutting across the lines of caste, class, gender and tribal affiliation, on the issue of displacement, livelihood and environment, making it a mass agitation. Thus what distinguishes this agitation from others of a similar nature is the mass involvement of all the people in this area irrespective of vertical and horizontal hierarchies. The sustained nature of the agitation against the NTR is to a large extent due to the mass involvement of the people, including the poorer sections. This participation of all sections can in part be explained by the commercialisation of agriculture which has yielded benefits for the rich as well as the poor classes (Patel, 1989: 604).

Localisation of the Struggle

The fact is that this agitation remained restricted to the Baliapal block and did not spread to the Bhograi block where thirteen villages were to be acquired in the revised scheme (as against the forty-five in Baliapal), it indicates the localisation of this struggle (Patel, 1990: 1238–1239). Further evidence of its specificity lies in the failure of the attempts to mobilise the Chandipur peasants and tenants against the use of the interim test ranges facilities for testing missiles. Features specific to the local people of Baliapal have facilitated the growth of the movement (ibid.).

Background of the Movement

The localisation of the struggle in Baliapal was a result of the consolidation of certain economic, political and social processes in one conjuncture. These are the topographical and historical developments that have restricted the growth of both large landholdings and absentee landlordism, excellent natural resources including fresh water supply throughout the year, the spread of cash crop economy and the growth of the market for rice, groundnut, coconut, cashew nut and *paan* (betel-vine). The specific nature of *paan* cultivation which made it possible to cultivate it on homestead land, and the significant role played by *paan* traders who were distributing knowledge of *paan* cultivation to the lower castes, who were also non-cultivator castes, were instrumental in expanding its production over large tracts of this land. So in 1985 Baliapal *paan* had a monopoly in the market of Banarasi patta.

The consolidation of these features was made possible by the increased demand for *paan* leading to a growth in volume of trade in Baliapal. With the integration of the local market into national and then the international one, these processes were more integrated. Two phases in class dynamics formed the background for the consolidation of these processes. The first took place in the early fifties when the landed peasants, the upper castes like Khandayats, Gouda and Raju introduced cash crop economy in this region, the immediate consequence of which were increasing land pressure with the conversion of common property resources into area for cultivation (thereby displacing the herders, the Gouda caste), usurpation of land that did not have clear land titles and the sale of land by small peasants. This process of consolidation of upper peasantry and the displacement of the small cultivators and other castes depending on common property resources received a setback in the late sixties onwards with the growth of cultivation and production of *paan*. The first stage in this development occurred when the outsider *paan* traders were eliminated and substituted by the Baliapal traders, they establishing direct links between the national and local market increasing the demand for *paan* in Baliapal. The upper caste peasantry diverted its efforts to the production of *paan*. In the seventies, when the demand for *paan* exceeded its local supply, efforts were made by (upper caste) *paan* traders to induce the non-cultivating lower castes to commence *paan* cultivation.

In the eighties, Baliapal was a region of intense economic activity and high productivity where five cash crops were grown. All available land was cultivated including homestead land for the production of cash crops. Earning was extremely high, a conservative assessment suggests that the annual flow of income from *paan* ranged from around 22 crores to 59 crores for the Baliapal block (*Economic Times*, 1988). The market had introduced possibility of mobility for the lower sections of the society and deflected the earlier process of class tensions to produce a collective interest in the continuation and expansion of cash crop economy, especially *paan* production. It is in this situation that the government announced its plan to take over the land for establishing a military project. Immediately, the *paan* traders organised the *Uttara Balasore Khepanastra Ghati Pratirodh Samiti* (KGPS) to struggle against the project and reverse this decision (Patel, 2001: 141–159). Thus the period of growth and the subsequent attempt by the state to hamper the process by taking over the land forms the background of the growth of the Baliapal movement.

The History of the Movement

The history of the Baliapal movement can be divided into three phases (Patel, 1989: 1381–1382). When the Oriya newspapers announced the government's decision to acquire land to establish NTR, the big *paan* traders initiated discussions to confront this move. Together with the big peasantry and supporters of the congress party, they set up the KGPS in December 1984. The first phase of the movement was inaugurated with the formation of KGPS.

Nature of the Movement

The second phase of the movement began with the reconstitution of KGPS, which was dominated by the small to medium sized *paan* traders, led by Godadhar Giri, a socialist. He was later joined by Gananath Patra, a member of the UCCRI (ML). Godadhar Giri believed in Gandhian tactics of non-violence whose emotional affinity with the locals fuelled mass mobilisation of the people. Patra's coming provided the organisational structure to the agitation, which was till then run by upper caste male KGPS leaders. Forefronts were organised by the students, the youth, the women and the fishermen people, and demonstrations were organised in the block, district and state headquarters. This phase of the movement was characterised by both creativity and a series of confrontation. Creativity of the movement involved mobilisation attempts through songs and poems. The involvement and participation of the people reached its peak with every family making up songs about its own involvement in the agitation.

Confrontation and Negation of the State

A series of confrontations with the representatives of the state at the local level insured (Patel, 2001: 150). The collector, who had come to negotiate, was gheraoed and not released for more than 24 hours, dharanas were taken out to the block headquarters and was organised in the district town (Kumar, 1993: 332). It was followed by formation of a 'Barana Sena' or suicide squad consisting of children upto the age of 15 in every village with a 'commander'. Goun Patra, commander of the suicide squad of Pratappur village, had under him more than 200 children and it was his responsibility to see that each boy was trained to meet an emergency situation. The children were taught that the 'sea' is ours and we shall sacrifice our lives but not hand over mother earth to the government (Ramdas, 1998: 85).

Barricades were established to restrict the entry of any official. In fact the 'threatened area' was made into a 'fortress' (Ravi, 1988). The KGPS took the decision to block the entry of revenue officials into the area by mobilising women and children to make a human barricade. Thus no revenue official was able to gain access to the area for a period of three years even when accompanied with para-military forces. Lastly in an operation termed 'Operation Baliapal' a strong police and para-military force with 8,000 personnels attempted re-entry to the area designed for acquisition. They found a bamboo gate constructed at its boundary impeding their movement. At the gate and on the road lay hundreds of women and children in peaceful protest offering Satyagraha. This confrontation lasted for 24 hours before the state government was able to ensure withdrawal of the force, but covert attempts at entry continued. The government retaliated by suspending all developmental work such as the maintenance and extension of the infrastructure like roads, transport and electricity systems and also suspended the implementation of the poverty alleviation schemes. For some time, even the supplies of kerosene and sugar were stopped. Even though, the law and order machinery in the form of a police post remained, people boycotted it effectively negating any presence of the state in the area (Patel, 1989: 604).

For the next few years the KGPS functioned as a *defacto* government, taking all the decisions and managing the barricaded area. Thus to manage this region a committee of 12 members was set up. This committee was to be guided by an assembly of 229 members consisting of representatives of all villages. The first decision of this committee was to construct a further set of bamboo barriers on the other road linking the region to the outside world. People were always prepared to perform non-violent Satyagraha of Gandhian ways. Baliapal closed itself and its people established a *defacto* control over their land. The movements committee became the 'government' and the enforcing law and order agency. Various committee members became involved in solving disputes in their various panchayats, in the process reviving an old institution called *vichar* through which local disputes, especially those relating to land and property, were being solved. The constitution of *vichar* and its proceedings marked the third phase of the movement that provided the context for the binding of various interests into a community, even as it created conditions for the decline of registered police cases and thus restricted the entry of the law and order machinery into the area (Patel, 1989: 1382).

Bheeta Mati – Environmental Dimension of the Movement

In the case of Baliapal movement the identity was constructed through the ideology of *Bheeta Mati* that brought out the environmental dimension of the struggle (Patel, 1990). *Bheeta Mati* is a word that can be loosely denoted to mean 'home', 'earth', 'soil', and the emotions rooted in these words (*The Samaj*, Oriya Daily, 1986: 5). This ideology converted a cultural sentiment for land into a political demand for the absolute right to its continued use through religious mythological tools. The fight was thus for *Sonar Maati* (golden land) and for the protection of *Maa* (mother) who were the symbols of *Prakriti* (nature). A fight was conducted by the entire community against the state which wanted to destroy all three: *Sonar Maati*, *Maa* and *Prakriti* (*The Dharitri*, Oriya Daily, 1986: 3).

Jatra – The Localised Way of Mass Mobilisation

This ideology of *Bheeta Maati* which formed the basis for the construction of identity of the actors of the movement was highlighted in the performance of *jatra* and the songs and poems sung by women as they work and protect the gate during the years of struggle. It was a mythological interpretation of the local issue through musical drama. To have a novel understanding of its impact on people's thinking we can discuss the theme of such a *jatra*.

The panchayat building in a Baliapal village was the main centre for the performance of the *jatra*. The performance started with the traditional blurring of conches. A small space is cleared for the musicians who start the programme, the small lanterns give light and the drums start. The surrounding noise decreases and a full-throated voice starts ringing and through the song tells the following story.

This is the story of Shiva and Parvati, says the Sutradhara, the narrator. When the story starts, Parvati disagreed with Shiva and is sulking while Shiva is trying to placate her. Why are you annoyed, asks Shiva? Parvati replies by singing a song (actors enter playing the roles of Parvati and Shiva)

I am extremely upset because my people on earth the Baliapalis are facing displacement. Oh Shiva, how could you allow the Rajiv Gandhi government to take over this land? This land which you have blessed by making it the most fertile land of the region, this land whose people you blessed by giving the technology of rice making, this land from whose people the rest of the world learnt how to make rice, this land which gives its people the best that earth, and its soil can give, this land which is blessed with mother and sons who want to protect their *bheeta maati*. Oh Shiva how can you allow the region that you have blessed to be misused?

The *jatra* continues and the actor playing the role of the then Prime Minister Rajiv Gandhi enters, when he sees Shiva quakes with fear. Rajiv Gandhi tries to convince Shiva but having seen the face of Shiva's wrath, he withdraws defeated. Later, Rajiv Gandhi announces the withdrawal of the project and the people of Baliapal start to cheer. This scene marks the end of the *jatra* (Vasudha Joshi, film).

It was the songs and the poems rendered by women and children which gave a sense of identity to their actions and their perception that the fate of Baliapal rested on their shoulders. Most of these songs and poems weaved personal biographical details together with the terms made popular by the movement like missiles, military options, nuclear club, Shiva, Parvati, the puranas, the peculiarities of rice production, cultivation of *paan*, the productivity of the region, the nature of its environment and bheeta maati. Bheeeta maati had a particular place in these songs because by this they were trying to protect the 'field'.

The Salient Features of the Movement

The movement was unique in many ways. Those are

- It was able to mobilise all people of the area thereby exemplifying a mass character,
- In spite of having obtained support from all political parties it maintained its independence from political parties,
- They have imagined its 'community', located it within a territory and suggested that it had a history going back to the puranas, whereas these people were recognised as a community. Thus it constructed a historical narrative of self-identification. It drew its creative intellectual resources from an analysis of its heritage and suggested that it retrieved indigenous knowledge to manage and maintain this movement,
- This movement used militant non-violence to confront the military and after its initial success took over civil control of the area,
- It used received networks and traditional symbols for mobilisation of the people.

What is distinctive of this movement is the fact that it was not only able to change the decision of the political managers but also lobby against the defence establishment. The notion of 'community' politics made possible the states recognition and response to civil society institutions which are legitimising a local democratic process (Patel, 2001: 153). As a result, it was able to affirm the agency of the people making them active citizens. The Baliapal region was earlier divided into discrete communities defined by class caste, gender, and tribal identities, between insiders and outsiders. Affiliated by regional perceptions separated between peasants and fisher people and political affiliation, like, congress supporters and Janata Dal supporters, there were closed ranks to form a community. This movement did not construct a primordial identity rather it built a language of solidarity between discrete castes and tribal groups. It has constructed an identity of itself as a 'people' and saw itself as a community. This community defined its identity and represented itself through the symbol of *Bheeta maati*, the struggle to define the people's right over their home and earth, their land and its environment.

The Chilika Bachao Andolan

The Chilika Bachao Andolan (Save the Chilika Movement) was a movement by the people for the people and of the people. Mostly fishermen, in the early 1990s successfully, resisted the Integrated Shrimp Farm Project (ISFP). The project, a joint venture of the Tata Iron and Steel Company (TISCO) and the Government of Odisha, for intensive prawn cultivation and export, posed a direct threat to the livelihood of fishing communities living around the lake. The fishermen were supported in their struggle by non-fishermen (mostly farmers, but some of them were also engaged in fishing), students, intellectuals and human rights activists. The lake, an otherwise quiet and scenic spot, was stirred by many voices of resistance opposing the Tata business house, the government and the development idiom that gives priority to the commercial use of local resources over their use for subsistence. The movement was episodic and uneven, with different streams of thought and action among which it was not always possible to achieve synchronisation. Yet, all these separate formations together gave the resistance the form of a movement. Thus, the Chilika Bachao Andolan (CBA) was a struggle of the poor against 'misleading development', a form of development which threatened to leave them destitute and exile from the land which supported them and coexisted with them for centuries (Seth, 1997: 250–252)

Geographical Location of Chilika Lake

Lake Chilika, situated in the eastern coastal part of Odisha is surrounded by Braillnagiri, Kanasa and Krishnaprasad blocks of Puri district, Tangi and Chilika blocks of Khurda district and Kholicot and Ganjam blocks of Ganjam. It is the largest brackish water lake of Asia. Its natural ecosystem is unique. Due to its distinctive features this lake has been designated under the Ramsar convention as a 'wet land of international importance'

(GOI, 2005: 256; Das, 1996). The lake has a length of 72 kms and width of 25 km, covering approximately 1,000 sq kms. It is the home of migrating birds of 158 kinds of species and commercially important species of the tiger prawn.

Socio-economic Importance

Chilika is home and earning source of 192 villages, dependent on fishing and particularly prawn fishing as their major source of livelihood. More than 50,000 fishermen and over two lakhs of total population depend upon the Chilika for their livelihood. Fishing has been the traditional occupation in the Chilika region for centuries. Fishermen, have had their right to fishing in the Chilika as early as the Afghan rule. The right was protected even by the British who aided the fishermen by setting up fishermen's cooperatives. Thus, Chilika has a rare and inspiring history of fish producers, cooperatives and village level democracy from early times (Samantara, 2000: 51).

A heterogeneous population comprising of both fishermen and non-fishermen belonging to different castes inhabit in a large number of villages around the lake. Fishing and agriculture are the two primary sources of livelihood. The fishermen belong to the lower castes and most of them are either landless or possess tiny landholdings. They are therefore entirely dependent on fishing. The non-fishermen belong to higher castes and are engaged in agriculture. However, a large number of them have also taken to fishing to supplement their income because land productivity is low due to salinity, erratic monsoon and lack of irrigation facilities.

Cultural Significance of Chilika

The scenic beauty of Chilika has drawn the attention of poets, both romantic and revolutionary and film producers. Socio-economic conditions of fishermen living around the Chilika, the manipulation of traders to sabotage the working of cooperatives of fishermen have been depicted in 'Chilika Tire' and scarcity of drinking water in the area in the film *'Swapna Sagara'*. Radhanath Roy, a renowned Oriya poet, has described Chilika as a storehouse of beauty in his poem, 'Chilika'. A similar description has also been made by Gopabandhu Das, a well-known Oriya social worker and nationalist leader in his poem *'Rail Upare*

Chilika Darsana'. Godabarish Mishra, in his poem, 'Kalijai' has described the real picture of the rural Odisha, the social and cultural links between the people living inside Chilika and those living around Chilika. The revolutionary poet Rabi Singh, in his poem, '*Ittahashaka too Pachare Bhare*', reminds us the about glorious past of a Oriya fighter, Krutbasha Patsani, who established a kingdom for three days at Banapur near the west bank of Chilika (Samal and Meher, 2003: 3319).

Ecological Significance

Ecologically, Chilika is a stupendous collector of water and sunlight. The solar energy is converted by the process of photosynthesis by grass and phytoplankton into food for brackish water fish and grass for cattle, in turn providing food and livelihood to the thousands of traditional dependents of Chilika. This is a well-balanced, sustainable, self-regenerating system needing no outside high cost and non-renewable inputs, not 'imported' dollars or fossil fuel or US-European technology. It is a system developed by years of experience of living in the region by the poor people of Chilika (Seth, 1997: 252).

Environmental Concerns

But the lake is facing the recent environmental perils of rapid situation, decreasing salinity of lake water and gradual lowering of depth of water etc. Human activities in and around the lake have posed serious environmental dangers to the lake. There are industries around the western part of the lake. A caustic alkali unit discharges its effluents directly into the lake causing problems of mercury accumulation in the lake ecosystem. Fertilisers used in the agricultural fields nearby also find their way to the lake during the rainy seasons. Apart from the industrial and agricultural effluents, the catchment area of Chilika has suffered badly from deforestation. This has led to soil erosion and silting of the lake. The problem is aggravated by the ongoing expansion of prawn culture bandhs (embankment) in the lake (Bogaeart, 1992).

The process of development undertaken by the government of Odisha, motivated by the keen desire to earn dollars ignored the environmental dangers facing the lake. Intensive prawn aquaculture not only threatened the existence of the lake but also adversely affected the large number of poor fishing people traditionally sustained through the lake. The Tata project exemplified the problem inherent in intensive prawn aquaculture, the model of production that proliferated in the 90s causing serious damage to the lake. According to R.N. Das, a Senior Scientist in the State Environment Department, people realised that indiscriminate prawn farming and siltation had greatly reduced the life of the lake (Sankar, 1992: 25–27).

Contextualising the Movement

In the colonial Odisha (Utkal), Chilika was owned by several owners including the government, Zamindars, Jagirdars and others. The Zamindars used to lease out fisheries exclusively to the local fisher folk. Even when Odisha was under the rule of the Marathas in the second half of the 18th century the local chieftains who controlled the lake leased out the fishery resources to the local fishermen living on the periphery of the lake. However, at the time of independence of the country, these local fisher folk were mostly indebted to the moneylenders having borrowed for fulfilling their social commitments and for purchasing equipment like country boats and nets. Through the development of means of communication, Calcutta provided the biggest market for fishery resources from the lake. So classes of middlemen were grown who functioned both as traders for the fisher people's catch as well as moneylenders for their day-to-day needs. Gradually these traders became exploiters and the fisher folk community virtually became their bonded labour (Patnaik, 2003: 55–65). During the 1950s, when the popular government was established, an attempt was made to free the fisher folk from acute exploitation and abject bondage from these middlemen through a scheme known as Chilika Reorganisation Scheme in 1959 that aimed at bringing the fishing community under the cooperative banner. The scheme was mainly intended to eliminate traders, intermediaries and moneylenders from the scene and ensure the payment of fair prices to the fisher folk in order to improve their socio-economic status. The fisher folk were organised under more than 50 prime cooperative societies and all these primary cooperative societies were integrated to a central or apex society. The apex body used to take all the fishery sources of Chilika on lease from the government and sub-lease them to the primary societies. The apex society gave loans to fisher folk to purchase equipment and would purchase their entire catch for marketing. Thus the exploitation of the middlemen ended and the condition of the fisher folk began to improve. However, this was short lived. After a decade or so, the condition of the apex society deteriorated due to lack of support from cooperative banks and bureaucratic control of the government. Gradually middlemen and traders again appeared on the scene. There was constant pressure on the government by the non-fisher folk of the locality that they are allowed to take a share of the fishery resources of the lake on the ground that they were also local inhabitants of Chilika (ibid., 58).

The year 1977–78, saw the development of prawns as an important export commodity. The name Chilika became synonymous all over in the name of prawns and money. The whole area became a virtual gold mine. And, with this transformation, the commercial invaders started appearing. First, the traders and middlemen, then the politicians with their musclemen, some big business families of Odisha through local middlemen and mafia, and finally, the big industrial houses, with the blessings of the state government, which was now very keen to usher in 'development' to the region (Seth, 1997: 251). In the early 80s, outsiders controlled a significant portion of Chilika's fisheries. Sometimes they made some fishery cooperatives their agents by depositing lease money with government on their behalf and advancing loans to their leaders. In this process, the fisher folk were gradually squeezed out of the resources with the money and muscle power of outsiders. The money and muscle power employed by the outsiders had led them to be called the 'mafia' locally (Patnaik, 2003: 58).

Since the 1980s, the lake has been witnessing increased subletting of leased out fisheries by the central and primary societies and illegal encroachment by non-fishermen and outsiders (Report of Fact Finding Committee, 1993). Large scale culturing of prawns resulted in widespread conversion of traditional fisheries into prawn culture ponds or gheries (barricade space). Culture fishery requires heavy capital investment but ensures big profit. It thus serves as a lucrative money making source for primary societies that sublet the fishery sources to other interested parties.

Background of the Movement

In 1984, the Ministry of Agriculture sanctioned a project for the establishment of a shrimp farm over an area of 300 hectares of land at Panaspara at a total cost of ₹ 17 crore. The site was then handed over to Odisha Maritime and Chilika Area Development Corporation Limited (OMCAD) by the government for implementation of the above project (Business Standard, 1988). The project could not be executed by OMCAD due to managerial problems. The project was revived subsequently as a joint venture of Tata and OMCAD in the form of Chilika Aquatic Farm Limited (CAFL). In 1986 the Odisha government under J.B. Patnaik, chief minister, through the OMCAD entered into a deal with the Tata business house to lease 600 hectares of land to Aquatic Farms Limited for 15 years. In 1987, the state government conducted a survey of the fish resources in Chilika without any participation of the fishing communities. A simultaneous move to undermine the fisher folk's cooperative society was also made. In 1990, the election of the board of directors of Balugaon Central Fishermen Marketing Cooperative Society (BCFMC) was postponed. Later on, this central society was dissolved and amalgamated with the Odisha State Fishermen Cooperative Federation Limited (OSFCFL); diluting the exclusive right the traditional fisher people had over the fisher resources of Chilika Lake. In the year 1991, the Government of Odisha signed an agreement with the Tatas for a semi-intensive prawn culture project called the Integrated Shrimp Farm Project (ISFP) and allowed the Tatas an advance possession of 400 hectares of land in Chilika (Mohanty, 2003: 182). The project consisted of shrimp farm, a hatchery, a shrimp feed mill and a processing plant. The total area covered by this shrimp farm was 400 hectares initially. A further 200 hectares were later leased out. The total project cost was estimated at ₹ 20 crore. The project was promoted on the ground that it would bring about the economic development of the region.

The farm posed a potential danger to the livelihood of the fishermen in area since their fishing fields would be squeezed. The ₹ 20 crore joint venture shrimp project of Tata and Government of Odisha also had the potential to inflict serious damages to the Chilika eco-system. The process which enables the Tatas to cultivate prawns in isolation kills the whole of Chilika lake. The technique entails the construction of an embankment with a width of 40 and height of 30 feet that would obstruct the natural movement of fish. The traditional fisher folk believed that the movement of the fish would be obstructed by the embankment built by the Tatas. It was also feared that the embankment would stop the drainage of water coming into Chilika from different rivers. The different fisher folk villages surrounding the area would be inundated for longer periods. A survey report of the then chief irrigation engineer Banabara Das noted that 35,000 acre of cultivable land in more than 80 panchayats of Kanas, Brahmagiri, Krushna Prasad blocks etc. will be inundated due to the back water effect of flood water that will get obstructed by the ring dam of this project. The large-scale inundation would lead to massive displacement of people, particularly local fisher folk from the affected region. The aquatic farms and embankments would also obstruct the local fisher people access to Chilika (Patnaik, 2003: 62). The Tata and Odisha government venture made local fisher people apprehensive about the ecological life of the lake and the future of their own livelihood from it. In addition, the fisher folk in small villages were also affected adversely by the fact that several fields on which they were able to catch fish for certain months in the year would now be denied to them after the construction of the embankment. The precarious nature of local livelihood became even more threatened by the recent move to lease fishing rights to persons or agencies other than those who have traditionally held rights as it was felt that higher revenue could be earned by the government in this way. In the wake of these developments; a powerful people's movement emerged in Chilika to protect local fisher-folk from commercial exploitation by big businessmen, to restore the people's right to livelihood and manage the lake.

Civil Society Assertion

Though the fishing communities had been resisting the commercial use of their resources and the consequent loss of control over their resources so that the mass mobilisation could not take place in Chilika till the ISFP took shape and threats it posed became more visible, imminent and gigantic. The people of the villages adjacent to the ISFP were aware of the project, but there was little awareness about the threats it would pose to their livelihood. In fact, the people anticipated getting a good bargain for the fish that they caught, as well as employment in the project. Thus, initially, only a few educated people in these villages were skeptical about the project. Later, an informal group of students from Utkal University, Bhubaneswar, who were actively involved in effecting social change, took the initiative to visit the villages and discuss the issue with the villagers. This student group played an important role in raising people's awareness and organising them against the Tata project during the initial years (Mohanty, 2003: 184). The student group comprised of young people pursuing ideas of social change, with the aim of making people conscious of injustices perpetrated on them by both society and the state. Later, a provincial level student's forum called *Krantadarshi Yuva Sangha* (KYS) was formed to mobilise youth against the Tata project. It's core comprised of students who were earlier members of that student group, and when they passed out of the university, joined the KYS. Thereafter it was decided that student group would function at the university level and KYS would work as a forum to mobilise youth against the project and the policy of the State.

The student activists, who worked relentlessly to raise awareness about the threats posed by the project, tried hard to persuade the local people to assume leadership of the movement which at the local level at least, was seen as a manifestation of people's initiative and strength. The point was to make people aware of their situation so that they could articulate the issue and claim leadership of the movement themselves. Gradually the students realised that local organisations could serve as an effective vanguard in the resistance against the project. Their grounding in local issues and the trust local people placed on them would help local organisations to carry forward the resistance more effectively. Steps were thus taken to involve the *Chilika Matsyajibi Mahasangha* (CMM), a mass organisation of 122 revenue villages in Chilika that works to protect the interests of fishermen (ibid., 185).

The united struggle of the student group and CMM led to the formation of a people's movement on 15 January 1992 at Gopinathpur village. So the fisher folk organised themselves to form a movement under the banner of the 'Chilika Bachao Andolan' (CBA) against the pattern of development which threatens peace, development, ecology and livelihood of the poor of Chilika, to protect it from commercial exploitation by big business operating under political umbrella, and to restore the people their right to livelihood in Chilika area (Seth, 1997: 252). In the protest movement against the Chilika Aquatic Farm, the CBA launched several actions such as *dharana* (non-violent strike), rally, *padayatra* (travel by foot), symbolic breaking of the farm embankments, and *gherao* of the State Legislative Assembly (Patnaik, 2003: 60).

The CBA organised movement to protect the lake, ecology and the large population of poor fisher folk. The Andolan which amplified the local struggle into a larger movement focused its attention against the nature of development fighting against the injustice of the states' appropriation of natural resources from the lake through industrial houses like Tatas. The popular movement attracted international attention due to several issues such as environmental degradation through intensive prawn aqua culture, deprivation of main support base for the livelihood of the poor local fishing communities, pollution of the lake environment by industrialisation etc. The CBA held the state as an illegitimate and repressive authority. It put pressure on the state through constructive, conscious strategies using the law courts, through the mass media and by mobilising the support of other intellectual elites. CBA was supported by many other civil society organisations, such as the *Ganatantrik Adhikar Suraksha Sangathan* (GASS), an organisation based in Bhubaneswar that works to protect the democratic rights of people and the *Odisha Krushak Mahasanga* (OKM), which works for the cause of farmers.

OKM gave a new dimension to the movement from 1992 by raising the question of the ecological health of the lake along with the impairment of livelihoods. So that all the villages around the lake were involved because they felt that if the Tatas were allowed to enter, other big business houses would follow suit for earning foreign exchange and large profits and the lake would die an early death in this process. The OKM at this juncture, under the leadership of Banka Bihari Das, its president, who was also the main activist of the CBA, gave the movement a great impetus by taking the matter to the Supreme Court (ibid., 63). All these civil society initiatives and formations gave the local people's protest the form of a powerful peoples movement that raised economic, social, legal and environmental issues related to the project

(Mohanty, 2003: 186). Some of the prominent issues that the movement drew attention to were:

- The land allotted to the ISFP was traditionally used by the neighbouring 26 villages for harvesting prawn; the shallow water collected during the monsoon was ideal for their natural breeding.
- The threats of flood and water logging due to the construction of the embankment on the Bhubania canal, which forms the outlet of the lake to the sea.
- The embankment would obstruct the movement of the fish and prawn from the brackish water to the sea during breeding season. This, in turn would hamper the nature and a generation of prawns.
- Long-term availability of fish within the lake would be adversely affected due to the pollution caused by protein feed chemicals and pesticides.
- The project had moved ahead without the mandatory Environment Impact Assessment (EIA).
- The land given on lease to the ISFP was classified as a reserved wetland and community pasture land. Leasing out the lake was therefore illegal, as it was not listed under property that could be leased.

The movement linked these issues with a central question on development and resource use. The Tata project is not the central point of attack of this people's movement. The prime focus of opposition is the policy of government towards its people, and the Tata project is only an instance of this policy.

Nature of the Movement

In the initial phase, since three or four villages were directly affected by the project, the movement was localised. The mobilisation against ISFP was confined to a few villages adjacent to the project. On 20 September 1991, the date on which the three-year lease to the central cooperative society expired, thousands of fishermen gathered in Bhubaneswar and protested in front of the Vidhan Sabha. Demonstrations, meeting, Dharanas and rallies at the project site and in the state capital summarise the movement activities during this phase. Since the movement at this phase was localised, the administration was able to suppress it.

In its second phase, the movement became more broad based since it evoked the support of all fisher folk of Chilika as well as a large mass of people of the locality and outside. The bureaucracy and the police now used brutal measures to suppress the movement. Nevertheless, the protest continued and the broader environmental issues pertaining to the project began to be addressed by the movement along with livelihood issues. The threats to the lake's fragile ecosystem and to the livelihood of fishermen were used to pressurise the government. In advocating the environmental aspects of the issue, emphasis was laid on India's commitment to the international community to preserve the lake. At the same time the government was interpreted on the legality of the project by invoking the *Land Settlement Act,* according to which Chilika is a 'reserved wetland' and therefore can't be leased to any individual or company. The Ministry of Environment and Forests issued an order banning further work on the project until an EIA study had been conducted. The Tatas assigned this task to the Water and Power Consultancy Services (WAPCO), which gave the project a clean chit, describing it as environment friendly with no possible adverse impact on the environment of the lake. The report was opposed and criticised by both the movement and the Union Ministry of Environment and Forests. The ministry much to the dissatisfaction of the Government of Odisha maintained that, the project could precede only after a proper EIA was done. While the Government of Odisha and the Union Ministry were engaged in this tussle and the movement was vociferously opposing the project, the Odisha High Court's judgment on the fishing rights of the fishermen in Chilika halted both intensive and semi-intensive prawn cultivation in the lake. After more than two years of struggle, The Tatas had to withdraw. This recognised the validity of people's protest against the project and reaffirmed the strength of people's collective resistance. The struggle of CBA exhibited the might of the fishermen and in its ideology it asserted the inseparability of ecological sustainability and social justice. It is an example of growing consciousness about the legitimacy of poor people's rights and the power of collective action. Thus the CBA, which started as a grassroots movement, became in subsequent years, an organised mass movement. It tarnished the false model of 'development' imposed upon the weaker masses by the state. It also tarnished the false image of the state regarding the protection of nature; rather it passed the message that the environment is best protected by the grassroots people. Although these people live sustainably on the ecology, still they are the best protectors of nature's treasure. So the goal of CBA was to protect both nature and people.

The Gandhamardan Movement

The environmental movement in the Gandhamardan Hills in Odisha against the ecological destruction for bauxite mining is very important in the history of environmental movements in Odisha. This movement drew its inspiration from the Chipko movement. The mining project of the Bharat Aluminium Company (BALCO) in the Gandhamardan Hills was being opposed (BALCO Hatao Andolan) by local youth organisations and tribal people whose life, livelihood and survival was directly under threat. The peaceful demonstration claimed that the 'project could only continue over their dead bodies'. The champions of their cause were the tribal people, living in the localities.

Background of the Movement

Gandhamardan bauxite project was being developed by BALCO as the captive mines capable of fulfilling the long term bauxite needs of its one lakh were per year. BALCO's Korba Aluminum complex at Bilaspur district of Chhattisgarh was getting its bauxite supplies from its captive mines at Phulkapahar and Amarkantak in Chhattisgarh. Due to the limitation of reserves in these captive mines, requirement of bauxite was estimated to be met from these two sources only upto 1985. The development of Gandhamardan bauxite deposit located at the junction of Sambalpur and Bolangir districts of Odisha was supposed to ensure a regular supply of bauxite at the rate of six lakh tones per year to Korba Plant beyond 1985 for almost the entire life of the aluminum plant (Pamphlet BALCO, 1983). BALCO officials found Gandhamardan as the most suitable, since its ore quality and occurrence were better than Amarkantak. They said that overburden was also much less in Gandhamardan and pointed out that the ore theme was much thicker, continuous and available within three metres. Mining of only 3 hectares per year on this reserve would feed nearly five lakh tones of bauxite every year to the Korba plant.

The bauxite deposit at Gandhamardan is the second largest deposit in the country with total ore reserves of about 213 million tons (*Indian Express*, 1987). BALCO was granted mining lease by the Odisha government in 1982 over an area of 9.6 sq kilometre which had an ore reserve of about 60 million tones of bauxite (ibid., 1987). The project envisaged an investment of ₹ 31.2 crores including infrastructure. It was scheduled to be completed within a span of 33 months beginning from 1 August 1982. The ₹ 750 crore integrated Korba Aluminum Complex of the public sector Bharat Aluminum Company could survive only if the proposed Gandhamardan bauxite project in Odisha would have come up within two years (*Indian Express*, 1988).

Social and Cultural Significance of Gandhamardan

The Gandhamardan reserve forest, with an area of around 300 sq km, situated on the borders of Sambalpur, Bolangir and Kalahandi district of Odisha, is a rich eco-system. Known as *Gandhagiri* in mythology and believed to be the *Gandhamardan* of the Ramayana, this hill is proved by historians to be the famous *Parimalagiri* of Buddhist literature, the plateau on which there was the international centre of learning, *Arimalagiri Mahavihar* cited in Hiuen T'Sang's reference as 'polo-molokili' (Misra, 1987: 124–144). There are two ancient temples on the northern and southern foothills of the plateau, Narsinghanath and Harisankar, in Sambalpur and Bolangir districts, respectively. They are situated near two perennial streams, the water of which is believed to be sacred. People from Chhattisgarh and Madhya Pradesh come to throw the bones of their dead elders into the Nursinghanath stream, called the *papaharan tirtha* (water that washes away sins). The local people believe that this is their Ganga.

Ecological Significance of the Gandhamardan

The richness of the Gandhamardan ecosystem is remarkable. Its water resources, with over 800 small perennial springs and many more rain-fed ones, supply water through 63 small streams to 17 large streams joining two rivers, the Ong and Suktel tributaries of the Mahanadi (*Hindustan Times*, 1987). Three streams, on their way downhill, form four waterfalls, 30 feet to 40 feet high. A partial vegetation survey of the slopes conducted by the Botanical Survey of India, more than two decades ago, recorded a diversity of 2,700 species of medicinal, quasi-medicinal and economically important plants and herbs (GOI, 1986). On the banks of the streams, ferns and lichens grow profusely. The department of forest sources claim that a rich variety of fauna exists, including mammals like the tiger, leopard, sloth bears, palm civet, junglet cat, wild bear, sam bar, barking deer, fox, jackal, wild dogs, red and black faced monkeys etc. All over these hills is a semiarid type of vegetation mostly deciduous. There are also semi-evergreen growths. The forest has no human habitation, due to the absence of habitable valleys, but is surrounded by the villages and towns of Jharbandh, Paikmal, Padmapur and Gaislet blocks of Sambalpur in the northeast, Naupara block of Nuapada district in the west and Khaprakhol and Patnagarh blocks of Bolangir district in the south. Most of the people in the villages of these blocks are farmers and agricultural labourers, depending directly and indirectly on the forest. More than 200 villages, with a population of around one lakh are directly dependent on the forest. About 30 per cent people of the area are completely landless, depending on daily wages and forest produce for their livelihood. They neither migrate to urban areas in large number nor work as bonded labourers. This is mainly because the forests supply them with subsistence needs and seasonal employment. Food is the most important link between people's subsistence and forests. About 30 to 40 varieties of edible roots and rhizomes are collected from the hill slopes. Not only the poor, but the rich too eat forest-based foods. The best example of these is the soft parts of the bamboo, called *kardi* and *hendua.* Primary health centres exist in all blocks and some panchayats, but the people only go there when ailments are unmanageable in the village. Minor ailments are mostly treated by the village *vaidyas* or practitioners of indigenous medicine found in the forest. Collection of minor forest produce is an important aspect of the economy of the landless, small and marginal farmers. Big landowners also sell these products from their trees.

Commercial Exploitation of the Gandhamardan

Commercial exploitation of natural resources systems can easily alienate people from this nature, consequently depleting the renewable resources of the area. The commercial exploitation of Gandhamardan dates back to pre-independence years by local business communities and Birla's Orient Paper Mill with the approval of forest department. But no conspicuous deterioration was noted. The first major indication of danger to this ecosystem came in 1971 with a government gazette notification that about 2 million tones of easily exploitable quality bauxite alumina was stored in the hill. Mica was also found there. In mid 1976, the Public Sector Bharat Aluminum Company (BALCO) applied to the Odisha government for a mining lease over 3584 hectares. In 1981 the Odisha government notified that 36 sq km of the Gandhamardan reserve forest was reserved for exploitation of bauxite in the public sector and a day later, a lease was hurriedly sanctioned to BALCO. In May 1983 the foundation stone for the mines was laid by the Chief Minister. A demonstration took place and his vehicle was stoned. Thus, though the project was started in 1983, after an investment of a few crores of rupees, work came to a halt following agitation by the local tribals due to ecological disturbance (Misra, 15).

Environmental Impact of the Project and Civil Society Assertion

Gandhamardan bauxite project was located in a reserve forest which was extremely rich in biological diversity, flora and fauna as well as medicinal and herbal plants of great economic value. So the project was going to have adverse impact on the biological diversity of the hill. These hills are the origin of more than 150 springs which fall into 22 major streams and four waterfalls. The local population in these hills as well as downstream is dependent for their water supply on these streams and have no alternative source when the streams get dried or polluted where the two possibilities accompany mining operations. The changed hydrological cycle would have adversely affected the irrigated cultivation. It would also have an impact on the vegetation and microclimate in the area. The total population in the area is about 50,000 who are predominantly tribal and their main source of sustenance is the forest produce. So a large proportion of the tribal population would have been adversely affected because of the forest destruction which is the base of their sustenance. The Gandhamardan hill range is a well known pilgrimage centre with sacred streams flowing. One of the streams, Kapildhara, is considered as sacred as the *Ganga* by the local people. Drying up of the streams and springs, held sacred by the local people, would have been a major catastrophe. Two famous temples named, Narsinghnath and Harisankar built around the 11th century are important pilgrimage centres where annual *melas* are held. The *Garuda* pillar of the Narsinghnath temple collapsed in August 1985 and the roof of the temple storehouse had developed cracks. Local people, therefore, apprehended that their sacred temples would get destroyed after the operations are taken up in the full earnest. Even though the mining operations were limited to an area of 107 hector only and an additional forest area of 55 hector had been acquired for allied operations and works, the environmental degradation would have taken place over a much larger area (Panda, 1986: 9–10).

Nature of the Movement

Since mining operation is an anti-forest operation and the forest is the core of tribal culture, it was therefore an anti-people operation. Loss of evergreen high mountainous range would have caused late rain or no rain and soil erosion ruining the harvest and bringing famine, which might mean dispersal of entire tribal community to live scattered on the mercy of their fortune. This would have meant making tribal poorest of the poor. Binghals and Kondhas tribal communities of this area lamented that there would be no wind and no rain, because their numerous gods and spirits especially clan deities and ancestral spirits in their peaceful sacred abode had been offended by the blasting of BALCO (*The Times of India*, 1988).

Thus when BALCO was preparing to mine bauxite from this densely forested Gandhamardan hills, which was intricately tied up with the survival of the tribals, instead of hugging a tree, these agitated tribals here hug the earth by lying down to obstruct the advance of jeeps and trucks of the public sector undertaking and they said that, '*Peethi mara petey nain mara*' (hit at our backside but not in the stomach) (Misra, 1987: 130). The tribals shouted, predominantly women and children, at seeing the vehicles of BALCO, which they called 'monsters'. They did not want these monsters to destroy the hills, which are their source of food, fodder, water and firewood. Apart from erecting permanent barricades, tribals refused to join BALCO's labour force.

The heterogeneous leadership of the agitation resented the project for its potential damage to forest reserve and claimed that it would affect 50,000 people, uproot a large number of rare medicinal herbs, dry up perennial streams, endanger the fauna, damage the ancient Narsinghnath temple which was 600 metres below the hill and leave a large number of people landless (Indian Express, 1988). People of the area expressed their concern over this issue by expressing their displeasure by filling a public interest litigation case in the Odisha High Court. In the meantime the idol of Lord Narsinghnath was stolen from the temple and people suspected BALCO's involvement.

In June 1985, a group of National Service Scheme (NSS) volunteers camped at Narsinghnath, went to the villages and lived with some families to understand their reactions more intimately. Some Sanghrasha Bahini volunteers managed to stay in the villages after the camp in August 1986, and the *Gandhamardan Surakshya Yuva Parishad* (Youth Action Group for Gandhamardan Protection, GSYP) was formed with the active participation of local youth (Telegraph, 1988). The GSYP discussed issues like deforestation, microclimate variation, silting of streams, dust pollution, the entry of frightened wild animals into villages because of blasting, in village meetings and workshops. The 'BALCO Hatao' movement gathered momentum through rallies, slogans and signature campaigns, which resulted in direct action like relay hunger pickets on the BALCO road to prevent vehicles from going to the mining sites, and boycott of the labourers working for BALCO at the cost of arrests and litigation. According to GSYP activists, as a result of BALCO's initial mining activities, nearly 66,000 valuable trees were uprooted, ruining the economic base of thousands of villagers. They pointed out that Gandhamardan was the only source of survival for one lakh tribals inhabiting in the area. The Parishad then turned to religious symbols to give a new thrust to the agitation against the project which threatened to deprive lakh of tribals of their source of livelihood and strain their unblemished environment (Misra, 1987: 131).

The anti-BALCO movement, spearheaded by the *Gandhamardan Suraksha Yuva Parishad,* compelled BALCO officials from visiting the Gandhamardan mining zone, the road to which was 'sealed' by the agitators sitting in *dharna* on the basis of rotation. They demanded scraping of the mining project on the grounds of protection of the environment and of temples and safeguarding of the economic interests of the population, which is traditionally dependent on the flora and fauna and water resources of the Gandhamardan hills (*Economic Times*, 1988).

During the road blocking, the local police and administration supported the company. They arrested and filed cases in the local courts against many people. As many as 1300, of which more than half were women, were harassed in this manner. Women were more involved in the movement than men. Initially, there was not much response from women. But when Sunderlal Bahuguna, the environmentalist visited the area in February 1986, and spent about five days there, he regularly addressed women. So that a rumour circulated that a saint from the Himalaya has come to see the devastations. He also met university students, staff and press reporters, which gave the movement strong encouragement.

In early 1986 a group of Oriya intellectual people, living in Delhi, organised the *Gandhamardan Protectional Committee* (GPC) and collected signatures to make an appeal to the Prime Minister. Some action groups like the People's Union for Democratic Rights (PUDR) and the Institute for the Study of Society and Culture (ISSC) visited the area and wrote their reports against the project (Indian Express, 1988). Many environmentalists urged to BALCO to examine the need for relocation of the proposed bauxite crusher plant at the site of the mines project on Gandhamardan hills so as to minimise dust and vibration on the hills (*Economic Times*, 1987).

Response of the BALCO

BALCO officials argued against the claims of the environmentalists who feared that mining activities will threaten rare medicinal herbs and wildlife in Gandhamardan. They dismissed fears of damage to the ancient Nursinghnath temple, 3.5 km from the mining site, saying that they had pledged ₹ 4 lakh to conserve and renovate the temple. Despite BALCO's claims, however, initial operations brought down the ancient *Garuda Stambha* of the Nursinghanath temple, disturbed the habitat of wildlife, and led to silting of perennial streams. This led to agitation of the people against the project.

Governmental Response

The then Prime Minister constituted a high-level experts' committee under the chairmanship of D.O. Nagchaudhary to assess the impact of the development of the Gandhamardan bauxite deposits on ecology and environment and the tribal population of the area. The Nagchaudhary committee recommended that the bauxite mines in the Gandhamardan hills should be opened immediately and suggested a reformulated environmental management plan to be reviewed every year and modified whenever necessary. At the same time it proposed for the adoption of 'humane concept' and 'principles of equity' while going for development projects. Thus the project came to a grinding halt after the company had incurred an expenditure of about ₹ 25 crores, following the agitation of the people led by GSYP. At that moment BALCO Chairman P.S. Rao calling for speedy clearance of the project stated that since extraction of minerals had to be necessarily undertaken, it could be done by causing the least ecological disturbance to the area. He suggested that part of the revenue earned could be ploughed back to ensure environmental restoration. Mineral exploitation and protection of environment had to go hand in hand and there had to be a balance between preservation of ecology and exploitation of natural resources. However, the people's resistance was so strong that the project had to be stopped and that proved the movement was a success because of the participation of people cutting across different caste, classes and gender.

The Case of Kalinga Nagar Movement

The Government of Odisha mooted the idea of developing a major industrial complex in the mineral-rich region of Dangadi, Duburi and Sukinda located in the district of Jajpur. The proposed complex has the capacity of producing 15 million tons of steel annually. The complex includes about 13 mineral based industries such as iron and steel, stainless steel, sponge iron and ferrochrome etc. Iron ore and chromites are the raw materials for these industries, which are available in plenty in the region. The state government has already signed a Memorandum of Understanding with nearly ten units spread over an area of 13,000 hectares of land. The major companies such as the Tatas, Visa, Jindal, Mesco and some others have already started their projects and a few of them are nearing completion. In pursuance of the MOU, the state government would grant mining lease to the concerned industrial units and provide them with land for setting up their industries. The state government has agreed to acquire land from the local residents as well as to look into all matters relating to displacement, rehabilitation and resettlement. However, all the efforts for industrialisation were met with violent protest movements with increasing frequency. Starting with the attack on the ADM of Jajpur and some policemen on 9 May 2005 during the *Bhumipuja* of Maharashtra Seamless Limited (MSL) (*The Prajatantra Saptahiki*, Cuttack, 15–21 January 2006) over two dozen incidents of industrial violence have taken place and the MSL had to withdraw. The tribal people inhabiting the region have repeatedly expressed their dissatisfaction over the payment of compensation, which ultimately resulted in loss of life of 13 persons who were from among the tribal community In the encounter that ensued between the police and the displaced people on 2 January 2006.

The compensation package was announced in 1994, according to which a land oustee was to be paid at the rate of ₹ 35,000 per acre through the Industrial Development Corporation (IDCO), a corporation of the Government of Odisha. Mediating between the State Government and the displaced people, the IDCO sold the land to the industries at a rate of ₹ 3,50,000 per acre. The compensation package was revised later in order to enhance the rate of compensation to ₹ 50,000 per acre (ibid., 4–8). The people complained that they were paid less and were being forced to lose their means of livelihood. The unfortunate incident of loss of lives of 13 persons not only united the tribal communities of the state but also attracted the sympathy and support of the tribal people from outside the state, giving rise to a complicated political situation and completely stalling the construction work of the industrial unit. The growth of pan-tribal unity is an emerging political phenomenon against the state political leadership (ibid., 6).

Nature of the Protest

Since 2 January 2006, the tribals of Kalinga Nagar have launched an indefinite economic blockade on the National Highway 200 at Madhuban Chhak. They are not prepared to work out any compromise with the State Government. So far all efforts of the government to appease the tribes have failed, and the present situation is characterised by a deep emotional overtone. The place where the 13 victims of police firing were cremated has been named as *Bir Bhumi* and on May 23, about 5,000 women from Odisha, Chhattisgarh, Jharkhand and Andhra Pradesh took out a rally and resolved not to lift the road blockade (*The Times of India*, 24 May 2006). Among other things the 7-point charter of demands of the *Bistapan Birodhi Janamanch* includes a complete halt to displacement in the area. The economic blockade has drawn the attention of the judiciary which has issued direction to the state government to take suitable steps to lift it as early as possible.

Outcome of the Movement

When the political climate is heavily charged with anti-government slogans and an unprecedented unity among the tribes of the state and the neighbouring states has emerged as a strong political force, the Tata Steel Company has announced a package. According to the scheme, every displaced family would be considered as a family of the Tata Steel and the Company would look into their all-round development. The Company would take stock of the social and economic conditions of the displaced families every month and all the families numbering about 700 would be provided with identity cards and their progress in matters of rehabilitation and resettlement would be monitored regularly. Further, the Company would give employment benefit to all the displaced families and also revise the compensation package after proper negotiation with the people. The Company has formed a task force which includes 7 tribal members to look into all matters relating to displacement and resettlement. The package, it is claimed, is the best in the country but so far there is no response to it on the part of the protesters (*The Sambad*, 17 May 2006).

The Anti-POSCO Movement

The South Korean steel major Pohang Steel Company (POSCO) and Government of Odisha signed Memorandum of Understanding to establish steel plant and construct captive port for the company at Jagatsinghpur district near Paradeep Port in Odisha on 22 November 2005. The South Korean steel major Pohang Steel Company (POSCO) created history in India for the single largest Foreign Direct Investment (FDI) of ₹ 52,000 crores (US$ 1,202.87 crores) in the year 2005. The total land requirement for the steel plant is 4,004 acres (1,62,03,487.30 sq metres). Out of the total 4,004 acres of land, government land is 3,566.56 acres and private land is 437.68 acres (Samantara, 2006: 5–7).

Socio-Economic Determinants of the Movement

The private land is the bone of contention and for which reason the local villagers have started their movement protesting against the POSCO project and the state government. It has to be allotted in the coastal area. The question is that, to giving land for the establishment of steel project has given rise to a dispute between the local villagers on the one side and the governments, both the central government and the state government, on the other side. In between these two sides, the POSCO is eagerly waiting to get the land so as to start the steel project. The land where the steel project is going to be set up is very fertile and is cropped twice in a year. Apart from rice cultivation and vegetables, the local villagers cultivate betel leaves by erecting betel-vines. This betel-vine cultivation *(Paan)* is very profitable and is also land specific. It cannot be grown in every land and requires specific soil, climatic conditions and also expert labour to grow it. The betel leaves from this village is transported to Kolkata, the eastern metropolitan city of India and to other parts of India. If the land is given to the project then the betel-vine labourers will certainly lose their livelihood (Samantara, 2007: 12–15).

Another group of people who would certainly lose their livelihood are the fishermen community. Due to the proximity to the Bay of Bengal (hardly 2 kms from the villages), a lot of the fishermen community live in the villages who are going to be displaced. They catch fish in the sea and sell their catch in the local markets and in the Paradeep port town, which is approximately 8 kms from the villages. These groups of fishermen community question that if we are to be displaced then can the government resettle us near the sea so as to continue our livelihood and also to preserve our ancestral traditional knowledge of fishing. Hence the people of the seven villages (Dhinkia, Govindpur, Nuagaon, Bhuyanpal, Polanga, Bayanal Kandha and Noliasahi), who going to be displaced due to the project, they will get sustainability of their life and livelihood. The POSCO project has three main things, first bring the captive iron ore mines from Keonjhor and Sundargarh districts, second the steel plant will be established in Jagatsinghpur district and lastly the private port will be constructed at the mouth of the Jatadhari River. In mining activity about 600 million tons of iron ore over 1,200 hectares in the Khandahdar forests of Sundergarh will destroy the forest-based livelihoods of several villages of the Paudi Bhuiyan Primitive Tribal Group. Madhumita Roy of Action Aid, Bhubaneswar, says, 'For families who have lived in Kandadhar's forests for generations, there will be no alternative livelihood. POSCO factories will be highly mechanised (*Outlook*, 2007: 15). The people living in 22 villages of three gram panchayats of Ersama block situated in the Ersamma Assembly constituency are likely to be displaced after the work starts. It is proposed that the company would be given mining lease of 600 million tons of iron ore for which a separate MOU has to be signed, even to the extent of permitting the company to export iron ore. Further the state government would acquire 435 acres of private land for the plant which involves displacement of 20,000 to 25,000 of people (*The Sambad*, 22 July 2006).

Background of the Movement

Soon after, people came to know about the establishment of POSCO, they began protests. People started awareness campaigns in the three gram panchayats that were likely to get displaced. The project affected three gram panchayats namely, Dhinkia, Nuaga and Godokujong of Kujanga Tahasil of Jagatsinghpur District in Odisha have formed the *POSCO Pratirodh Sangram Samiti* and under the banner of this committee, they are continuing their struggle to block the entry of the steel plant in that locality. They have been relentlessly and non-violently resisting the take over of their resources for the establishment of a mega steel plant and a port by the Korean steel plant of POSCO. In the latest attempt of the Odisha government to undermine the anti-POSCO agitation, the president of the PPSS, Abhay Sahu, was arrested on 12 October 2008. His arrest once again brings to public attention how the government has become brazen in favour of POSCO's interests, and is increasingly overt in using repression and intimidation to silence people's democratic voices. While the state government has an obligatory duty to contain the spreading communal violence at the moment, it has rather adopted the age-old tactics to divert public attention from its inability and unwillingness to do so by arresting Abhay Sahu in a desperate bid to intimidate all democratic peaceful protest. Despite the repression unleashed on them, the villagers and their supporters have stood their ground and have further intensified the protest, refusing to part with their land and soil. People said that the undemocratic measures taken by the state to crush people's peaceful movement needs is widely condemned and it is time for all concerned citizens to strengthen the collective protest against such repression. The convention is aimed to consolidate people's strength into a collective in order to contribute to the process of protest for forceful acquisition of lands and natural resources in the name of 'development' which lead to loses of right to livelihoods. However, over 20,000 people from around 15 nearby villages have opposed the project, saying it would take away their homes and livelihood. On the other hand the POSCO says that the plant would affect only 500 families but would create thousands of jobs.

Spirited Protests

However police have not been able to arrest the people because the villagers have organised themselves and blocked all the roads to their villages. Check gates are created, 24 hours patrolling is carried out, every vehicle passing into the village is checked, interrogated and if it belongs to the State government or the POSCO Company than they are denied entry to the village. Daily meetings of the villagers and those offering solidarity are held near the Dhinkia village market, are well attended and addressed by women, many of whom are from dalits and tribal groups. The protests are likely to be intensified further as Company in the State is putting Odisha government under pressure to invoke repression and hand over the necessary land to POSCO. The livelihood movements in Odisha have originated from the Kashipur and Kalinganagar massacre as a symbol of anti-mining peoples' movement which they fight for their right to livelihood.

Supporters of the Movement

It is to learn that people from Maharashtra, representing the Mahamumbai Shetkari Sangharsha Samiti leading the struggle against Reliance Company's Raigadh SEZ project and Lokshashan have circulated the report and collecting relief for Dhinkia people.

One team from Janahastakhep would be visiting the area on 10 December and one team from Bhubaneswar-Cuttack would be visiting on 8 December. Examples of mass movements are the CPI(ML) New Democracy, SUCI, CPI, *Bistapan Birodhi Janmanch,* Sukinda, *Posco Pratirodh Sangram Samiti,* Dhinkia, *Prakrutika Sampad Surakhya Parishad,* Kashipur, *Vedanta Viswavidalaya Birodhi Sangharsa Samiti,* Puri, Anti-Mittal Movement, Patna(Keonjhar), *Gandhamardan Surakhya Andolan*, Lower Sutkel Anti-Dam Movement, *Paschim Odisha Krushak Sangathan Samannaya Samiti* (leading the Hirakud Water Movement), *Niyamgiri Surakhya Samiti* (Anti-Vedanta Movement of Kalahandi), *Basti Surakhya Manch,* Bhubaneswar, *Lok Mukti Sanghathan*, Jharsuguda, *Loka Shakti Abhijan* (Odisha), *Jatadhari Banchao Andolan*, Ersama (movement against POSCO's Drawing of water from Jobra Barage from a distance of 100 km and POSCO's private port at the mouth of Jatadhari), *Loka Pakhya* and some NGOs. These organisations come from across the state and represent the mass movements and political forces for opposing establishment of companies, displacement, SEZs and industrialisation in the name of development. Jointly they staged a day long Mahadharna in front of the state assembly where more than 15,000 persons participated and declared that the struggle against POSCO is their own struggle and they shall take the message across the state.

Response of the State Government Towards People's Movement

The Naveen Pattnaik government declared that the construction of the proposed POSCO steel plant project shall start on 1 April 2008 (the Odisha's Foundation Day). However, the Chief Minister, Shri Naveen Pattnaik said that 'we will discuss with the people and then go ahead with the project'. People of the anti-POSCO movement claim that, the Government of Odisha in the interest of the company, by using force and money has been able to convert some of the villagers to pro-POSCO people and has decided to make all efforts to create rift amongst fellow villagers like, the divide and rule of the colonial British. All this was being done to break the people's movement against the POSCO project and enter into the area, which they have not been able to do for the last 30 months. The whole operation was organised in the same way as was employed by the CPI(M) government of West Bengal in Nandigram. The goons in the evening of 29 November 2007 threw bombs at the protester's tent at Balitutha, where the protesters were sitting on a 24 hour vigil for the last 2 months. The vigil was meant to not allow the police, POSCO and *Prashasan* (Administration) to enter their villages (PPSS, 2008). This was the people's way of protesting the proposed acquisition of their 4,004 acres of land for establishment of a steel plant and a private sea port in the river mouth of Jatadhari for their livelihood.

The local administration has close collaboration with the Ersama MLA, who is aspiring to become a minister in the State government. Incidentally the present Collector of the Jagatsinghpur district Mr Pramod Kumar Meherda was the Collector of Rayagada district, where the Kashipur Movement, has been going on for the last 13 years against the proposed Utkal Alumina bauxite mining and Alumina plant of the Birlas. Local MLA has expressed that 95 per cent of the local people are interested in the POSCO plant and only a handful of people with vested interest are opposing. He said that out of 4,004 acres of land to be acquired by the POSCO only about 500 Acres is private land and the rest 3,500 Acres is government land where the people have been growing beetle leaves, however, the beetle leaves farming is no more profitable and people are actually leaving the profession. All these statements are trying to create a favourable public opinion for the POSCO project by the government.

Movement Against Vedanta in Lanjigarh

About the Niyamgiri Hill

The district of Kalahandi is one of the least industrially developed parts of the state. It has special characteristics of backwardness and a special project of the central government called KBK (Kalahandi, Balangir and Koraput) covering three former backward districts of Odisha and is under implementation. In the recent past, the districts attracted a lot of attention of the media due to outbreak of famine, drought, starvation and incidence of extreme poverty of the masses leading to sale of babies.

The Niyamgiri Hill of Kalahandi district has a bauxite deposit of 1,950 lakh tons. Niyamgiri is a hill range, about 250 sq km in area. The Niyamgiri Hill is also known as the Niyam Dongar. From socio-cultural, anthropological as well as geographic point of view, this is a single hilly area; but from administrative point of view, the area comes under three districts viz. Kalahandi, Rayagada and Koraput. As per sociology and social anthropology, Niyamgiri Hills are better known as the country of *'Dongaria Kandhas'*. *Dongaria Kandha* is one of the primitive tribe in India and they belong to the scheduled tribes of the State. *Dongaria Kandha* tribe depends on Niyamgiri Hill for their livelihood. The name *'Dongarias'* is derived from *'dongar'* meaning hill areas. If one claims to be a *Dongaria Kandha*, he must reside in the Niyamgiri hills and possess land of his own, and pass on to his posterity (Daspattnaik, 1984: 26). The *Dongaria Kandha* have a distinguished heritage, because of their dress style, mode of living, indigenous skills, cultural pattern and social system with nature and forests. Both culturally and ecologically, the Niyamgiri hills are extremely rich and significant. The most important thing is that, the Niyamgiri Hills are the source of Vansadhara River and Nagavali River. It also has some of the most pristine forests in Odisha, and is home to a number of vulnerable wildlife species including tiger, leopards, sloth bear, pangolin, palm civet, giant squirrel, mouse deer, langur, sambhar etc. It is also on the path of migration corridor of elephants. In view of its ecological importance, it was declared as nature conservation/game sanctuary and also was proposed as a Wildlife sanctuary in the working plan of Kalahandi Forest Division. The State Wildlife Organisation has a proposal to declare this area as South Odisha Elephant Reserve.

The Proposed Mine on the Top of Niyamgiri Hill

Niyamgiri hills belong to the Eastern Ghats. Vedanta Alumina Limited, a subsidiary of M/S Sterlite Industries Limited (SIIL) is going to mine bauxite deposit from the Niyamgiri hills jointly with Odisha Mining Corporation Limited (OMC) as per the lease agreement signed between VAL (Vedanta Alumina Ltd.) and Odisha Mining Corporation (OMC) in October 2004 (the MOU was signed by SIIL and Government of Odisha on 7 June 2003) (*The Samaj*, 2004). SIIL would set up an Alumina Complex, which includes 1.0 MTPA Alumina Refinery Plant, 3.0 MTPA of bauxite mining and 75 MW Captive Power Plant at Lanjigarh in the district of Kalahandi at an aggregate investment of approximately

₹ 4,000 crore. The estimated life span of the mining is 23 years. The proposed mining site is located on the top of Niyamgiri hills. The total forest area required for mining is 672.018 hectares, out of which 660.749 hectares (98.32% of total mining area) will be diverted for mining and other ancillary activities of the project. The proposed mining area is situated on Niyamgiri Reserve Forest of Kalahandi (South) Forest Division and Khambesi and Nimagiri PRF (Proposed Reserve Forest) and Jungle Block (Protected Forest) of Rayagada Forest Division. In addition, IDCOL, Odisha (Odisha Industrial Infrastructure Development Corporation Limited) has already acquired 775.5 acres of land from 6 villages namely Kinari, Borbhatta, Bandhaguda, Kothadwar, Bundle and Sindhabhal to lease out to Vedanta Alumina Limited required for setting up a 'Alumina Refinery Plant' at Lanjigarh, which includes 64.55 acres of village forest (Samantara, 2004: 27).

Niyamgiri area is covered with wide range of hills and peaks. The dense forest contiguity is from around Devagiri in Rayagada district to the Niyamgiri forest (on the border of Rayagada and Kalahandi districts) and further into the forests of Karlapat and Thuamal Rampur in Kalahandi district. It then turns south connecting the Tikiri-Lilligumma and Gumma forests, and then to the Narayanpatna forests in Koraput district. Thus this forest links the forests of Kandhmal district with the forests of Rayagada, Kalahandi and Koraput districts. Recently, the Proctological Society of India during a survey found that Niyamgiri was among the four major spots of Odisha where medicinal plants were found in abundance and in rich diversity (*The Samaj*, 2002).

Protest Movement Against the Vedanta

Recently, the Vedanta Alumina Limited has started its work for setting up a plant at Lanjigarh and mining of bauxite from the Niyamgiri hill. While efforts are being made to change a predominantly rural economy and hilly area into a major industrial complex, the people have been strongly resisting the work of setting up of the plant and mining of bauxite. A mass movement has been organised since 2004. On 7 April 2004 the '*Niyamgiri Suraksha Samiti*', an organisation was formed to protect the forest, land, water and their livelihood, while thousands of tribal of that area are members of the organisation. Their slogan is 'Vedant *Hatao*' (remove Vedant). The people's causes have been taken up by another organisation known as the '*Green Kalahandi*'. The '*Niyamgiri Suraksha Samiti*' has been formed by the local people to resist leasing out of the hills to the company on the ground of protecting the environment (*The Times of India*, 2006). The Niyamgiri has a number of perennial hill streams, which are useful for agriculture and for the purpose of drinking water of the tribal people living in the foothills. It is also the source of the river Bansadhara that flows through Andhra Pradesh. The hill is a place of worship of the people belonging to the '*Dangaria Kandha* tribe'.

The people of two villages namely Kinari and Bolbhatta displaced and resettled in the foothill of Niyamgiri are not at all pleased with their new environment. The people protest against the use of ground water by the Company in a drought-prone area. For their cause, they have also sought the participation of political leaders of the neighbouring Andhra Pradesh. The local Congress leaders and the CPM are active in the movement. The agitating masses point out that the Company has a plan of giving employment benefit to only 286 persons (*The Sambad*, 2006).

The proposed alumina project of the Vedanta group at Lanjigarh has provoked a political controversy between the ruling BJD and the opposition Congress. While the supporters of the BJD claim that the project will not only bring development in the area but will also generate employment. The opposition Congress Party points out the possible adverse impact on Niyamgiri's biodiversity and loss of livelihood of the *Dangaria Kandha*. The reports of Supreme Court committee and different scientific organisations have worked out the adverse implications of the project. A tribal leader and President of the *Niyamgiri Suraksha Samiti*, Daisingh Majhi says, 'Niyamgiri hills, popularly called Niyam Penu (God) are considered as the mother of the tribals, and such emotional issues should be kept above petty politics'. Further he adds that the tribals are bothered about the area's forests, natural springs, wildlife and livelihood resources. The parties should not indulge in politics over the nature's gift (*The Times of India*, 2006).

The Niyamgiri hill range abounds with streams. More than 100 streams flow from the Niyamgiri hills and most of the streams are perennial. Niyamgiri hills have been receiving high rainfall since centuries and drought is unheard of in this area. Some of the major streams that originated from Niyamgiri hills include Vamsadhara, Nagavali, Sakta Nallha, Barha Nalla etc. It provides drinking water and the agricultural fields of millions for people in the state. Similarly, another important river, known as 'Nagavali', also originates from the Niyamgiri hills as well as the Bijipur hills of the Eastern Ghats near Lanjigarh.

Socio-cultural Importance of Niyamgiri

It is more important to examine the socio-cultural aspects of the life of the indigenous tribes in Niyamgiri since they have developed, practised and nurtured their life and livelihood patterns around forest. They believe themselves to be the descendants of Niyam Raja and hence consider (being 'royal' descendants) wage labour as derogatory to their culture. Therefore they do not prefer to work as wage labourer for outsiders. However, they do work for other members of the community either in exchange of some nominal wage, or labour; but in that case also the employee-employer relationship does not exist and they treat others as their equals. The *Dongarias* consider that the right to cultivate hill slopes has been conferred to them by Niyam Raja and changed since each *dongar* plot is haunted by an ancestor spirit who helps in bumper growth of crops (Daspatnaik, 1984: 26). The *Dongaria Kandha's* economy and its major sources of livelihood are directly related with Niyamgiri forests. They collect various types of forest products and sell it to nearby weekly *haats* (market). Thus, when the government hands over such lands for mining, a whole socio-economic and ecological tradition will be smashed.

Impact of Mining Bauxite on Niyamgiri

Prior to assessment of impact of mining on Niyamgiri hills and livelihood of the indigenous, it is needed to understand the process of mining. Mining in Niyamgiri hills, which is one of the most ecologically biodiverse areas of the state with its wide range of flora and fauna, rivers and streams defies logic and reasoning. It becomes even inhuman and anti-conservative when one sees gross undervaluation of the close interaction between the local tribes especially the primitive tribe '*Dongaria Kandha*' with the nature and other forms of life in Niyamgiri.

Impact on Flora and Fauna

The proposed mining area is located on a plateau on top of Niyamgiri hill. The alumina refinery plant is situated at the footstep of Niyamgiri hill near Lanjigarh. The approach road to the proposed mining site and conveyors belt for transporting of ore from the mining site to refinery plant passes through very dense and rich forests. Secondly, as it is open cast mining, it will generate high noises during excavation, drilling, transportation, blasting and crushing operations. Thirdly, it will also pollute the air through emissions from various sources like drilling, blasting, transportation and crushing operations. The constant traffic on the road by the heavy machinery and trucks, continuous operation of machineries, blasting, influx of outsiders and run-off water from the mining site during the monsoon season would destroy the rich ecosystem of Niyamgiri hills and lead to the loss of livelihood of the indigenous, which is the main cause of vulnerability of people.

The impact of the industrial activity and influx of outsiders is already visible in shape of quarries on the edge of the Niyamgiri Reserve Forest and the felling of trees in many parts of the area. The location of the rehabilitation colony has been decided while totally ignoring the interest of the people. It is just few metres away from the Niyamgiri Reserve Forest. Adverse impact of this colony and the labour force staying near the forest is already visible.

Impact on Local Tribal

The Niyamgiri hills, which are going to be adversely affected by the proposed bauxite mining project also, happen to be home to *Dongaria Kandhas*, one of Odisha's most distinctive and traditional tribes. Their social, economic and cultural life is closely interlinked with Niyamgiri hills. Most importantly their lives and identity are confined to the Niyamgiri hills. If the project is implemented, the *Dongaria Kandha* will lose their precious home, livelihood, culture and heritage and ultimately would be left without identity.

Summary

A review of above movements, provides us with a clear picture of the nature and emergence of social movements in Odisha. A common thread which covers each of these movements is that these are protest movements which revolve around livelihood rights and are often projected against either government or the industrial capitalists. However many of the protest movements have been undertaken by the tribes of Odisha having the core idea of livelihood and right to use natural resources which they have been using for their survival since time immemorial. The emergence of such movements really makes it more clear that nationalist project of development is antithetical to tribal development project. In the process of undertaking development projects the government is in a way marginalising the already marginalised section of our society. The analysis of movements in Odisha also makes it clear that people's agency or mass participation can bring change in society, which is obvious from the movements like Baliapal, Chilika Bachao Andolan and so on.

4

Profile of Kashipur

The research work has been conducted in selected villages of Kashipur block of Rayagada district in Odisha. But before presenting an in-depth profile of Kashipur block it would be important to highlight in general some important features of the state of Odisha. The state of Odisha is located between 17E 50' and 20E 34' of the north latitude and between 81E 24' and 87E 29' east of Greenwich having a land area of 1,55,707 sq km (Odisha Development Report, 2002: 01). The state comprises of 4.74 per cent of India's total landmass with a population of 36.81 million (Census of India, 2001). This accounts for 3.57 per cent of the total population of the country. On the basis of physical features the state can be divided into four physical zones viz. the Northern Plateau, Central Tableland, Eastern Ghats and Coastal Plains. Apart from this the state can also be divided in terms of various developmental indicators into three regions i.e. Coastal region, Northern region and Southern region. For administrative purposes the state was divided into thirteen districts but in the year 1992 the then government decided to create some new districts for convenience in administration. Now the state consists of thirty districts. The fieldwork for the research work was conducted in Kashipur block under Rayagada district which was formerly a part of the undivided Koraput district.

The demography of the state is basically rural in character. According to the 2001 Census the state has the largest percentage of rural population among all Indian states. Nearly 85 per cent of

Odisha's population lives in rural areas (Odisha Development Report, 2001: 01). Odisha is primarily an agrarian state where a significant population depends on agriculture for their livelihood. Table 4.1 presents a sectoral composition of different occupations to the total Gross State Domestic Product (GSDP). The table shows that in line with the trends in other states, there has been a decline in the contribution of agriculture from 34.16 per cent in 1993–94 to less than 30 per cent in 2004–05. Again, in line with all India trends, there has not been a corresponding decrease in the proportion of the population working in agriculture, which declined much less from 74 per cent to 72 per cent in the same period as shown in the table.

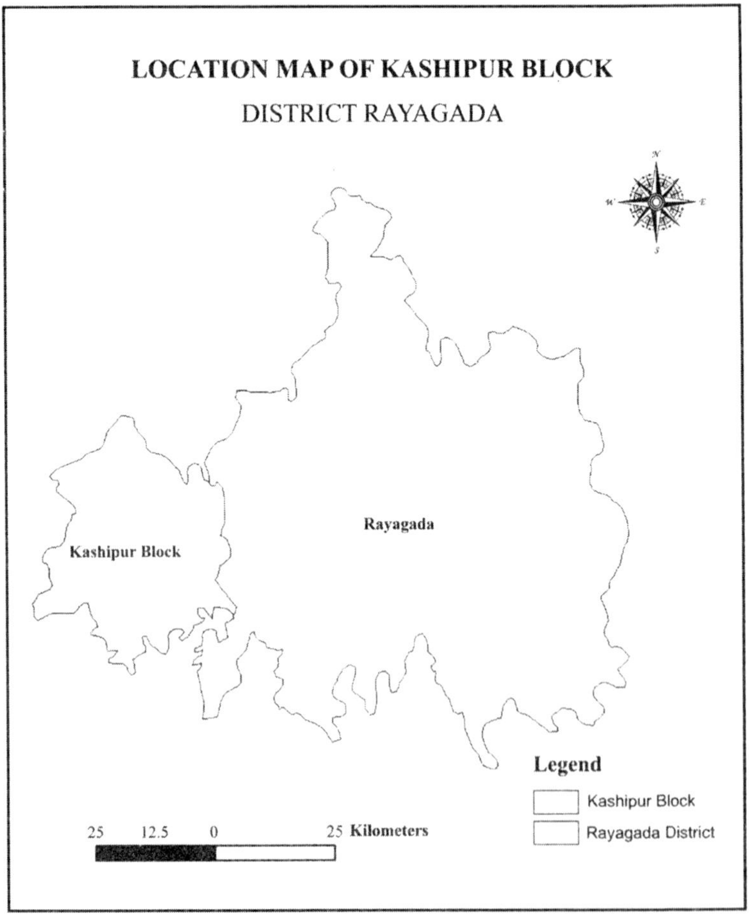

Table 4.1

Sectoral Composition (%) of GSDP, at 1993–94 prices

	1993–94	1999–2000	2004–05
Agriculture	34.16	24.80	21.43
Forestry	3.47	3.04	2.42
Fishing	2.20	2.22	2.15
Mining	5.12	7.22	9.83
Primary	44.95	37.28	35.83
Secondary	19.78	21.26	19.58
Tertiary	35.27	41.45	44.59

Source: Food Security Atlas of Rural Odisha, 2008: 19.

The growth rate of agriculture in Odisha only reiterates this story of stagnation in production. In the period 1994–2005, agriculture grew at just 1.83 per cent, forestry at 1.90 per cent, and fishing at 4.96 per cent. Fishing, however, is concentrated in the coastal region. Thus, the only agricultural sub-sector that did grow was in the already better off coastal region as shown in the Table 4.1. The sectors of the state economy that grew substantially were mining in the primary sector, and the overall in secondary and tertiary sectors. But this growth is concentrated in urban areas. There would of course, be spin offs from this urban

Table 4.2

Distribution of Operational Holdings and Area Operated by Size Class of Landholdings in Rural Odisha

Size Class of Operational Holdings (Ha)	% of Operated Area				% of Operational Holdings			
	1961–62	1971–72	1981–82	1991–92	1961–62	1971–72	1981–82	1991–92
Less than 1.01	39.42	54.52	54.45	59.99	6.97	18.60	17.02	22.09
1.01–2.00	22.92	25.78	26.11	24.34	12.51	27.32	26.48	30.16
2.01–4.00	19.65	13.90	14.08	12.02	20.73	27.06	26.16	27.87
4.01–10.00	13.66	5.25	4.63	3.36	31.04	21.56	17.84	16.20
Above 10.00	4.35	0.55	0.73	0.29	28.75	5.46	12.50	3.68
All Sizes	100.00	100.00	100.00	100.00	100.00	100.00	100.00	100.00

Source: (a) N.S.S. Report 17th Round (1961–62); (b) N.S.S. Report 26th Round (1971–72); (c) N.S.S. Report 37th Round (1981–82); (d) N.S.S. Report 48th Round (1991–92).

development, both in terms of remittances by workers of rural origin, and in terms of increasing employment opportunities and thus also overall wages. Therefore it is important to understand the agrarian structure of Odisha in general. Table 4.2 shows the agrarian structure of Odisha in terms of operational landholdings and its distribution in rural Odisha.

Table 4.2 clearly indicates that the marginal farmers having land of 1 hectare or less comprise 60 per cent of the total landholdings. Small farmers comprise 24.34 per cent while small and marginal farmers' together account for about 84 per cent of the total operational holdings. Thus it can be said that marginal farmers who have landholding of less than one hectare dominate the agrarian structure of Odisha. Within the agriculture dependent population too, there has been an increase in the proportion of agricultural labourers. Odisha has a remarkably high proportion of agricultural labourers. There are very few states in the country where the percentage of agricultural labourers to all workers exceeds that of cultivators; Odisha is one of them. However, among the states with dominant (more than two-third) workers engaged in agricultural activities, Odisha (39%) ranks after only Bihar (51%) and Andhra Pradesh (48%), where the agricultural labourers outnumber cultivators, pointing towards high levels of landlessness. Agriculture provides employment to more than 75 per cent of the workers in as many as 15 districts in Odisha. However, in almost all these districts, the majority of the workers are employed as agricultural labourers. There are only seven districts in the state where the number of cultivators exceeds that of agricultural labourers and most of these districts lie in the agriculturally developed coastal belt, except Malkangiri. All the KBK districts have more than 80 per cent of their workers in the agricultural sector, the bulk of these are labourers. This is a pointer towards the extreme vulnerability of these populations. Not only is the proportion of agricultural labourers higher, the wage rates in this region are also the lowest in the state, with an average daily wage of just ₹ 33, while that of the coastal plains is more than ₹ 50 (Food Security Atlas of Rural Odisha, 2008: 56).

Odisha is also a state with very high incidence of poverty. In some regions of the state the incidence of rural poverty is very high. Table 4.3 explains the picture of poverty concentration in different regions of the state.

Table 4.3

Region-wise Rural Poverty Ratio in Odisha, 1983–84 to 2004–05 Year

Region	*Years*				
	1983–84	*1987–88*	*1993–94*	*1999–2000*	*2004–05*
Coastal	57.90	45.30	48.40	31.80	27.4
Northern	75.20	61.00	45.80	49.80	59.1
Southern	80.80	83.00	68.80	87.20	72.7
Odisha	65.29	55.58	48.56	48.01	46.9

Source: Food Security Atlas of Rural Odisha, 2008: 14.

There is a clear regional concentration of poverty in Odisha. Poverty is highest in the southern region followed by the northern region. In the coastal region, the incidence of poverty at 27.4 per cent is actually just below the all-India rural figure of 28.1 per cent. Poverty in the northern region is as much as 30 per cent points higher at 59.1 per cent. But it is the southern region that has a massive incidence of poverty of 72.7 per cent. Significantly, both of these are the highest for any region in India. Of the three regions, poverty actually increased between 1993–94 and 1999–2000 in the north and south, while it decreased in the coastal region. Further, the north and south together account for almost 75 per cent of the state's poor.

But, even within the poorest Southern region, it is not as though all social groups of the population are equally poor. Table 4.4 shows the region-wise concentration of rural poverty among different social groups. In both the Southern region and in rural Odisha as a whole, the proportion of STs (Scheduled Tribes) in the poor is much greater than their share in the population. The STs are 28 per cent of all rural Odisha households but 43.3 per cent of rural poor households. The incidence of poverty among the STs is 75.8 per cent in rural Odisha as a whole, and as high as 82.8 per cent in Southern Odisha. Thus, a social dimension accompanies the regional dimension of poverty, with the STs accounting for a larger share of the poor and having a high incidence of poverty. The proportion of the SCs (Scheduled Castes) in rural poverty, 19.0 per cent, is a little more than their share in the rural population, 18.2 per cent; while the incidence of poverty among the SCs is close to 50 per cent. The STs and SCs together account for 62.3 per cent of the rural poor, while they account for 46.9 per cent of rural households as shown in Table 4.4. Thus, the regional and social dimensions of poverty manifest themselves in the fact that poverty is highest in the southern region and most prevalent among the STs, with the SCs also doing quite badly overall. In the Southern region, even the OBCs (Other Backward Classes) and 'Others' have a relatively high incidence of poverty of 64.7 per cent and 44.1 per cent respectively.

Table 4.4

Region-wise Poverty Rates by Social Group for Rural Odisha (2004–05) [%]

Region	*ST*	*SC*	*OBC*	*Others*	*All*
Southern	82.8	67. 2	64.7	44.1	72.7
Northern	72.8	64.4	48.6	33.9	59.1
Coastal	67.7	32.8	24.4	19.0	27.4
Rural Odisha	75.8	49.9	37.1	23.5	46.9
Rural India	44.7	37.1	25.8	17.5	28.1

Apart from this let us look at the district-wise concentration of rural families who are below poverty line according to the 1997 survey as shown in Table 4.5.

Table 4.5

District-wise Distribution of Rural Families Below Poverty Line (on the basis of their occupations) in Odisha as per 1997 Survey

S. No.	*Name of the District*	*Small Farmers*	*Marginal Farmers*	*Agro-Labourers*	*Rural Artisans*	*Total BPL Families*	*Total Rural Families*
1	Angul	9.37	28.58	15.39	1.42	59.36	100.00
2	Bolangir	11.05	17.93	21.26	1.09	61.06	100.00
3	Baleswar	8.87	21.26	42.96	0.63	73.72	100.00
4	Bargarh	11.28	18.14	28.02	2.09	60.38	100.00
5	Bhadrak	9.73	29.06	40.49	0.43	66.70	100.00
6	Cuttack	6.30	19.45	18.37	3.92	52.38	100.00
7	Dhenkanal	6.61	24.67	26.92	0.73	62.63	100.00
8	Gajapati	4.96	5.86	22.51	0.72	61.38	100.00
9	Ganjam	3.01	4.73	17.60	1.17	55.00	100.00

Contd...

...Contd

10	Jagatsinghpur	1.26	28.26	20.81	2.24	52.75	100.00
11	Jajpur	7.18	23.53	23.37	3.23	60.40	100.00
12	Kalahandi	12.29	15.03	26.03	1.13	62.71	100.00
13	Kendrapara	7.71	23.53	24.39	4.71	59.89	100.00
14	Kendujhar	18.32	7.27	1.61	27.61	76.96	100.00
15	Khurda	5.94	9.52	20.77	2.00	59.17	100.00
16	Koraput	14.85	22.84	35.69	1.14	83.81	100.00
17	Malkangiri	24.68	30.17	23.68	3.34	81.88	100.00
18	Mayurbhanj	11.57	33.96	27.85	3.46	77.74	100.00
19	Nuapada	13.23	38.60	24.55	1.49	85.70	100.00
20	Nabarangpur	36.81	16.16	40.70	5.29	73.66	100.00
21	Nayagarh	11.86	32.27	21.23	4.94	67.91	100.00
22	Puri	10.34	22.63	23.66	1.50	69.13	100.00
23	Rayagada	7.97	18.99	34.81	3.41	72.03	100.00
24	Sonepur	9.20	17.80	40.69	1.91	73.02	100.00
25	Sundargarh	15.86	29.87	17.35	2.13	65.22	100.00
26	Phulbani	12.11	25.62	25.63	1.07	78.42	100.00
27	Boudh	20.65	30.55	24.16	2.32	80.20	100.00
28	Sambalpur	16.07	18.41	26.00	1.95	59.78	100.00
29	Deogarh	15.97	16.55	32.05	1.48	78.79	100.00
30	Jharsuguda	7.03	21.52	6.42	0.80	49.02	100.00
	Total	11.02	20.90	24.91	3.24	66.37	100.00

Source: Panchayati Raj Department, Government of Odisha.

From the Table 4.5 it may be seen that in the state of Odisha in 1997, 66.37 per cent of rural families were living below the poverty line. The rural poor are agricultural labourers, rural artisans, marginal farmers and small farmers who together form the rural BPL families. The district-wise analysis shows that Jharsuguda district had the lowest percentage of rural poor families i.e. 49.02 per cent, who were living below the poverty line, whereas, the highest percentage of rural poor families is 85.70 per cent in Nuapada district.

The KBK Region

As the study area falls under the Koraput-Bolangir-Kalahandi (KBK) region it is necessary to throw some light upon this region. The KBK region comprising of three old undivided districts i.e.

Koraput, Bolangir and Kalahandi, has caught global attention for its very low level of living and chronic poverty. These three districts are now divided into 8 districts including Rayagada district, inhabited mostly by Scheduled Castes and Scheduled Tribes, with high incidence of poverty. Out of 80 Community Development (CD) blocks as many as 53 blocks (66.25%) are considered the most backward blocks of Odisha (Odisha Development Report, 2002: 318).There is also a wide variance in the levels of poverty amongst the poor.

Table 4.6

Literacy Rate of KBK Districts (2001)

District	Popu-Density	Literacy Rate					
		Female (%)	Rural (%)	ST (%)	SC (%)	Total (%)	Female (%)
1	2	4	5	6	7	8	9
1 Koraput	134	49.96	83.19	49.62	13.04	35.72	24.30
2 Malkangiri	87	50.00	93.13	57.43	21.35	30.53	20.90
3 Nawrangpur	194	49.81	94.22	55.03	14.10	33.93	20.70
4 Rayagada	118	50.66	86.11	55.76	13.92	36.15	24.60
5 Bolangir	203	49.59	88.46	20.60	16.90	55.70	39.50
6 Sonepur	232	49.08	92.61	9.80	23.60	62.84	46.20
7 Kalahandi	169	50.00	92.50	28.65	17.67	45.94	29.30
8 Nuapada	138	50.19	94.34	34.71	13.62	42.00	25.80
KBK Districts	153	49.91	89.95	38.41	16.25	43.33	29.10
Odisha	236	49.30	85.01	22.13	16.53	63.08	50.50

Source: Panchayati Raj Department, Government of Odisha.

Note: Popu-density means population density (persons/sq km).

The KBK districts account for 19.80 per cent population and over 30.60 per cent geographical area of the State. About 89.95 per cent people of this region still live in villages. It has a lower population density of 153 persons per sq km in comparison to 236 for Odisha. The tribal communities dominate the demography of this region. As per 2001 Census, about 38.41 per cent people of these districts belong to the Scheduled Tribes (ST) communities and 16.25 per cent populations belong to the Scheduled Castes (SC) communities. Literacy level of this region is not only below national average but also below state average. Female literacy is only 29.10 per cent.

Education is an essential factor to improve the quality of life and to develop the human capital. It is found that despite economic backwardness the development gap of the literacy rate of population in Odisha is not so low when it is compared with the average literacy rate of population at the national level. However, this table shows that at the inter-district level it is noticed that the backward tribal and highland districts like Rayagada, Koraput, Malkangiri and Nabarangpur have comparatively lower level of literacy rate 36.15 per cent, 35.72 per cent, 30.53 per cent and 33.93 per cent respectively.

As per the 1997 census of BPL families, about 71 per cent of the total families are identified as BPL families in this region. District-wise information about the number of BPL families as per 1992 and 1997 census are summarised in the Table 4.7.

Table 4.7

Families Below Poverty Line (BPL): 1992 and 1997

S. No.	*District*	*Census 1992*	*Census 1997*
		Per cent (%)	*Per cent (%)*
1	*2*	*7*	*10*
1	Kalahandi	85.77	62.71
2	Nuapada	83.64	78.31
3	Bolangir	75.82	61.06
4	Sonepur	62.29	73.02
5	Koraput	86.59	83.81
6	Malkangiri	84.81	81.88
7	Nabarangpur	90.56	73.66
8	Rayagada	86.04	72.03

Source: As per 1999–2000 NSS data (Manoj Panda, 2002)
Panchayati Raj Department, Government of Odisha.

On the basis of the above table, we can see that in the KBK region 71.40 per cent of population is living below the poverty line and district-wise the Koraput district has the highest population living below the poverty line. If you compare to Odisha and India as a whole then we can imagine the condition of the KBK people. The KBK districts have been historically rich in forest resources. Though the people have been using these forests very intensively but they eke out their livelihood from these resources only.

Profile of Kashipur

Kashipur block is situated between 82E 42' and 83E 18' east longitude and 19E 3' and 19E 32' north latitude. Shaped as a parallel gram of irregular sides, it is bounded in the west and north by the Kalahandi district in the east, Rayagada block and in the south, Dasamantapur block of Koraput district (Koraput, 1966: 439).

After merger of states in 1948, Kashipur, which was a Zamindari in ex-Kalahandi state, formed part of the newly formed Kalahandi district. In 1952 the Zamindari was abolished. As the communication facilities with Bhawanipatna, headquarter of Kalahandi district, had some inconveniences, it was decided to transfer the Kashipur police station covering the Zamindari area to Koraput district. As a result it became a part of Koraput district from 1 August 1962 (ibid., 1966: 439). However, because of the reorganisation of districts of Odisha, it became the part of Rayagada district after 2 October 1992. The Kashipur block is one of the eleven blocks in the divided districts of Rayagada. Kashipur is situated to the southern part of the Rayagada district with geographical area of 1,505.90 sq km. There are 412 Revenue villages and 109 Hamlets divided into twenty Gram Panchayats (GPs) (Kashipur Block Report). The total population of the block is 1,21,086, of which STs are 74,646 (61.64%), SCs are 24,216 (19.99%), and others are 22,224 (18.35%) (2001 Census). The literacy rate of Kashipur block is 19.15 per cent.

Topography

The topography of Kashipur block consists of rugged hills and intervening valleys with a few level stretches. The mountain system in the eastern part of the block forms the watershed between the Nagavali and the Indravati rivers. The highest peaks are along its east in the hill ranges called *Kutrumali, Sasubahumali, Kodingamali* etc. *Kodingamali* on the southernmost point of the Tahasil has an elevation of 4,182 feet. *Tangri Dongar* is next having a height of 4,031 feet. Another important peak *Indragiri* is in the east of Kashipur block headquarters. To the west lies *Baphalimali Parvat,* the highest point of which is 3,588 feet

(Odisha District Gazetteer, Koraput, 1966: 439). This hill consists of rich reserves of bauxite.

Rivers

The most important river of the block is Golagada, which rises from Sasubahumali hill near Kashipur village towards south. It has a number of mountain streams and its main tributary is *Kandabinda Nalla* that flows near *Baphalimali Parvat*. The *Golagada* falls into the Indravati river, on the border of Kalahandi district near Katikhaman village of Kashipur block. All the rivers of Kashipur block are non-perennial in character. So they completely dry up or have less flow of water during the dry season. But during the rainy season they suddenly rise to the banks discharging enormous volume of water.

History

The early history of Kashipur can be known from two copper plate's inscription files. One of which is in possession of the Maharaja of Kalahandi and the other one is with the ex-Zamindar of Kashipur. The Maharaja of Kalahandi submitted the copper plate to the Ministry of the State, Government of India in May 1949 for claiming the Zamindari of Thuamul Rampur in ex-Kalahandi state as his personal property (Odisha District Gazetteers, Koraput, 1966: 442). The other plate was submitted by the Zamindar of Kashipur to the political agent of Chhattisgarh State, Raipur, in 1937 (ibid., 1966: 442). It has been said that Maharaja Kumar Sri Kesai Singh, the Zamindar of Thuamul Rampur of Kalahandi state fought with the father of Budha Biswambhar Deo and installed him as the Raja of Jeypore. In return Biswambhar Deo gifted four *garhs* namely, Kashipur, Chandragiri, Bissamgiri and Mahulpatna to the Maharaja of Kalahandi. It was also settled that Kesai Singh would pay 700 rupees per annum as *Malguzari* to the Maharaja of Jeypore (ibid., 1966: 442). It is known that the *garhs* of Kashipur, Chandragiri, Bissamgiri and Mahulpatna, which formerly belonged to the Maharaja of Jeypore were gifted by Biswambhar Deo to Maharaja Jugraj Deo of Kalahandi because of some military help in 1712 A.D. Later Maharaja Jugraj Deo presented these four *garhs* to Kesai Singh who was the Zamindar of

Thuamul Rampur and Deopur. Elliot also said that the Raja of Jeypore ceded the four *garhs* to the Raja of Kalahandi (ibid., 1966: 443).

After Kesai Singh, his eldest son Govinda Rai became the third *Patraja* of Thuamul Rampur, and another son Udaya Singh became the manager of that Zamindari, who was popularly called '*Thatraja*'. Under Fokir Singh, the son of Jay Singh and the grandson of Kesai Singh, Mohulpatna became a separate Zamindari in 1778. It is also said that the dispute continued between the *Rajas* of Kalahandi and Jeypore over the ownership of Kashipur. The '*Thatraja*' of Kashipur was Baidyanath Singh who was the fifth descendant of Udaya Singh, the first '*Thatraja*'. In 1869 the '*Thatraja*' was placed under the feudal control of *Raja* of Kalahandi. Thus Baidyanath Singh became the first Zamindar of Kashipur (ibid., 1966: 443–444). *Ranee* Suryakumari Devi, widow of Baidyanath Singh had managed the administration of Kashipur after his death in 1885 and at that time his son Udit Pratap was a minor. During the tenure of Udit Pratap Singh the settlement of Kashipur was undertaken in 1913 and he died in 1918. Rudra Pratap Singh the son of Udit Pratap Singh was the last Zamindar of Kashipur (ibid., 1966: 444). The Zamindari of Kashipur having the title of '*Thatraja*' would sometimes act as an independent ruler. But at other times they would act as subordinate chief of Thuamul Rampur Zamindar (*Patraja*). The Kashipur Zamindari was traditionally divided for administrative purposes into a number of units like:

- Uperbissi or Uprabissi with headquarters at Kashipur.
- Munusbissi also called Baphalabissi with headquarters at Chandragiri, the foothill of Baphalimali hill, lying towards the west of Kashipur.
- Hungringbissi with headquarters at Sunger lying towards the east of Kashipur.
- Mandibissi with headquarters at Mandibissi lying towards the north of Kashipur.

Health Care Systems in Kashipur

This section deals with the health care services and facilities provided by the government and the responses of the tribes. It examines the health care services and argues on the basis of fieldwork that Government's health care facilities in this area are in a very poor condition. The poor tribal are suffering from various communicable and water borne diseases. The entire block is malaria and diarrhoea prone area. The government hospitals/health centres have failed to provide adequate health facilities to the needy. At the same time people cannot afford to go to private hospitals. If members of the indigenous people are suffering from any disease, first they try to ignore or do not prefer to go to hospital. The reason is that they are not provided medicine in government hospital and they have to buy it from the chemist shop and most of the time the doctor is found absent.

Their economic condition is very bad as most of the tribal depend on daily wage, hence they cannot manage the extra expenses on medicine other than food expenses. In most of the cases to avail medical treatment they mortgage their belonging, take loan from private men/moneylender with high interest rate and sometimes it makes them bonded labour. The government is well aware of this situation but nothing has been done for the tribal people. In Kashipur block, there is one Community Health Centre at Kashipur block headquarter, six Public Health Centres (PHCs), 31 ANM Health Sub-Centres and 170 Anganwadi Centres (AWCs). The Community Health Centre at Kashipur has a single doctor, which is against the sanctioned strength of four. Now government has posted the doctors on contract basis, but in many places they have not joined. The ANM Sub-centre and AWC are providing first aid services to the people. There is a single doctor in the Kashipur hospital. Hence in case the doctor is on leave or in any other official work, the health service gets paralysed. Ultimately it is the people who suffer.

The tribal population constitute 61 per cent of the total population. The SC constitutes 20 per cent and the rest are Paikas, and Goudas, belonging to backward communities, who are agricultural classes. The Sahukars (village moneylenders) have been living in most of the villages, who are outsiders and belong to forward castes. Many *Kumutis* and *Marwaris* have settled in the township areas and are engaged in the business activities in rural as well as urban areas.

Kashipur is a hill tract and drought prone area. Agriculture is the main source of livelihood for the people of Kashipur. The land quality is not good and irrigation is almost non-existent. Most of the people are landless, who either do sharecropping in others' land or work as wage labourers. The land possessed by the tribal are very little and of bad quality. They practice burn-slash cultivation. The other backward classes and forwards communities hold the best quality land.

Education in Kashipur

Education is the vehicle of development, without education all round human development is not possible. Keeping in mind the importance of education and to improve the literacy of the tribal people, the Centre and the State government have been undertaking many programmes and policies. In Kashipur block, there are four High Schools and 183 Primary Schools. However, it was found that schools are with single teacher and most of the time teachers are not regular. Parents do not send their children to schools owing to chronic poverty and ignorance. The little children also form part of their economic activities, who look after the cattle and the small children. The provision of hostels in each GP for 40 students is not able to accommodate many poor children as one GP comprises of 20–40 villages. After the primary education, many are deprived of higher education, as there are only four High Schools in the whole block, one each at Tikiri, Gorakhpur, Kashipur and Dangasil. Out of these Gorakhpur and Dangasil are having ST/SC welfare hostels.

A person learns from her/his natural environment, from the salt of her/his soil, helps her/him learn the art of living or growing food grains, learn her/his own culture, around their environment where they live. Social responsibilities do not constitute education according to the dominant paradigms. People who have learnt all these things are dubbed as illiterate, uneducated in the modern education system. As a result, they suffer from terrible inferiority complex, which drives them towards a sort of mental poverty and they lose faith in their own way of living. Secondly, prevalent education system tries to entrench the idea in their mind that their language is not useful for them to be integrated to the national mainstream, so they need to learn a Standard Language. Let us see the status of education in Kashipur. The word 'absence' is the hallmark of education system in Kashipur, be it school, teacher, or students. Most of the teachers do not come to the school but draw their salary. At some places they employ proxy teachers paying two hundred to three hundred rupees per month. At other places where 5/6 teachers are required only 1 teacher is posted. The biggest problem is that teachers coming from outside do not understand their language or their lifestyle. Thus they fail to instil any interest in them to study anything. Till today we see hardly 10 to15 matriculate or 5 to 10 graduates in an entire Panchayat (in every five to six thousand population). In some Gram Panchayats like Sunger, Odajore, Munusogaon, Chandragiri, Mandibisi and Godibali, it is very difficult to find even 2/3 graduates. This shows the sincerity and condition of education in Kashipur block. Nevertheless the fact that the target for education is not achieved, so some people talk of reform in education system (operation blackboard, joyful learning, night schools' scholarships, free primary education etc.). Committee after committees are set up, reports prepared and experts employed, just to show that state is really concerned for the people. What is the mystery behind this concern?

To minimise the dropout rate, the government has launched the mid-day-meal (MDM) scheme which is the best programme, as it provides nutritional support to the poor students. Mid-day-meal is functioning in all the villages of Kashipur block. Head master of the school is in charge of mid-day-meal and accountable to higher authority for any explanation. It is given only in working days in the school at recess period. It is a known fact that in most of the villages mid-day-meal is not given regularly. Whereas there is village level committee called Village Education Committee (VEC) which constitutes of 10 members including the head master of the school who is the member secretary of the village education committee in every village. This VEC is a powerful body of the school and without the signature of the President of the committee the teachers cannot draw their salary. But the reality is that, this committee is playing no role as it is neither looking at the functioning of the school nor at the mid-day-meals. It is because of the illiteracy of the people. The fact is that tribal often face various problems due to lack of quality education.

Rajiv Gandhi and the New Era of Development

During 1985–86, Kashipur faced a terrible drought. Deaths due to severe starvation were reported in both local and national media.

Then the late Prime Minister Rajiv Gandhi visited Kashipur to see the problems of people by his own eyes. This ushered in a new era in the history of Kashipur block. Development plans were chalked out. The International Fund for Agricultural Development (IFAD) came in to develop agriculture in the area. In the name of agricultural development, it introduced coffee plantation and sericulture. Earlier in their *dangars* where they used to grow *alsi, mandia, kandul* etc., now they were taught to grow coffee and mulberry for the benefit of traders and capitalists. IFAD also suggested for development of roads and communications to bring the people to the national mainstream. So roads from Tikiri to Kashipur via Kucheipadar and Dongasil, railway line from Rayagada to Koraput via Tikiri, were constructed. Kashipur is a willy-nilly forest area with rich natural resources. It has become the centre of national attention since last 10 years. The main reason is that, the rich deposit of Bauxite mines for which one after the other private sectors, corporate and multinational company are trying to establish Alumina Plants, to which local communities have been strongly opposing. Kucheipadar village near by 12 kms away from Tikiri police station is a place proposed for establishment of the Alumina Plant of Utkal Alumina International Limited (UAIL). There is another village known as Sunger that is about 20 kms away from Kashipur block headquarter, where the L&T Company has decided to establish the Alumina Plant. There is a third village with the name of Kansariguda about 10 kms away from Tikiri police station, where the Aditya Birla Company has decided to set up another Alumina Plant. There has been strong people's agitation against the establishment of all these Alumina Plants. From 1993 onwards one company after another company has decided to establish the Alumina Plant in this area, and then the people of Kashipur realised as to what is the real motive behind this International Funds for Agricultural Development (IFAD) in Kashipur area.

The PDS in Kashipur Block

Three bodies run the PDS in Kashipur block: the Civil Supply Corporation, the Department of Food and Civil Supply and the District Cooperative Banks. The mid-day-meal schemes and the food for work programmes are managed by the District Rural

Development Agency. To bring an end to the corruption by private dealers, Gram Panchayat took over distribution of food grains from 1994. In Kashipur block, the Inspector of Supplies and Marketing Inspectors are functioning as Departmental Storage Agent. The Targeted Public Distribution System (TPDS) was introduced in May 1997. Under this scheme, 16 kg of food grains (rice) per BPL family per month is being issued at highly subsidised rates of ₹ 4.75 per kg. Despite a very heavy subsidy burden, the TDPS has come in for severe criticism from various quarters including many state governments. It has been argued that a scale of ration of 10 kg per month per BPL family is grossly inadequate. So it was increased to 16 kg per month. Under the Annapurna Scheme, senior citizens of 65 years of age or above who though eligible for old age pension but are not getting the pension are covered under the scheme on the basis of 10 kg of food grains per person per month that are supplied free of cost. And the Government launched in 2000, the Antyodaya Anna Yojana (AAY) for the poorest of the poor. Under this scheme, 35 kg of food grains are distributed to each eligible family at highly subsidised rates of ₹ 03.00 per kg for rice in Kashipur block. Some of the facts regarding the price and the working of PDS in Kashipur block are as follows.

Sugar is being issued to the BPL families only. As per the instructions of the government the BPL families are entitled to get 2 kgs of sugar per month at ₹ 13.50 per kg. The consumption of sugar by the BPL families in this district is poor. The zonal sugar deport is situated at Jeypore. Due to heavy expenses on transportation charges of sugar to different block points of this district, the storage agents are reluctant to lift the sugar every month; of course there is poor demand of the sugar by the BPL families. Kerosene oil is allotted to Rayagada district. As per Government instruction, 4 litre of kerosene oil is being supplied to the consumers of rural areas per a ration card per month. But people are getting only 1/2 litre a month and the rest of it goes to black market.

Awareness of Citizens

The association of people with some governmental activity or programme is proclaimed as public participation. People associate themselves with the administration and governmental programmes through expression of opinions about the action of the government. This type of participation must be based upon knowledge without which it becomes meaningless.

If support or criticism is well informed, it will be neither meddlesome nor harassing to the administrator. For this however, the prerequisite is the availability of accessibility to correct and sufficient amount of information to the eager and competent public. Hence, the participation of the people depends upon the level of awareness and magnitude of their interest in administration and governmental programmes. It is needless to say that awareness of the facilities of the programmes will not only generate an interest in them but also make them avail benefits to a large extent and increase people's participation in it. So a study of the awareness of the individual is necessary for the study of participation. Most of the people however come across the programmes and policies of the educated people, teachers of the villages and some decent political leaders. Lack of education, poverty and cultural backwardness are mainly responsible for their lack of awareness.

The political leaders, like ward members and Sarpanch play the crucial role of communicators to the villagers in the grassroots level. Again the Panchayat Samiti plays an effective role in block administration. The people of Kashipur say that, there is closer relationship between the political leaders and the officials. Citizens don't have trust and confidence upon political leaders. People feel that, they will get more help and support from the political leaders but once the election is over, people do not get anything from the leaders. The villager is still not exposed to mass media like radio, newspapers or television. Thus accessibility of the respondents to mass media is limited and official machinery is not in a position to meet the information demand to the extent desired in order to generate the required feelings that, there are varieties of measures implemented by the government for their advantage through block administration. Advantages are taken by the sarpanch and panchayat secretary. In the name of the Gram Sabha, Polli Sabha in the villages or gram panchayat and Village Level Committees (VCLs), the workers, representatives, the sarpanch or the Mukhia is enjoying the benefits. The Food for Work Programmes, Swarnajayanti Gram Swarojgar Yojana (SGSY), Sampoorna Grameen Rozgar Yojana (SGRY) and now the National Rural Employment Guarantee Scheme (NREGS) are the major rural development programmes of the government which have not been implemented properly in Kashipur block. These programmes are being implemented through the Gram Panchayat with direct supervision of the block authority. Implementation of these programmes has greater importance both for the region and the people due to two reasons namely, its support to get food security for the rural poor and its help in the building of rural infrastructure. These works are not supposed to be given to contractor as it is strictly forbidden. The concerned village's workers the community level are doing the works. No individual person is allowed to take the work. In every village there is a Village Labour Committee (VLC). It is consisted of all the labourers (BPL cardholders) of the village who are registered in NREGA, headed by a team leader called Village Labour Leader (VLL). Work order is issued in the name of the VLL on behalf of village labourers and he will see the work. Selection of works are being made on the basis of Palli Sabha and are approved in the gram sabha held at the panchayat level twice in a year. It is revealed from the fieldwork that in reality the works are not done by the VLL. No doubt the work order is issued in his name but the contractor is doing the work indirectly. For the official purpose the VLC is fully answerable to the concerned high officials for the work. Whereas the profit of the works goes to the pockets of contractor, this is happening with the full knowledge of all the concerned officials, starting from the top to bottom. So now the central government has taken initiative to stop the corruption. Hence it has made the provision that all the wage payment of the workers will be made through the SBI account or post office account.

Near about six months in a year, the poorer families depend on forest for their livelihood. Some of them depend on wage labour. The source of labour varies from agricultural employment to construction works to government employments. Though a substantial fund is spent in employment generation programmes by the government, it is found that government employment is hardly a dependable source of income/employment for the people. It was found that in most of the cases including Food for Work, the project has been contracted to private persons, who almost inevitably cheat the people of at least half their wages. Sometimes wage is paid in terms of grain, in which case, the labourers do not even avail a means of measuring whether they have received their due or not, and complaints to the BDO hardly brings any response. Contractors have become powerful despots in the tribal regions with subtle backing from the administration, as the administrators also get percentage from the contractors and cheat them in the payments for the various governments' work. As they live in the neighbourhood of the tribal people, they also subdue the tribals with threats of sheer physical violence. There is little recourse for the tribal people in such cases, as the money power of these contractors, is enough to win over any law keeping forces that the region might have. If people resist, and insist on higher wages than the contractor is ready to bring labourers from neighbouring villages to work. Any aggression on the part of the resisting villager is efficiently quelled by counter violence.

5

Livelihood and Environmental Movement in Kashipur

> The Gandhian version of the simple life in its focus on manual labour in the village as the supreme form of human society and rejection of industrial culture as violent, competitive and destructive of nature. Gandhi had concerns that were focused on the economic and political, the restoring of the livelihoods and dignity of villagers. (Guha, 2000: 24)

Koraput district was known for diseases, bad weather and tigers. An image was actually promoted by the tribals as it helped preserve the beauty of this landscape. The mountains, the forests and valleys were keeping away outsiders, but then a new era of 'railway' was born 12 years ago when the government laid the Rayagada-Koraput rail tracks. This track was called the 'lifeline' of south Odisha, but was actually built to export the bauxite, iron ore, limestone and the forest produce.

To see the movement in a proper perspective, an insight into the region is essential. The Kashipur is a block in the Rayagada district of Odisha. From Rayagada towards Koraput after a distance of 32 kms one will arrive at Rupakana square. Then from here if one moves towards right again for about 32 kms, one arrives at Kucheipadar village. This is the place proposed for the establishment of the Alumina Plant of Utkal Alumina International Limited (UAIL). The people of this entire area are against this proposed Alumina Plant as it is going to uproot them. There is another village nearby known as Sunger, which is about

20 kms from Kashipur block headquarters. This is the second village where the L&T Company has decided to establish Alumina Plant against which the people have been struggling to protect their life and livelihood. There is another village called Kansariguda, which is about 10 kms away from Tikiri police station where the Aditya Birla Company has decided to setup another Alumina Plant for which a strong public resistance has already set in.

Social Composition and Natural Resources

Kashipur is a dense forest area, rich with different flora and fauna, inhabited by majority of tribals that constitute 62.64 per cent of the total population; mainly Kandha, Jhodia and Penga communities of tribes reside in this area and the dalit community who comprises 19.99 per cent of the total population. Their identifiable sources of income are agriculture, occasional wage labour and collection of forest produce. It needs to be noted that in this area both dalits and tribal people do *dangar chasa* (shifting cultivation). The details of the social composition of the people are given in the Table 5.1, like the total population, scheduled caste, scheduled tribe and the literacy of the population.

Natural resources such as forest, water and land are fundamental to all life forms, these are, much more than money and economic infrastructure, for the base of survival. The large numbers of rural poor communities depend on natural resources in their locality to meet most of their needs for livelihoods. Their material livelihood and economic sustenance largely depend on it. In Kashipur block, most of the tribals, dalits and rural poor population directly depend on land-based occupations like forests, *podu* cultivation, wetlands and marine habitats for their basic needs and requirement with regard to water, food, fuel, housing, fodder and medicine as well as ecological livelihoods and cultural sustenance. Given this close interdependence of humans and their environment, it is not surprising that the culture of tribal societies is so greatly influenced by their environment. They seek inspiration, knowledge, spirituality and aesthetics within their natural surroundings.

In Odisha, as elsewhere, vital resources like land, water and forests had, for centuries, been controlled and used collectively by

Table 5.1

Total Population, ST, SC and Total Literacy Rate in Kashipur Block

Total Population (TP)			*Scheduled Caste*			*Scheduled Tribe*			*Total Literacy*		
TP	*Male*	*Female*	*TP*	*Male*	*Female*	*TP*	*Male*	*Female*	*TP*	*Male*	*Female*
1,21,086	59,867	61,219	24,216	12,043	12,173	74,646	36,668	37,978	23,189	17,701	5,488
100%	49.44%	50.55%	19.99%	49.73%	50.26%	61.64%	49.12%	50.87%	19.16%	76.33%	23.66%

Source: Census of India 2001.

village communities thus ensuring a somewhat sustainable use of these renewable resources.

In the above table we have seen that the male population is 49.44 per cent and the female population is 50.55 per cent, the tribal population including the Kandha, Jhodia and Penga Paraja has 61.64 per cent, among them male is 49.12 per cent and the female is 50.87 per cent, thus it has a tribal dominated block. The SC constituted only 19.99 per cent, their male is 49.73 per cent and the female is 50.26 per cent and the rest are other castes namely the Paika, Gouda, Khandayat and Brahmin. If we see the educational systems, it has very low, only 19.16 per cent. Therefore Kashipur is one of the underdeveloped blocks in Odisha.

Once upon a time, Kashipur was a land of dense forest and perennial springs, and in its lap human communities were living. They depended on land and forest and practiced hunting and gathering to meet their basic needs. In the course of time, their lands and forests became the property of the state, in other words, nature turned into property, the State became its owner. Odisha government created a series of laws in subsequent years to exercise control over nature particularly forest. As a result, people were debarred from their birthright to use forest for their survival. Once state becomes the owner of the nature, it arrogated the role of the protector of the jungle. It also becomes solely responsible for its proper use and also for the present and future of the people who depend on it. Barring a few places, *dangars* are completely naked, no trees, no animals. The government, squaring on the responsibility, is accusing people for deforestation, but all have been sacrificed in the name of national development and national interest. J.K. Paper Mill at Rayagada is a monstrous monument of this process. The loss of forest resources has become the biggest bone of contention for local communities dependent on it. After destroying the forest resources based life patterns of the people, the state has taken up various schemes to show its concern for the people. It tries to establish its welfare character by introducing various welfare schemes. The state government has made itself indispensable both through its coercive power and welfare measures.

In what follows below I have mentioned in the Table 5.2 about the rural, urban population and the main workers in the Kashipur block.

In the table it is seen that the total main workers are 51.29 per cent, the male is 53.09 per cent and the female workers' population is 46.90 per cent. From the table, it can be concluded that the total male workers (51.29%) depend on daily wage labours and natural resources for their livelihood.

Table 5.2

Rural-Urban and Main Workers Percentage in Kashipur Block

Areas	*Population*	*Male*	*Female*	*Total Main Workers*	*Male*	*Female*
Total	1,21,086	59,867 (49.44)	61,219 (50.55)	62,111 (51.29)	32,979 (53.09)	29,132 (46.90)
Rural	1,21,086 (100)	59,867 (49.44)	61,219 (50.55)	62,111 (51.29)	32,979 (53.09)	29,132 (46.90)
Urban	000	000	000	000	000	000

Source: Census of India 2001.

Note: Parenthesis in the bracket is percentage.

Photo 1

One of the Nala on Baphalimali hill

Photo 2

South Eastern area of Baphalimali hill

Cultural Significance of Baphalimali Mountain

The area is inhabited mainly by *Desia Kandha* tribes, along with *Paraja*, *Jhodia* and dalits communities and other backward communities. *Baphala Budhi*, who stays on the Baphalimali hills is the reigning deity of the tribals of the area. She stays on the plateau of Bapahalimali which is proposed for mining bauxite. A cairn of stones marks this place where *Kandhas* carry out prayers and sacrifices to appease the deity. There used to be grove of trees at this location. *Baphala Budhi* is a central focus of the *Kandha* cosmology, and permeates the whole life and culture of the local tribals. The tribals have many collective festivals for *Baphala Budhi* on Baphailimali. It takes place every year after the harvesting is over or at the time of *Pausa Purnima* called '*Malichega*'. The *Pausa Purnima* is called *Tokimora* by the local people. This festival is celebrated for seven days, starting from Thursday and ending on Wednesday and the *Malichega* festival takes place on Tuesday including *meriah* sacrifice offered to *Baphala Budhi*. *Baphala budhi* is seen as being both magnanimous and angry and can wreak retribution on those who anger her. Tribal people say that, earlier human sacrifices used to take place to appease *Baphala Budhi* on Baphailimali (at Jenabasa). Now buffaloes and lambs are sacrificed to appease the *Budhi.*

The digging of holes for mining survey on the plateau and the regular visit by officials and company people evinced reaction by the tribals who are scared of the reaction of the deity to this profanation of her abode. For instance, the *Jaani* (tribal priest) of the area pointed out 'now the deity is getting angry, *Budhi* is getting angry, our lives are in anxiety, how can we live here'. We went there with coconut and pigs, and we told her about our helplessness in stopping the digging work. The deity whenever she feels disregarded eats the disobedient person. The deity said (in *Jaani's* dream) 'they are ruining my abode, where shall I live? What shall I eat?'.

The governments, the company and other social activists or academicians have never mentioned about the cultural and religious value of the tribals of the area. The implications of mining site in Baphailimali hill should not be overlooked because the tribals of this locality are religiously very attached to this hill. So any research work should take a holistic view rather than considering the issue only from economic grounds.

Natural Resource

The Koraput district and major portions of these areas are hill tracts covered with forests where Non-Timber Forest Products (NTFPs) form an important source of subsistence and livelihood in the tribal's life. Again, at a time when agriculture has become a losing proposition, where output fluctuates violently from year to year along with frequent droughts, NTFPs have sustained not only the tribals but also other forest dependent communities in Koraput district. But strangely the locals overlook the strength of NTFPs in combating poverty and food crisis. Thus, not only in Koraput district, but in the entire state the poverty alleviation programmes have a land based approach i.e. it aims at increasing the agricultural production and income generation activities centring agriculture. Besides it gives some importance to occupations relating to collection, processing and marketing of NTFPs. Here it may be noted that the large scale land alienation process in Koraput district has failed to resolve the poverty issue on a long term basis. In such a situation, forest produce and NTFPs in particular have all along been a vital source of subsistence and livelihood for the rural poor and tribals in the districts and particularly in Kashipur block. Again, it may be noted that the collection of NTFPs acquires special importance as most of them generate income and food for the poor households in the leanest season.

Over the last 13 years the Government of Odisha has been trying to clear all the people out of the areas for establishment of Utka Alumina International Limited. Most of the affected people in this case are the tribals and dalits i.e. extremely poor indigenous people, who are below the poverty line and outside the Indian caste systems.

A similar forced displacement of people happened from 1981 onwards at NALCO, India's biggest bauxite mine and refinery, which is so near to UAIL that its people are familiar with the results: unacceptably low compensation rates, exclusion of many affected communities, and substantially under-estimated assets, resulting in conversion of independent and self-reliant small farmers into paupers now living in slums.

The people of Kashipur affected by UAIL have learned from NALCO and many similar projects in the Koraput district like upper Kolab hydropower project, Indravati hydropower project and HAL; however, that displacement has always led to poverty. Hence in Kashipur block most of the tribal and dalit people who were directly affected by the UAIL were rejected compensation. Police forcing the tribals into accepting compensation have resorted to lathi-charges, tear-gassing, imprisonment, torture and shooting that resulted in death of three tribals at Maikanch village on 16 December 2000. This Maikanch massacre was repeated again on 2 January 2006, where twelve tribals were shot dead by police in the Kalinga Nagar massacre to make way for Tata Steel Corporation.

Work on the UAIL site is racing ahead; at the time of my last visit in August 2009, there were dozens of heavy machines leveling the refinery site, the ore-rail spur was almost completed, quarries and borrow pits were active, and a high boundary wall surrounded most of the site.

Hindalco and Alcan's partners have withdrawn from the project and sold their shares. India's Tata conglomerate sold out in January 1999, and Norsk Hydro in March 2004, because unacceptable violence persists to this day, combined with many violations of Indian and Odisha laws. Alcan presumably asks itself if it should also withdraw, as its two major partners have already done.

Displaced people have repeatedly seen that displacement swiftly changes independent self-sufficient communities into paupers or slum dwellers. UAIL states that there are 1,750 'property holding' families, and 1,900 families would be affected by the company. But many potentially affected people may not hold property. Only a very few tribals have their own paper titles to the lands they have used for centuries.

UAIL says that land acquisition, the rehabilitation and resettlement programme are 'progressing well' for 148 families. Ramibeda village was bulldozed and the people were told to move into what may be a rail construction camp. The displaced people have not been given title deeds, and they suspect they will soon be uprooted yet again and evicted elsewhere. On the other hand, police is shooting, lathi-charging and tear-gassing the groups of tribals.

Photo 3

Indravati Catchment area from Baphalimali hill

UAIL states that they have documents showing support from elected representatives from all but one of the 'official project affected' villages. Affected groups have not been provided with any evidence of this statement. While the Baphalimali Hills area is

Photo 4

People collecting the Shiadi leaves from the forest and selling in the market

to be allocated to mining, assessments by various groups reveal that the requirements of 2,610 hectares of land, including 1,000 hectares of cultivable land for the factory and wastage dump alone, will cripple the livelihoods of most settlements in the area. In fact, many villages stand to lose 70 per cent of cultivable land and will not even be considered displaced, rendering the people virtually landless. Tribals have been warned that few jobs will be open to them, mainly as construction labourers or menials.

Consultation is mandated by the Panchayat Extension to Scheduled Areas Act (PESA) of 1995 in such cases of land acquisition, compensation, resettlement and rehabilitation programmes. UAIL claims that three villages 'consented' in December 2004. As this was shortly after the police killings of tribals in Maikanch, one cannot be certain if such consent was freely given. In contrast, at least twenty five affected villages are against the project, five of whom passed resolutions opposing UAIL (PSSP, 2006). The rights of people over their resources, livelihoods and democratic ways of life will continue to be threatened.

In addition, the state government helps industry in two powerful ways. First, Government of Odisha offers handsome subsidies to investors in the form of guarantees, tax concessions and investment subsidies. Second, Government of Odisha acquires tribals' lands on behalf of the company. The fact that buying or selling tribals' land is illegal under the constitution seems to be overlooked by Government of Odisha. The rates paid by Government of Odisha also are far from replacement cost, further impoverishing the tribals.

Sources of Livelihood

The tribal livelihood is primarily dominated by natural economy, where market plays a minimum role. This is not to say that the market has not penetrated into their system, rather especially in last 50 years because of various developmental efforts tribal system has come under the domain of market economy. This has resulted in gradual degradation of their resource base i.e. their control and access over land, water and forest. In many places because of development projects and also due to the operation of formal as well as informal land market forces, tribals have lost control over land. Again, due to the peculiar process of development their control over water resource is on decline. They have come to a situation where they are in possession of sloppy lands (in most of the situation it is viewed as encroachment though they are enjoying these lands for quite a long time). The productivity of these lands is low and the agriculture is subsistence oriented.

The tribal's socio-economic system is based on forest. Their culture as well as livelihood's support system is closely linked with forest. From the forest the tribals collect timber for house construction, fuel wood, wild tubers, leafy vegetables, mushrooms and different kinds of NTFPs. Definitely a part of them is exchanged for meeting the cash requirement of the household but most importantly a major portion is used for consumption purpose. The part that is exchanged in the market for meeting the household requirements is normally made either at the doorstep or in the village *haat* (weekly market). These commodities are exchanged for other essential commodities or sometime for cash. The merchants are petty traders at the village level, who pay unfair price to the households. In a sense the market is highly exploitative.

Thus looking at the importance of NTFPs on the lives and livelihood of poor tribals the Roy Burman Committee (Roy Burman, 1982), that was set up by the Planning Commission on Forests and Tribals in India headed by B.K. Roy Burman, has recommended that collection of Minor Forest Produce (MFP) for food and cash income should be conceded as the right of the tribal families without restriction. It is pointed out that MFP is also important for non-food purpose in the tribal economy, like for house construction and grazing, the committee recommended collection and marketing of MFP.

Livelihood in Kashipur

The people of Kashipur mostly depend on agriculture, occasional wage labour and collection of forest produce. People in this area particularly tribal and dalits do *Dangar* cultivation. *Dangar,* literally, means hilly areas for slash and burn cultivation. Each village has a traditionally demarcated area of *dangar* for the use of the people of that particular village only. This land is also distributed among villagers. Their main expenditure is on food, festivals and medicine. From April to October, malaria takes a virulent form and so also gastroenteritis during rainy season, hardly any family remains untouched by it. From their identifiable income source of a family, 5/6 members can at best survive for six months. Then how do they survive for remaining six months? In Kashipur hardly migration takes place due to shortage of food or non-availability of work. Tribal communities like, Kondha, Paraja, Penga Paraja, and Jhodia Paraja generally do not prefer to migrate but some landless dalits migrate seasonally. Their food culture will explain how they manage. '*Mandia Peej*' (gruel prepared out of ragi) is their staple food. They also add some rice and maize to it, especially, in rainy season. Rice and 'suan' (name of cereal) come next in their food habit. Their food pattern largely depends on seasonal agricultural and forest produces. Besides this, they grow various types of pulses and oil seeds like, *Kandul, Masur, Mung, Chana, Alsi,* Castor, Mustard etc. Wherever water facilities are available, they grow maize 2/3 times a year (most of the villages are situated near a perennial spring). Maize harvested during October–November is stored by hanging them from the ceiling of the roof. For rainy season they collect tamarind and its seed. They also collect kernel of mango seeds to prepare '*Peej*'. They grow

Photo 5

Women collecting fire wood from the forest

Photo 6

Potter boy going to sell their pots in the market

various kinds of roots and tubers in their kitchen gardens and also collect all sorts of greens from the jungle. During the last decade vegetable growing has picked up. Throughout the year they get something from their natural environment. But the fundamental thing about their livelihood is that nothing remains surplus. They do not desire to produce more than that of their needs. Their mode of cultivation, mainly *dangar* cultivation which requires hard physical labour, does not allow any scope for surplus production. If one argues for surplus production, they say 'if we work 24 hours, then when will we eat, dance and make merry?'. This simple approach to life leaves no room for greed, hoarding and profiteering. But this culture of non-hoarding/non-surplus production fails to meet the problems at the time of natural calamities and also of exploitation.

Livelihood Systems of Tribal

An indigenous forest dwelling community has been living amidst the hill and forest. The economy of the tribal is based on forest even after several changes have taken place in the structure of their ecosystem and economic pursuits. Their main sources of livelihood are cultivation, shifting cultivation and collection of minor forest product. Besides, practising paddy cultivation, raggi cultivation and collection of minor forest product, they have depended on hunting and food gathering mode of economy as the source of their livelihood. Some of the tribals work as agriculture wage labourers and some work as labourers in construction work like, National Rural Employment Guarantee Act Programme.

Economy is an important constituent of the community's life and plays a crucial role in the formation of the cultural and social structure of the society (Vidyarthi and Rai, 1976: 93). The economic activities of a community are visualised in its social and cultural framework. Each community has its own way to meet its basic needs for the survival of its members, which are fulfilled from its 'resources base' available in the immediate environment

The socio-economic and cultural structure of indigenous communities is different from that of the mainstream, advanced communities. It is need-based, community-based and cooperative in nature. Even after modernisation and globalisation enter into the tribal areas, the wider prevalence of cooperative labour system is still functioning among many indigenous communities all over the Koraput district. The tribals of Kashipur believe that, the forest is the storehouse of their needs, so the exploitation of resources is on daily use basis. They do not exploit the forest for greedy purposes.

Forest is regarded as the mother of indigenous people. They have developed a symbiotic relationship with the forest, which manifests in every aspect of their livelihood. The socio-economic and cultural practices of these communities closely revolve around the forest life. Forest is the centre of indigenous people's livelihood. Their economy is entirely based on forests. They collect fruits, tubers, stems, honey, leaves, flowers, the raw materials for agricultural requirement, household needs etc. from the forest. It shows their greater dependence on forests. Forest fulfils all the socio-religious, cultural and economic necessity of the rural poor people. Hence, the forest is very important to the indigenous people as a living space, as a resource base and as the harvest ground of a specific socio-cultural identity. It appears that the existence of tribal communities without the forest is impossible (Behera, 2000: 292).

The religious life of the indigenous communities does have a very close link with the forest. Forest is the sacred ground and ritual site of tribals. In tribal religious tradition, some parts of the forest are preserved as sacred groves which are protected by the communities themselves as prohibited areas. Sacred grove is worshipped by the tribals as they believe that sacred grove is solely inhabited by supernatural spirits. People do not dare to cut the trees due to the fear of disturbing the spirits. This has been the practice of the tribal people of Koraput district to conserve their forest and natural resources for their livelihood. In Kashipur block, on the hilltop of the Baphalimali, where UAIL mines have started, one of the caves is there. Inhabitants of near about 42 viliages around Baphalimali hill gather there to worship their god and sacrifice animals during a festival called *pousa parva* (pousa festival). Also, some people of the *Gouda* caste (OBC) at the time of rainy season take their cows and buffalos to the hilltop and stay up till the completion of harvest season. Along with cultivation, it is the main occupation of the *Gouda* caste people. Where will they go if the mines start working? What will happen to the religious practices of the tribal people around Baphalimali hill?

Photo 7

Researcher with Sumani Jhodia is in the left and Mukta Jhodia in the right

Photo 8

Old age woman collecting fire wood from the forest

Role of Forest Produce in Rural Livelihood

This section focuses on the nature of dependence of poor households on forest in Kashipur block of Odisha. As mentioned earlier, NTFPs play a crucial role in rural livelihood. It not only supports their consumption requirement but also plays a crucial role in providing employment and income during the leanest season.

The study is heterogeneous in the sense that people from various caste groups reside in this area. The landholding pattern is skewed and there is a substantial section of landless households in these villages especially belonging to SC and ST. For analytical purpose the households have been divided into five categories i.e. landless, marginal farmers, small farmers, medium farmers, big farmers and their dependence on NTFPs have been looked into. The following are the major findings of the study. The contribution of NTFPs to the BPL household's income is between 20 to 45 per cent.

- In Kashipur block it was observed that collection of NTFP was a major economic activity for the households below poverty line.
- However, simultaneously it can be observed that the income from the major NTFPs i.e. *Mahua* flowers and *Sal* leaf, *Kendu* leaves, *Shiadi* leaves and *Jhadu* increases with the size of landholdings. This is because the large landowners are able to harness these produces from the trees in their private lands.
- A significant fact is that in terms of income covered from NTFPs women's role is more as compared to men because women including girl children do most of the NTFP collection.
- The role of NTFPs in enhancing economic equity is also strengthened by the fact that for the most disadvantaged sections like widows and old people, income from NTFP collection is very often the main income source.
- Another important finding is that among the major NTFPs, *Mahua* flower, *Sal* leaves, *Kendu* leaves, *Shiadi* leaves, *Jhadu*, and Mango available in Kashipur block play the most important role in supporting household income particularly that of landless and marginal farmers.

Minor forest produce (MFP), i.e. all forest products other than wood, plays an important role in the rural economy. MFP items are important raw materials for cottage, small and village industries and contribute to national economy through export and import substitutes. MFP forms the major economic activity of livelihood for majority of the rural people and particularly the tribal. Tribal economy depends upon the forest, its produce and access to it. The tribal have some specific right and concessions in forest produce and access there too. However, their rights and concessions are said to have skewed with the changing forest management system ever since the British government took over the management of forests. The National Forest Policy (1988) empathically lays importance on the policy of protection, generating and optimising collection of MFP along with institutional arrangement for marketing of such produce. It also envisages family oriented schemes for improving the economic status of tribal beneficiaries. Collection of MFP is conditioned by availability, marketability, access to forest and various other constraints. The tribals traditionally used to collect many items which were necessary for their day-to-day sustenance. Mentioned below are the respondents of the studied villages.

Table 5.3

Villages Directly Affected by the Company near Doraguda Village

Name of the Villages	*No. of Respondents*	*SC*	*ST*	*Women*
Tikiri	08	04	04	02
Osapada	06	02	04	02
Bagrijhola	10	04	06	03
Ramibeda	06	00	06	01
D.P. Colony	10	05	05	03
Koral	10	04	06	03
Dimundi	10	04	06	04
Kendukhunti	10	10	00	04
Kucheipadar	12	04	08	04
Total respondents	82 (100)	37 (45.12)	45 (54.87)	26 (31.10)

Proposition: For the convinced of the present study the collected data has been divided into two analysis part, that is Table 5.3 and 5.4. Total number of sample is 160 households, of which 82 households are directly affected by the proposed MNCs and 78 households are partially affected. Out of 82 total households, 45.12 per cent scheduled caste and 54.87 per cent scheduled tribes are directly affected by the proposed factory. Of the factory affected are mostly women that are one-third. People those who are partially affected by the proposed alumina factory in absolute number are 78, of which 35.89 per cent scheduled caste and 64.14 per cent scheduled tribes are going to be partially affected by the project. In general, it has been seen that women were the most vulnerable with the proposed factories.

Table 5.4

Villages Partially Affected by the Company Around the Baphalimali Hills

S. No.	*Name of the Villages*	*Total Respondents*	*SC*	*ST*	*Women*
1	Paikakupakhal	08	05	03	03
2	Dandabad	06	00	06	02
3	Dangeskhal	08	05	03	03
4	Maligaon	06	02	04	02
5	Maikanch	10	05	05	04
6	Andirakancha	08	03	05	02
7	Kanchaguma	06	02	04	02
8	Cheptaghat (K)	06	01	05	01
9	Kendumundi (K)	08	03	05	03
10	Durmushi (K)	06	02	04	02
11	Maligam (K)	06	00	06	02
	Total	78 (100)	28 (35.89)	50 (64.10)	26 (33.33)

Note: K villages belong to Kalahandi district.

In Table 5.3, those villages are shown, whose inhabitants can be called as the 'displaced persons' (DPs) by land acquisition. This Table 5.4 also includes others like 'project affected persons' (PAPs) from whom the project acquired land or other livelihood without moving them away physically from their habitat. Here the project has been acquiring only land and that is the people's livelihood but leaving their houses untouched (Fernandes, 2004: 1191), though somehow they are getting compensation money. However, in Table 5.4, the inhabitants of those villages are shown who are not directly displaced by the company. Their lands were not acquired by the company. But company activities made them leave their places. They can be called 'forcefully displaced persons' (FDPs) although the company did not displace them forcefully. Their day-to-day livelihoods are dependant on the Baphalimali hills, because they have been living in the foothills of the

Baphalimali hills. The tribals, the dalits and the marginalised people who have depended on the forest for centuries, the takeover of their lands for mining, industries and hydropower projects has effectively deprived them of their sources of livelihood; they have traditionally depended on non-wood forest produce for their sustenance. In Odisha the government supported mining companies, huge industries and the construction of multi-purpose power projects which uprooted thousands of people, many of them were indigenous tribal people, dalits and other marginalised communities who have been dispossessed of their lands. In Koraput district alone, over 1,00,000 tribals were dispossessed of their land, including the forest on which they have depended for their livelihood (Fernandes and Raj, 1993; P. Sainath, 1996). Odisha had acquired 40,000 hectares of land for industries from 1955–1995 but there are plans to acquire more than 1,00,000 hectares of land in a decade (Fernandes and Asif, 1997: 69–70; Fernandes, 2004: 1192). It means that the 1,40,000 hectares of agricultural lands has been acquired by the companies, so the lands are out of cultivation; and as its consequence, the occupation of farmers has changed from cultivation to daily wage labour and the social status of the people has also changed from middle classes to manual working classes. In general, Indian society has an upward mobility through the industrialisation, but here we are witnessing the downward mobility of the people in the Indian society. So the question is development for whom? Thus here, the development work is not for the farmers, the poor, the tribals, the dalits, and the women.

Food Gathering

Food gathering economy is the simplest form of economy started by the earliest men in the prehistoric times. Tribals collect food from the forest, use the timber to construct their houses or make different types of implements. They collect firewood and different objects from the forests required by them for a variety of purposes. Economic activities among the tribals are organised along the line of nature's method of operation. When the lands are well endowed with forests, the tribal could depend on surplus food grain from slash and burn, roots, shoots, tubes, wild vegetables, preserved animal meat, fruits and dried and powdered seeds such as mango kernel and tamarind seed to meet their food requirement during the lean season. MFP may be further classified into flowers, fruits, edible leaves, roots and tubers, and edible herbs. Among the flowers, *Mahua* seems to the most popular one. It has almost become the symbol of the tribal diet all over the central belt where it is available from Rajasthan to western Odisha, through Gujarat, Maharashtra, Bihar, and Madhya Pradesh (Fernandes, 1988). Emphasising the importance of the *Mahua* tree in the lives of the Kharia tribes who are spread over Bihar, Madhya Pradesh and Odisha, Vidyarthi and Upadhyay (1980) observed that while the flowers of the *Mahua* are used for preparing tasty dishes by the *Dhelki* and *Dudh Kharias*, the hill *Kharias* use them more for fermenting and preparing liquor. Similarly, leaves, bark and flowers of the Sal are part of tribals' food and medicine. The same thing is happening in the tribal areas of Koraput district in general and Kashipur in particular. It is found that 70 per cent of the tribal economy is based on forests. The most prominent among these are mango, jackfruit, jamun, *mahua, sal, kendu, tentuli, harida, bahada, siadi leaves, jhadu*, lac etc. Besides produce that could be collected directly from the trees and underground, there are also items such as honey on which some of the tribes depend. Collection of honey and other non-timber forest produces are important sources of income for the tribal for their livelihood.

Hunting

The animal hunting varies in the Kashipur region. The men of the *kondha* tribe traditionally practised hunting with the use of bows and arrows at the time of *Chaita Parava* (chaitra festival). Dogs are used for tracking and killing. On the occasion of *Chaita Parava,* the men go for hunting and the women drink alcohol. It is the traditional culture of the tribes in Kashipur areas. However the animals such as hare, deer, rabbit, snakes etc. and birds such as wild fowl, falcon, peacocks, forest hen etc. are hunted for food. Vidyarathi and Upadhyay (1980), Sinha (1982) also mention about the animal hunting of the Kharia tribes in Jharkhand and West Bengal respectively. Collection of fuel is practically a day's work which is usually done by the people. The women and girls usually leave home early in the morning and come back in the evening with firewood on their heads. Besides being the main source of fuel for cooking, the forest is also one of the main earning sources where the collected firewood, on the next day is sold in the market particularly in Kashipur and Tikiri.

Forest and Medicine

Ethno-botany, a term coined in 1896 by Harshberger, refers to the study of the relationship between people of primitive societies and their environment. In the report of the Roy Burman committee on the forest and tribals, it was noted that, it has been possible for the tribal community to survive for generations with a reasonable standard of health because of forest. Forest provided their food, medicinal herbs and plants which they have been using for treatment of diseases (Roy Burman, 1082). Health and treatment among the tribal particularly the forest dwellers are also very much connected with the environment particularly the forest ecology (Chaudhari, 1991: 9–16). The wide varieties of medicinal herbs are available in the forest. In the study of the biogas of Madhya Pradesh, in which 120 tribal villages were covered, it was revealed that the use of 242 species as is medicines and 112 species as food (Brij Lal, 1988: 5). Punam Kumari has mentioned

Photo 9

Young women taking drinking water from the Gadagada river

that, the educated *mundas* in Chhotanagpur refer to their system of medicine as '*Horopathy*', the term *horo* being the munda version of homo i.e. human being. She has listed 52 species which are used in common ailments such as cough and cold, nausea, stomach disorders, jaundice, urinary infections, leucoderma, fever, eye infections, and against snake bites (Punam Kumari, 1990: 2–4). Pal and Banarjee (1973: 28–32) have listed 29 plant species that are used for hair and scalp reparations among the *kondha* and *soura* tribes in Ganjam, Phulbani and Koraput districts of Odisha. The tribals traditionally depend on forest for medicinal plants which are used for the treatment of diseases. Due to industrialisation and big dam projects in Koraput district many of these medicinal plants or animals are not available today.

Photo 10

Tribal man practicing traditional weapon, bow and arrow

Forest and Flora

The type of forest found in this block is invariably mixed forest, with or without bamboo. In the peripheral areas of Kashipur block the Sal trees have been reserved. *Sal* is the principal species on the intermediate slopes and hills. These forests are found in Sunger, Chandragiri, Mandibisi, Godibali, Sikarpai gram panchayats and the Baphalimali hill areas of the Kashipur block. The principal species commonly found are *Asan, Dhaura, Jamun, Kendu, Bahada, Harida, Kusum, Kasi, Bija, Champa, Mohua,* Mango, *Tangan,* Peepal etc. During the monsoon months a variety of edible fungi and indigenous medicines are also available.

Language and Religion

Oriya is the principal language of this region and the Oriya script is in use. Tribals of Kashipur block speak a dialect called '*Desia bhasa*', which is the common dialect of the tribal belt of the undivided Koraput region. The *penga bhasa* and *Jhodia bhasa* do not have a script of their own. Among the tribal communities Kandha, Penga Paraja and Jhodia are the most populated communities. They have their own community's *bhasa* (dialect), namely, *jhodia bhasa* for the Jhodia communities, *penga bhasa* and *kondha bhasa* for the Penga Paraja and Kondha communities respectively, but their common language is *Desia bhasa*. This dialect has been practised from generation to generation through informal ways of local conversation. No doubt *Desia bhasa* is the tribal dialect having its origin from tribal people but the local Scheduled Caste (Dombo) people are also using this dialect, not only in conversation with tribal people but also at their home. Moreover *Desia bhasa* is the homely language of both SCs and STs, which is different from Oriya language.

Most of the people belonging to this region are primitive tribes. They have their own religion and primitive local deities are prevalent among the tribes. Though they belong to a unique religious group based on the nature, officially they are included in the Hindu fold. Some are converted into Christians, who constitute a small population group.

Festivals

In Kashipur block the '*Chita Parav*' (the spring festival) is most popular among the tribals of Kashipur. The other important festival of the tribes is '*Pousa Puranima*'. In the western region of Kashipur a popular festival known as a '*Toki-Mara*' (sacrificing girls) is celebrated. Bali Jatra is another festival of the block. '*Ghanta Parva*' is festival of both the tribes and non-tribes, which is popularly observed in Kashipur village, Tikiri village, Champajodi village and Jamaguda village. Due to the impact of outsiders and modernity, nowadays so many other Hindu festivals like, Dashehra, Holi, Deepavali, Sivaratri etc. are also celebrated.

The Market

It is clear that the process of production in the marketplace is primarily meant for direct consumption of producers. In such a scenario, the role of an impersonal institution like market in their life is bound to be limited. People buy few things like salt, kerosene and cloth which are not locally produced from nearby weekly markets. The use of cloth has specifically increased during the last two decades and that is much less compared to other areas. Besides weekly market, one can find small grocery shops in few villages generally run by *Shundi* and in cases by few dalits. The dalit women carrying big basket on her head contains items like salt, *gudakhu* and dry fish who sells them moving from village to village. People exchange their items like maize, ragi and *kandul* with those items. Use of soap and other commodities are very less. A very few people have items like cycle, transistor and T.V. One can easily deduce from this that market is yet to create a big space in their life. Their needs are also very less. Their *dangars*, jungles and springs are bountiful to fulfil their needs. These are the source of their life and livelihood. Each village to a large extent is self-sufficient. Their world of need is limited to their village where they live with dignity. The outside world has little meaning for them. They hardly need the State, Government or market to run their life. But the relative isolation is breaking. Market and state are forcefully entering into their life creating new demands and dreams. The irony of this phenomenon is that neither they meet those demands nor the market process can realise their dreams.

Food Pattern in Kashipur

Besides rice, the most important staple food of the indigenous people of kashipur is '*mandia pej*'. The *mandia pej* is the gruel prepared from *mandia* (ragi) with small percentage of rice. They also prepare a food by mixing different types of green leaves. The green leaves are called '*sag*'. It has many varieties such as *papal sag, kumunda sag, bhaji sag, ghurdi sag, kailari sag, girel sag, sursu sag, mandia rab and roots such as rani kanda, cheranga ganda,* napa kanda etc. They collect all these roots and leaves from the nearby forest. Rice is considered the main food in this region but *mandia pej* is used frequently because the paddy harvested by an average family gets finished within 4 to 6 months. Nowadays, people prefer to use rice due to the availability of rice through public distribution system. The traditional indigenous people get sufficient animal protein from their frequent ritual sacrifices and offerings. Every local ritual is usually followed by sacrifices. Other sources of animal protein like, rats, snakes, rabbits, wild birds, deer etc. are occasionally available in the tribal houses.

The food patterns of the tribal in Kashipur block have undergone visible changes. Factors accountable for this are: impact of the lifestyle of the upper caste (Sanskritisation), modernisation, education, migration, economic development, changing pattern of agriculture, development of horticulture etc.

Table 5.5

Distribution of Rural Households According to Ownership of Land

MPCI Groups	*0 Acres*	*0–2 Acres*	*Above 2 Acres*
Up to 100	12	9	5
100–150	15	7	8
150–200	14	10	7
200–250	11	9	9
250–300	10	7	5
300–350	08	8	6
Total	70	50	40

Source: Field Survey.

Note: *MPCI – Monthly per Capita income groups.

From the above table it can be inferred that 70 households out of 160 households interviewed are without any land i.e. 43.75 per cent. Again 38.25 per cent i.e. out of 160 households has marginal land up to 2 acres and 25 per cent has above 2 acres of land. A direct relationship between ownership of land and income cannot be established since income from land depends on other factors, the most important being irrigation. Many households depend on agricultural labour and forest produce for most of the time of the year. In Dandabad, Maligam, Cheptaghat and Kupakhal villages the wage rate is ₹ 40–45 per male worker *(coolie)* and as well as for female worker *(reja)* in governmental work, but in private land the wage rate is 8–10 kg of paddy per male worker *(coolie),* and 6–8 kg paddy for female worker per day and the employment days per year is very limited.

It can be derived from the above mentioned facts that the general standard of the living of the people is very low. Average landholding is very little and avenues of employment are too little. There would be only a dozen persons or so with a monthly income of ₹ 500. Low castes, people particularly, the tribals, dalits and other backward castes *(Gouda and Paiko),* hardly get rice to eat. They mostly depend on *Mandia* (raggi), which is a crop found generally in the hilly areas. It is also cheaper than rice.

Most of the people are dependent on forest and natural resources. In fact natural resources are the main sources of the livelihood of the villagers. For 3–6 months in a year they are engaged in hunting and gathering of natural resources and rest of the 6 months they get engaged in shifting cultivation *(Danger chash or Podu chash).* Being upland and rain fed areas during excessive rainfall the soil gets eroded and it becomes difficult to do the cultivation, as there are no good irrigation facilities. Generation after generation they are engaged in the task to make the land ready for agriculture, but the outcome is virtually very low. For an acre of land only 7–8 quintal of paddy can be cultivated. In addition to this, the lands are in the hands of non-tribals. Landlords and moneylenders have exploited the tribals. It is found that most of the rural households do not possess land and those who have it is less than 3 acres. Now as far as labour work is concerned a daily wage earner is getting a low wage that is not more than 40 kg in government works and 8 kg paddy in private works. Thus the average landholding being very little, the earning out of employment is limited. The protein content in their food should be taken seriously as they get protein from forest *(jungle)* or domestic animals and they are unable to supplement their diet with milk or pulses.

Wage Labourer and Government Programmes

Across the villages that are studied here, the daily wage for agricultural workers does not go beyond ₹ 45 and in kind, not more than 8 kg of paddy. In most instances women receive ₹ 35 and men received ₹ 40 to 45 in government sponsored developmental programmes. About six months in a year, the poorer families depend on natural resources and wage labour. The source of labour varies from agriculture employment to construction works to government employments. Though a substantial fund is spent in employment generation programmes in the government, it is found that government employment is hardly a dependable source of income for the people. It was found that in most of the cases including the National Rural Employment Guarantee Scheme, the projects have been contracted to private persons, who always cheated the people of at least half their wages. Often wage is paid in terms of grain, in which case, the labourers do not even get means of measuring whether they have received their due or not. Complaints to the BDO hardly bring any response. As the contractors live in the neighbourhood of the tribal people, they also subdue the tribals with threats of sheer physical violence. There is little recourse for the tribal people in such cases, as the money power of these contractors, is enough to win over any law keeping forces that the region might have. Those contractors are the supporters of the company in Kashipur block. Any protest on the part of the resisting villagers is efficiently quelled by the company.

A large number of respondents fall under the category of landless, insecure tenants and those owning marginal plots too small to support a family constitute the poorest of the poor. Thus it is inferred that land distribution in the panchayat is still not even and because of this there is economic disparity among the people.

Along with occupation, the income level of the respondents is also considered, as during these days cash money is the determinant of the economic standard of living. The economic level of the respondents shows that only 70 per cent of the rural people are earning ₹ 1800 annually which shows the deplorable economic conditions of the rural people. Moreover, the number of family members too affects the economic condition of the village. It is seen that in the panchayat under study, joint family system is still in existence. From the survey it is found that the size of the family is large, whereas 35 per cent of the families have less or 5 members, and 65 per cent of the family have more than 5 members. The findings with regard to the personal socio-economic characteristics of the rural people under study reveal that by and large they have less educated, less property, more family members, lass savings and less employment opportunities. So they are more dependent on natural resources.

Livelihood Movement

There are an innumerable number of grassroots environmental movements (GEM) in India. In the Kashipur block the movement is typically made up of community members joined together to act on livelihood issue rather than environmental, which directly affected local livelihoods. The organisation is highly differentiated according to size, structure, organisational skills and capacities, motivations and goals, ideological and cultural orientations, and legal status.

The environmental protest movement based in the Kashipur block is much more likely to express direct concern with daily livelihood and development issues. Environmental movements in the Kashipur block have two distinguishing characteristics: the movement is supported and participated by the local tribal and dalit people who are small and marginal farmers, agricultural labourers and others who have been engaged in daily livelihood. As far as the leadership is concerned, they are from the tribal communities and from the Kucheipadar village itself. Present convener of the PSSP, Mr Bhagaban Majhi is 7th class educated. Under the umbrella of PSSP, Kashipur people's movement has been going on since last fourteen years. If we see other movements, the leaders came from the non-affected areas. They are upper dominant caste and educated people. But in Kashipur movement, the leaders are local tribals, dalits most of whom are uneducated people. This struggle is linked to sustainable objectives. It is organised around livelihood and local area development objectives. The protest movement to have these arrangements protected or supported is often framed around claims about the value of traditional indigenous and ecological knowledge, moral and cultural themes. Furthermore, there are often religious grounds for mobilising to protect sacred or culturally significant areas.

People have experienced in the NALCO area of Damanjodi, Sunabeda, upper Kolab and Indravati that the episodic environmental incidents such as flooding, drought, industrial accidents, and outbreaks of water borne disease produce environmental vulnerability. These incidents, especially in their most severe manifestations, affect everyone, but the poorest and most resource-dependent people are typically the most vulnerable.

The people's movement in Kashipur block is concerned with livelihood and natural resources issues rather than issues related with environment. Here, it is found that the Kashipur movement basically, this is people's movement; local victims or project affected people initiated this movement. They are working for themselves, planning the strategies, suffering for it and they are enjoying its results, whatever it may be. So for the people of Kashipur block, this movement was not started as an environmental movement but it was basically about their rights to livelihood, life with dignity and over natural resources, which they have been using for centuries. A similar study by Kusum Karnik is about the forest dwellers of Bhimasankar wildlife sanctuary. Here, people got organised under the *Ekjoot Sanghatan;* they began their agitation to sustain their relationship with and control over their forests (Pawar, Patil and Sulunkhe, 2005: 27–28). The Chipko movement was not started as an environmental movement. It began as a people's movement for their right over natural resources. But later on some scholars started calling it an environmental movement (ibid., 30).

At least 58 numbers of streams both seasonal and perennial have originated from the Baphalimali hill and merged with the Indravati river basin. A large number of villagers depend upon these streams for agricultural, domestic and other daily purposes. The villagers grow paddy, wheat, mustard, vegetables and a number of crops depending upon this stream water. Mining will disrupt the flow of these perennial springs and lead to drying up of the streams affecting the livelihood and water supply for thousands of people. The streams of this location – the *Khanda Bindh nadi* and the *Goda gaada nadi* – are flowing in this area, which lead to the Indravati river.

Trees of the Dandabar reserved forest would be lost and the forest is located in the Baphalimali foothills. About 13 villages come within 2 km distance of the mining lease, with Durmushi being the closest village. Without massive reorientation and training, it is just not possible to employ the uneducated tribals from the local villages in such a mine which is totally mechanised. Local tribal culture based on subsistence agriculture, hunting and gathering doesn't lend itself to working in mechanised mines.

This implies that all the talk about employment to local people will vanish into thin air. However, the local people will bear the cost of the influx of sophisticated outsiders into this remote tribal area. As has happened in other such areas, incidents of prostitution and several diseases may increase. It is apprehended that the local tribal people might not be able to compete with the outsiders and end up as second class citizens as it is visible in the NALCO area of Damanjodi. So 14 years of protest movement promoted an awareness of their commitment to the land and forest and their relationship to it.

Modernisation and industrialisation led to a reduction in the levels of inequality, domination and exploitation within the region and caste. Industrialisation has been accompanied by rapid urbanisation. On the other side modernisation, urbanisation and industrialisation have also disrupted the traditional relationship that prevailed among the *Kandha, Jhodia, Paraja, Dombo* and the various other backward communities of the Kashipur block, bringing them into increasing conflict with one another. The disparities within each caste group have also increased. The major cause is the rapid degradation of the natural resources which is increasingly demanded for industrialisation. The villagers particularly in Kashipur block depend on forest for house construction, for the manufacture of agricultural implements such as seed drills, plough, mats, baskets, some roots and leaves, firewood etc. A large community of basket weavers depends entirely on bamboo for its livelihood, and most of the tribal communities depend entirely on *Shiadi* leaves and firewood, that they sell at the market for their livelihood. So the tribal people have faced mixed up environmental damage, which led to loses of livelihood resulting in social injustice.

The sustainable resource used is not in the immediate interest of our elite. However, it is very much in the long term interest of the masses, because their livelihood has always been closely associated with the well-being of the rural communities. They suffer, if the level of groundwater falls drastically or if the firewood is no longer available in the nearby forest. They suffer, if the streams are polluted and can no longer provide drinking water for masses and their cattle. They suffer, if the bamboos and trees are destroyed, which are available in the forest which they need for their livelihood.

Society would orient itself to sustainable use of natural resource only when the long term interest of its masses come to decisively influence development polices in India. That is supposed to be happening in the democratic, egalitarian country like India. People need development but without destruction of the natural resource. All the development projects should be mandatorily examined from the point of environmental costs and benefits as well as social costs and benefits. We should have the Gandhian version of the simple life in its focus on manual labour in the village as the supreme form of human society and rejection of industrial culture as violent, competitive and destructive of nature. Gandhian concerns were focused on the economic and political restoring of the livelihoods and dignity of villagers (Guha, 2000: 24).

> Broadly speaking, these conflicts have set in opposition, on the one side, social groups who have gained disproportionately from economic development whilst being insulated from ecological degradation ... and on the other, poorer and relatively powerless groups ... whose livelihoods have been seriously undermined through a combination of resource flows biased against them and a growing deterioration of the environment. (Gadgil and Guha, 1994: 119)

Impact on tribals: A large part of our natural resources lay in the hilly areas as the major rivers originate from the mountains; most of the development projects have been executed in those areas. These areas are the place of habitation of the tribals – the most disadvantaged sections of the society. Thus, a significant number among the displaced people are the tribals, and other economically marginalised rural people, who depend upon the natural resource base for their livelihood. The Twenty-ninth Report of the Commissioner of Scheduled Castes and Tribes (1990) says that even though tribal people are roughly 7.5 per cent of the population, over 40 per cent of those displaced till 1990 belonged to these communities. A report of the Official Working Group on Development and Welfare of Scheduled Tribes during the Eighth Five-Year Plan (1990–1995) on the rehabilitation of tribal people, based on a comprehensive study of 110 projects, has concluded that of the 1.694 million people displaced by these projects, almost 50 per cent (8,14,000) were tribal people (Government of India, 1993).

The most serious consequence of development-induced displacement for the tribal people has been the dispossession of land, both agricultural and homestead, along with the loss of their traditional occupation. The tribals are deprived of compensation and rehabilitation benefits as per the Land Acquisition Act, 1894 (as amended in 1984) because they do not possess any legal documents to prove their ownership right on their land that they occupy and earn their livelihood from for centuries together.

Multiple displacements: A number of studies across the country have documented multiple displacements of people. Successive displacements of the same families from one place to another occur following the execution of development projects in those areas. The displaced people of Rihand dam, Hirakud dam and Hindustan Aeronautics Limited (HAL) are some of the examples in the country. In the early 1960s, the displaced people of Rihand dam had to face displacement from their new place of habitation for the second time in 1970s because of the coal mining projects, and again for the third or fourth time in mid-1980s due to the setting up of a number of industries. In each time of their displacement, they were progressively pauperised (Lokayan and Environmental Defence Fund, 1987 quoted in Thukral, 1989). Similarly, the displaced people of Hirakud dam, who were resettled in the mid-1950s in the upper catchment areas of the reservoir, faced displacement for the second time in 1980s due to the Ib Thermal power project that came up there, and again in 1980–1990s due to the Ib valley coal mining projects. The displaced people of HAL, who were relocated in the early 1970s, were evicted for the second time in 1980s due to the execution of Upper Kolab dam project. They apprehended further displacement due to the establishment of naval armament deport and agricultural farm coming up in the area (Pandey, 1998a).

6

Environmental Movement, State and Civil Society in Kashipur

> The craze is for what they call labour-saving machinery. Men go on 'saving labour' till thousands are without work and thrown on the open streets to die of starvation. I want to save time and labour not for fraction of mankind but for all. I want the concentration of wealth, not in the hands of a few, but in the hands of all. Today machinery merely helps a few to ride on the backs of millions. (Mahatma Gandhi, *Hind Swaraj*, 1938: 8)

This chapter seeks to discuss various perspectives on people's protest movement in Kashipur block. It also analyses people's views on the movement and focuses on origin and development, difficulties, police repression, the leadership of the movement, supporters of the movement and participation of people and gender dimension. This chapter deals with the background of the movement, nature of the movement, contextualising the movement, songs and dances, the localised way of mass mobilisation, organisation of the movement, demand for right to information, role of NGOs in the movement, role of media, response of the state and administration, the constitutional and environmental issue, some facts about the companies and some of the important events of the movement in Kashipur block.

Background of the Movement

The Kashipur block of Odisha is one of the poorest regions in the country and has often caught the media attention, for the unusual scale of deaths due to starvation, malnutrition and diseases. Needless to say, this underdevelopment has been a cause for much fund inflows into the region through various developmental programmes and projects. Unfortunately, only a marginal percentage of this has actually been used in developmental works and the impact of much of this is quite invisible. Therefore, the Government of Odisha (GoO) thought of a better alternative by inviting private sector investment in the region for Bauxite mining and processing. In the process, the lands of the tribal are being acquired in the name of 'national interest' and 'public purpose', for a 100 per cent exports oriented alumina plant and for bauxite mining (*Swabhiman*, 16–8–2004).

The development projects have raised questions of equity, fairness, justice and dignity, in the matter of distribution of benefits and burdens. Today the project affected people are no longer in a mood to suffer displacement along with its concomitant attributes like occupational degeneration, social disorientation, pauperisation, loss of dignity and often getting cheated of the compensation amount, which serve to make the experience a trauma. This has given rise to protest movements in Kashipur block. An interesting feature of the growing protest movement has been the fear of loss of livelihood of the people and the creation of a national awareness of the problem by the academicians and social activists. The protest movements of the displacees have played a major role in loss of livelihood and displacement becoming key issues in the debate on development of Kashipur block. The presses, the activist groups, the NGOs, the academicians, the social workers, researchers and the judiciary have combined together to not only educate masses about the problem but also to build up a national consciousness (Government of India, 1996; Kothari, 1996; Goyal, 1996).

The scheme has its advantages, the hills of Kashipur have very rich deposits of Bauxite and the land and labour value in the region is cheap, water is available from numerous perennial streams, and infrastructure for transportation and communication has been built up. A railway line providing the link between the mining area and Vishakhapatnam, as well as Bhubaneswar, the closest seaport has been constructed and all weather roads providing communication to all the areas being prospected are coming up. It is against this decision of the government, that a powerful people's movement has been started in the Kashipur region which questions the authority of the state that has deprived the tribal of their rights over hills, forest and land, which are the only source of their livelihood. The tribals of Kashipur are still struggling to protect their sustainable land and natural resources against the onslaught of multinational companies and the state. The champions of their cause are the very people, living in the localities (Samnatara, 2000: 33).

The Constitutional and Environmental Issue

The Constitution of India, 1950, did not include any specific provision relating to environment protection or nature conservation. Presumably, the acute environmental problems being faced now in the country were not visualised by the framers of the Constitution. However, the past five decades have witnessed two major developments in this connection. The first development took place when the Constitution (Forty-second Amendment) Act, 1976, was adopted in the mid-seventies. Specific provisions relating to certain aspects of the environment, more especially for the protection of the forests and wildlife in the country, were incorporated in Part IV – Directive Principles of the State Policy and List III, the Concurrent List of the Seventh Schedule of the Constitution

The mining leases given to various aluminium companies violate the letter and spirit of the Constitution of India. Particularly, the area where the lease has been given falls under the Fifth Schedule of the Indian Constitution. The Supreme Court of India in the case, *Samatha vs. State of AP, 1997,* categorically held that transfer of land by any means including lease by the government to a non-tribal is not permissible under the Fifth Schedule. But the government of Odisha maintains that this judgment is not applicable in Odisha and it has been transferring the land of the tribals of Kashipur to industries.

Even the Panchayat (Extension to the Scheduled Area) Act (PESA), 1996, states that before any land acquisition, particularly in the scheduled areas, it is imperative to consult *gram sabhas* (Village Councils) and involve them in decision-making. The state initially refused to consult the *gram sabhas* and started land acquisition from the people. Lately *gram sabhas* were conducted to fulfill legal requirements, those were exercises flouting all norms and obtaining consent through force. A striking example of this is that of the village of D. Karal, where the village was cordoned off and the *gram sabha* meeting was conducted in the intimidating presence of heavily armed police and district officials who had been openly campaigning for the setting up of the industrial units. People were prevented from speaking at the meeting; the minutes and decisions recorded were not read out to the villagers, and the people present were asked to sign on blank papers, as people of that area claimed.

Environmental problems in India arise from a number of proximate or surface causes:

- Economic growth has necessitated a corresponding expansion in energy availability for industrial, agriculture and domestic purposes. There has, till recently, been little regulation of the environmental impacts of such expansion.
- The level of environmental literacy is low, especially amongst decision makers, and there is a gross under-valuation of the economic and material values of the environment.
- The policies and programmes of the Central and State Governments have not incorporated environmental principles, with the result that many development projects have been conceived for short-term gains without considering their long-term ecological and social impacts.
- The growing human populations are making increasing demands on natural resources resulting in the exploitation of resources in an unsustainable manner.
- The general indifference of the industrial sectors on aspects of environmental safety and protection has led to the spread of unavoidable air, water and soil pollution.
- The inability to convert the oft-repeated rhetoric of growth with equity into reality and the neglect of the livelihood needs of the tribals and rural people have resulted in persistence of real poverty (including scarcity of resources).
- The uncontrolled consumerism of the upper classes, which seems to be completely oblivious to the limits of resource use, has put serious pressure on natural resources.

But while these are the proximate or immediate causes, the fundamental factors behind the crisis are deeper.

This environmental crisis is causing enormous disruption of lives and livelihoods, threatening the collapse of its entire life-support system. The poor and unprivileged classes of humans and the other non-human species unfortunately have to bear the main brunt of these environmental problems. Ironically, the crisis is rooted deep in social, economic and political structures, more specifically in relations of inequity of three kinds (Kothari, 1995):

1. *Intra-generational inequity:* Hierarchical relations between classes, castes, races, communities, countries and sexes, within one generation, create conditions for ecological destruction. Those in power are able to dictate the use of the majority of resources regardless of consequences on others, while forcing the powerless to depend on and further degrade meagre resources. This has been the case with land, for instance, in societies with a tremendously skewed ownership pattern.
2. *Inter-generational inequity:* Entire generations of human beings, as yet unborn, who will depend on the same resources that we do have, will have no voice in decisions regarding these resources. This generation's overexploitation of water, land, soil, and biodiversity, will leave little for future generations, except abundant toxic wastes, barren wastelands, polluted water bodies, and a handful of past species that have thrived on human wastes.
3. *Inter-species inequity:* Humanity shares the earth with a mind-boggling diversity of life forms, perhaps up to 50 million species of plants, animals, and micro-organisms. This explosion of biodiversity is not only a source of wonder, but the very bedrock of human existence. Yet, simply because we have the right, we have considered it our right to colonise ever increasing spaces on earth, driving out thousands of species. Over one fourth of all biodiversity is threatened with extinction in the next few decades, unless we can drastically change the way we deal with the earth.

Inequities in the relations between people and countries have also allowed the imposition of unsustainable and destructive models of 'development'. The process of 'development' has been characterised by the massive expansion of energy and resource-intensive industrial and urban activity, and major projects like large dams, commercial forestry, mining and chemical-intensive agriculture (CSE, 1999). The resource demand for the economic progress of a minority of people has led to the narrowing of the natural resource base for the survival of the economically poor and powerless. This has happened either by direct transfer of resources into cities and industrial complexes, or by the destruction of life-support systems for rural communities everywhere.

Nature of the Movement

The movement began with the reconstitution of *Pakrutika Sampada Surakshya Parishad* (PSSP), natural resources protection committee, which was dominated by the small to medium sized of tribal farmers, led by Krushna Saunta, resident of Kucheipadar village. He was later joined by Laxman Majhi from the same village. Since 2003, Bhagaban Majhi has been leading the movement, who is also from the Kucheipadar village. He generally believes in Gandhian tactics of non-violence. Bhagaban Majhi's coming provided the organisational structure to the agitation. Women were leading the front, the students, the youth, from the tribals and the dalit people closely associated with the protest, and demonstrations were organised in the block, district and state headquarters. This phase of the movement was guided by both creativity and series of confrontation. Creativity of the movement involved mobilisation attempts through songs and dances. The involvement and participation of the people reached to the peak with every family making up songs about its own involvement in the agitation.

Some of the Important Events of the Movement

- 1 January 1993 – The18 member team met the then Chief Minister Biju Pattanaik and demanded cancellation of the project. For some time company activities slowed down but again it was in boom.
- December 1994 – Villagers of Kucheipadar snatched away instruments of survey team and set fire on their camp.
- 1995 – Protest against L&T gained momentum in Sunger area. Protestors destroyed the camp of the survey team. Police arrested 15 protestors. The case is yet to be finalised.
- 14 February 1996 – Formally the PSSP was formed in a mass meeting. Many important leaders of various people's struggles participated in it.
- March 1997 – Company floated an NGO, Utkal Rural Development Society (URDS) to win over people through

developmental work like distribution of plants, construction of roads etc. PSSP opposed work of URDS and did not allow it to work out anything and protestors destroyed the resettlement colony of the company.

- 5 January 1998 – The barricade was raised to stop the entry of the company at Kucheipadar village. Police tried to break the barricade forcefully and resorted to lathi-charge and lobbed tear-gas which injured nearly 50 people including 12 women.
- December 1998-January 1999 – The 15 days foot march was organised to coordinate all the agitation of the area from Laxmipur to Baphalimali.
- 8 February 1999 – The call for united struggle of Kashipur and Laxmipur was given in a massive meeting at Tikiri.
- 1999–2000 – All developmental activities of the company were stopped and at many places they were destroyed.
- 16 December 2000 – Police gunned down 3 tribals (Damodar Jhodia, Abhilash Jhodia and Raghunath Jhodia) and injured 8 others in Maikanch village.
- 20 December 2000 – A road blockade was organised at Rapkana chowk in which 5,000 people with their traditional weapons participated. The success of the programme gave a new life to the movement.
- 30 January 2001 – In protest against Maikanch firing, an 'Oath March' from Maikanch to Kashipur was organised with the slogan, 'We are not afraid to die, we will not leave our land' – taking this oath 10,000 people with their traditional weapons went to march from Kashipur to give a befitting reply to the killer government. Many people from various struggle movement of Odisha participated in it.
- 17 September 2001 – A charter of demands was placed before the government to solve the problem of starvation death where they demanded for irrigation facility through check dams and mobile medical team to provide them with health and hygienic support.
- November 2001 – The survey work of Sterlite Company in Sasubahumali area was failed.
- March 2002 – With the support of local tribal people, the survey work at Thuamul Rampur of Kalahandi district was opposed.

- 28 May 2002 – Demanding cancellation of all bauxite projects in KBK (Koraput, Balangir and Kalahandi) districts, a big rally was organised at Tikiri.
- 1 December 2004 – Police lathi-charged a group of people, as they were protesting the construction of a police outpost in D. Koral village. Eight people were injured including two women were arrested and taken to jail in Rayagada.
- 12 March 2008 to 11 June 2008 – People from 24 villages gathered and locked the main gate of the plant side of the company and started rally hunger strike in front of gate. It was a peaceful and non-violence way of satyagraha.
- 16 June 2008 – Near about 5,000 people from company affected 24 villages organised a rally at Rayagada district headquarter and submitted a memorandum to the district collector.

Contextualising the Movement

It was in the year 1993 that for the first time the people from Kashipur block came to know about the UAIL, a multinational company consisting of Indian Aluminium Company Limited (INDAL), Tata and Hydro Aluminium of Norway which have decided to establish an Alumina plant in Kashipur (PSSP Documents). Alcon, a Canadian company is involved in bauxite mining. Alusuisse, a Swiss Company is supposed to provide technical support. The Aluminum refinery complex has been proposed to be set up at Doraguda, a village near Kucheipadar. The initial estimated investment is ₹ 2,400 crores. The Bauxite for their refinery would be mined from the Baphalimali hill, about 25 kms away, and transported via conveyer belt to the refinery. This plant initially targeted approximately one million metric ton capacities, which would subsequently be expanded to three million metric tons capacities (ibid.: PSSP). In the year 1995, the people came to know about the second proposed alumina plant in the area, L&T, in collaboration with the ALCOA of America, planning an initial investment of ₹ 1,500 crores which proposes to have its refinery in Kalyansingpur in Rayagada district. The Bauxite would be extracted from Kutrungmali plateau in the bordering Kalahandi district. Various other plateaus like Sigimali etc. in its vicinity are also being prospected. Due to protest from the local people in the beginning of 1996 the company did not take any initiative to start the project. But towards the end of 1996 the company again set up a camp near Sunger village to resume its activity (*Samaj*, Oriya Daily, 01–12–1996). In 1998, people came to know about the third alumina project proposed to be established by Aditya Birla Aluminium Company at Kansariguda village in Bankam Panchayat of Kashipur block. For this plant the Bauxite from the nearly Kodingmali hill has been proposed to be exploited. In the recent years the Sasubahumali bauxite mines in the area had been sold out to BALCO to increase its selling price (*Sambad*, Oriya Daily, 15–05–2001). Sterlite Company of India has purchased 51 per cent share of that public sector company. The proposed projects for mining and processing of Bauxite are 100 per cent export oriented.

They are planned along the border areas of Rayagada and Kalahandi districts, which are characterised by a high percentage of tribal population and a fragile ecosystem always rendered more vulnerable by extensive deforestation. Hence, for that reason, the tribal people or the other residents are not permitted private possession rights over major portions of the land as it has high gradients, on the grounds of loses of livelihood, ecological instability and environmental protection. In the Table 6.1, the three displaced villages by the company, shows the number of SC, ST and other caste.

Table 6.1

No. of Families Displaced due to Establishment of Company

Name of the Villages	*ST*	*SC*	*OC*	*Total*
Ramibeda	41	—	—	41
Kendukhunti	—	55	—	55
D. Koral	—	86	01	87
Total	41	141	01	183

Source: Tahasildar Office, Kashipur.

The above table reflects the acquisition of agricultural land and home from the 183 families of three villages. They are now rehabilitated nearby the company area, in which 22.40 per cent are from the tribal communities, 77.04 per cent from the dalits and only one family means 0.54 per cent are from the other caste. In Kendukhunti and D. Koral villages, only SCs were resided before displacement but more people had been rendered landless.

Table 6.2

Villages and Category-wise Private Lands Acquired by the UAIL (per acre)

S. No.	Name of the Villages	No. of Land Losers of ST	Area Acquired of ST	No. of Land Losers of SC	Area Acquired of SC	No. of Land Losers of OC	Area Acquired of OC	Total No. of Land Losers	Total Area Acquired
1	Tikiri	—	—	02	3.20	32	22.19	34	25.45
2	Gokhulmunda	70	47.19	9	1.50	27	60.28	106	108.97
3	Osapada	38	8.26	13	12.53	74	46.84	125	67.27
4	Makapadar	45	51.49	2	0.88	—	—	47	52.37
5	Bilamala	88	42.11	2	3.02	—	—	90	45.13
6	Bagrijhola	56	68.87	21	7.24	23	10.76	100	86.87
7	Bhitarmuchukuni	70	96.77	2	10.65	42	37.46	114	144.88
8	Ramibeda	205	165.03	1	0.84	24	11.53	230	177.40
9	Tikirapada	6	12.70	19	21.67	180	348.58	205	382.95
10	Raimachapurunapadar	—	—	22	1.66	18	11.34	40	13
11	Koral	41	92.88	284	334.18	7	21.56	332	448.62
12	Dimundi	87	195.04	141	289.21	2	0.66	233	484.89
13	Paikakupakhal	4	1.15	18	4.89	10	0.62	32	6.70
14	Kanchaguma	—	—	—	—	10	4.54	10	4.54
15	Kodipari	38	14.80	—	—	—	—	38	14.80
16	Naringijodi	14	7.78	1	0.30	10	0.22	25	8.30
17	Ratachuan	26	4.99	—	—	—	—	26	4.99

Cont'd...

...Cont'd

18	Lundrukona	6	2.52	1	2.12	7	0.41	14	5.05
19	Jogiparitunda	—	—	—	—	35	7.00	35	7.00
20	Andirakancha	19	7.69	2	1.10	3	0.16	24	8.95
21	Anbiligatatunda	45	21.97	8	2.75	10	6.45	63	31.17
22	Hatikhaman	1	0.98	1	0.41	39	10.66	41	12.05
23	Peringini	10	5.73	19	4.44	—	—	29	10.17
24	Gaimundatunda	6	0.94	6	0.75	13	1.97	25	3.66
	Total	875	848.89	574	703.34	566	603.23	2,009	2155.46
	Percentages	43.55	39.38	28.57	32.63	28.17	27.98	100	100

Source: Tahasildar Office, Kashipur.

The agricultural lands of the villages of Kendukhunti and D. Koral belong to ST communities of nearby villages.

Table 6.2 shows the villages and category-wise private lands acquired by the Utkal Alumina International Limited (UAIL) and numbers of land losers.

According to the above table, 24 villages may be directly affected by the company. Here 43.55 per cent of tribal populations are getting directly affected by the company. It has acquired 39.38 per cent of tribal's land, 28.57 of the dalit are losing 32.63 per cent of lands and 28.17 per cent of other castes namely Paika, Gouda and Shundi have lost their 27.98 per cent of lands. In the beginning, it was informed by the companies that only 183 families of three villages namely Remibeda, Kendukhunti and D. Koral are going to be displaced because of the establishment of the plant. But this was only the tip of the iceberg. In fact, when the villages were identified to distribute the compensation money then only the people came to realise the hidden agenda of the company. This project (UAIL), if it takes on, will directly affect more than 25,000 indigenous people (PSSP Documents). The resistance is, therefore, on the grounds of displacement and encroachment upon their livelihood and life patterns. According to a survey conducted by a voluntary organisation of Andhra Pradesh known as IDEA, which is working in collaboration with NORAD of Norway, it has been estimated that as many as 43 villages are going to be directly and indirectly affected by the plant through displacement (Samantara, 2000: 38). At the same time, a Delhi based organisation TARU has submitted a report suggesting that about 87 villages are likely to be displaced (ibid., 44). Reports suggest that 90 per cent of local tribal are going to be affected by this project (ibid., 47). In this study it is found that, 24 villages are going to be directly and indirectly affected by the company through displacement and livelihood, somehow they are getting compensation money. But another 42 villages of Maligaon and Adri gram panchayats from Thuamul Rampur block of Kalahandi district and Munusogaon, Chandragiri, Kodipari and Maikanch gram panchayats of Kashipur block of Rayagada district are going to be affected directly and indirectly by the company through forceful displacement and loses of livelihood. Hence, it is a great betrayal of the trust of the people because the project, which is ostentatiously, a project for the welfare of the tribals turned out in reality a carefully calculated conspiracy to deprive the tribal in order to promote the interests of the company.

Ultimately, the tribal and dalit people will be deprived of the fruits of development done in this area because they are to be displaced. Projects like these seem to be selling the resources and the lives of the people for Companies' interests, and in the process making refugees of its own people. As per the official claim, the scheme demands over 2,000 hectares, necessitating the loss of three villages, and land in which 12 villages have legal claim. Numerous other villages will lose their access to common resources, such as a posture and water, which will bring a significant blow to the subsistence economy of the region. People estimate that the livelihoods and agriculture in and around 100 villages in the area would be irreparably damaged (*Dharitri*, Oriya Daily, 10–10–2003). If the proposed alumina plant begins, above two thousands of tribals and dalit household will lose their home, livelihood and cultural life. Consequently, near about 3,000 acres of the agricultural land and forest area will be disappearing forever, tribal and dalit farmers will become manual workers and the ecology will be destroyed. Table 6.03 shows the village wise government lands acquired by the UAIL Company in acres.

According to this table, the UAIL Company acquired governmental lands from 26 villages of 518.25 (24.04%) acres. These lands belong to the village communities, like the cremation ground, village's *Thakurani Mandir* (temple), *Dhangadi Basaa* and *Dhangada Basaa* (the youth dormitories, *Dhangadi Basaa* means the youth girl's dormitory and the *Dhangada Basaa* means the youth boy's dormitory, where the youth girls and boys meeting centre respectively), village communities centre, school buildings etc. All this land has been taken care of by the village people. If the government lands are acquired by the company, then the above things will be destroyed, so the traditional tribal culture will be destroyed. In the DP colony, only school building is there and there no places for other activities.

The process of extraction of alumina from bauxite is an extremely hazardous process. After the extraction of one ton of alumina, the rest 6.95 materials are treated as wasteful effluents, which are dumped at the site. The most hazardous material of these wasteful products is 'red mud'. To extract one ton of alumina it creates 1.2 tons of red mud which is thrown into a specially constructed pit and as a result of this red mud it creates pollution in the nearby water resources and agricultural field

(Samantara, 2000: 40). The ore extraction process for Bauxite would produce huge amounts of dust. The subsequent operations of transportations, grinding, granulimatric sorting would raise even bigger amounts of dust. The water run off from the ore pile would carry a toxic substance that is likely to mix in the surface run off from these areas, and also infiltrate the groundwater reservoirs with acidic solutions.

Table 6.3

Villagewise Government Lands Acquired by the UAIL (in acres)

Name of the villages	*Land aquired*
Tikiri	0.56
Gokhulmunda	0.14
Osapada	0.40
Makapadar	1.65
Bilamala	17.42
Bagrijhola	68.30
Bhitarmuchukuni	81.25
Ramibeda	37.56
Tikirapada	23.69
Raimachapurunapadar	14.81
Koral	59.81
Dimundi	60.24
Paikakupakhal	66.48
Kanchaguma	0.59
Kodipari	0.50
Naringijodi	6.84
K. kupakhal	23.28
Lundrukona	6.16
Jogiparitunda	2.13
Andirakancha	22.28
Anbiligatatunda	5.94
Hatikhaman	4.36
Peringini	0.95
Gaimunatunda	1.90
Dhuturapas	4.20
Gadalaghat	6.81
Total	518.25

Source: Tahasildar Office, Kashipur.

Some Facts About the Companies

Odisha possesses 69.7 per cent of the total bauxite deposits in India that are mostly accumulated in KBK districts. About 2,130 lakh ton bauxite is deposited in the Gandhamardan areas (Bolangir-Sambalpur) and the rest is in 5 adjacent blocks of undivided Korput and Kalahandi districts. About 1,957.3 lakh ton is in Baphalimali and 810 lakh ton in Sasubahumali of Kashipur block, Rayagada district, 860 lakh ton in Sijimali and 400 lakh ton in Kutrumali of Rayagada-Kalahandi district, and 914 lakh ton in Kodingamali of Laxmipur block of Koraput district. Bauxite is also deposited in Ghusurimali and Sijlimali of Dasmantpur block of Koraput district and in Niyamgiri hill of Lanjigarh block of Kalahandi district. This is a vast bauxite zone, which constitutes a sizeable portion of KBK area.

The Utkal Alumina Project will source bauxite through open cast mining from Baphalimali of Kashipur block. Bauxite will be transported to the plant site at Doraguda village of Kucheipadar Panchayat (25 km from mining area) through conveyor belt. Alumina will be exported through Visakhapatnam port of A.P.

Utkal Alumina is a joint venture. In 1992, INDAL, TATA, Hydro (Norway) and ALCAN (Canada) were associate partners of the venture. Hydro and TATA have withdrawn from the project. HINDALCO of Birla India has replaced INDAL. Earlier the production was scheduled to begin by 2002, but it was rescheduled for 2005.

The plant at Doraguda village will directly affect 10,000 people of 24 villages of Kucheipadar, Hadiguda, and Tikiri Panchayats (for plant, red mud pond and ash pond). But the company claims that 147 families of 3 villages will be affected. In the foothills of Baphalimali, 42 villages of Chandragiri, Maikanch, Munusogaon and Kodipari Panchayat of Kashipur block and Adri and Dandabad Panchayat of Thuamul Rampur block of Kalahandi district will directly be affected by the open cast mining at Baphli mali. But the company claims that not a single village will be affected.

In the year 1995, L&T started survey work in Sijimali and Kutrumali of Kashipur-Thuamal Rampur blocks of Rayagada-Kalahandi districts. The proposed plant was to be set up at the village Kusumsila, Sikarpai Panchayat, Kalyansingpur block of Rayagada district. Due to strong opposition of the people the company work has stopped. Recently, Sasubahumali has been leased to Sterlite Company. Villagers of 5 panchayats around the mali vehemently opposed the survey team and did not allow them to survey.

Under the banner of '*Khadualmali Surakhsya Vahini*' people of eight panchayats of Thuamul Rampur block of Kalahandi district are protesting against bauxite mining. Similar voice of protest has been raised against Sterlite Company in Lanjigarh area (specifically in Botlima and Lanjigarh panchayat).

Sites of Movement

The fact is that this agitation remained restricted to the Kashipur, Laxmipur and Dasamantpur blocks of Koraput and Rayagada districts and did not spread to the other blocks in these districts. The Baphalimali hill which is the concentration of bauxite mines from which the utkal Aluminum has proposed to exploit the ore is situated near the large multi-purpose irrigation dam known as Indravati hydropower project. The catchment area of this Indravati river and the hills of Kashipur block from which have generated the water sources of Indravati. At a cost of more than 1,000 crores this project has been constructed to irrigate the perpetually drought affected areas. Once mining starts in Baphalimali hills, it will not only drain out the water resources but also will produce silting which will dry up the dam and as a result the whole Indravati Project will die an unnatural death (*Swabhinam*, Oriya Fortnightly, 16–08–2004: 8). The contamination from L&T project is similarly likely to feed into Nagavalli river. The effluents of the plant will pollute the water resources of this river which is the lifeline of Rayagada district. Recently, Bagirijhola minor irrigation project was constructed for the ostentatious purpose of irrigation of the agricultural land. Now this irrigation project is going to be handed over to the Utkal Alumina project depriving the local people of their right to water for irrigation (Samantara, 2000: 45). Not only that, the mining of Baphalimali, Sasubahumali or Kuturmali hills will turn more than 100 villages into desert and about 32 rivers will dry up and will be polluted. The temperature is also likely to rise. So the proposed alumina projects will destroy the *Prakrutika Sampada* (natural resources) of that area (*Swabhiman*, 01–09–2004: 5). So, the people of Kashipur have demanded the issues of livelihood and life with dignity.

This may go under the garb of development, but the destruction of people's livelihoods, the degradation of the environment causing the breakdown of fragile ecosystems, should make one pause to ponder, over whether this development is not more violent than many a war. In spite of this, the Odisha government pretends as if there is no problem for the tribals of the area and behaves almost like a business company. These indigenous people have now been enlisted as a business commodity by the government of Odisha. There is strong disenchantment against the government. Among the tribal women, Mrs Lachhama Majhi says, 'We have been living for generation and generations under the lap of nature. If we are evicted from this place by the company, we will turn out to be beggars on the street, we will not leave our homeland'. An illiterate tribal women, Mrs Alai Majhi who is in the forefront of the struggle says, 'Your governments, you collectors, you Tahasildar have not given us this forest, land, rivers and the treasure under the earth, we have got these as the gift of the nature and have been enjoying for thousand years together since our forefathers and it will continue also for future generations. The governments have taken away the natural resources, land, forest and livelihood from tribals, so people would not allow the company and they will fight to save their motherland till death'.

After 13 years of this movement against the companies and the state activism, the state policies geared toward capital-intensive industrialisation and modernisation in that areas which, increased poverty among the rural poor, the tribals and the dalits in the Kashipur block. Some political leaders believed that they had a state mandate to highlight the contradiction between state policies and practice and to demand accountability. Such structural contradictions were recognised and articulated by a 'new social class' of young, educated, urban and rural men and women, influenced by radicalised factions of the left and Gandhian movements (Meyer, Whittier and Robnett, 2002: 68). The new actors like, social activists, some NGOs, academicians have been organised including the impoverished i.e. urban, rural and tribal people. Their focus, influenced by the *sarvodaya* (well-being of all) movement (Gandhian movement), was total revolution, involving re-examination of not only unjust economic relationships but also unequal social relationships between the upper and lower castes, as well as between men and women. Workers, peasants, tribals, and students, both men and women, organised mass protests demanding that the state should live up to its promise of eliminating poverty. In this period of popular unrest, the initial phase of the women's movement, comprised of poor urban and rural women organised by middle-class women, and it emerged around issues of survival and gender inequality in affiliation with tribal movements and movements of peasants and workers (Meyer, Whittier and Robnett, 2002: 68). The focus of the livelihood movement of Kashipur block, like most of the other movements, has been a challenge to the development plans of the state, which had abandoned the agrarian self-sufficiency vision of Gandhi.

During 1985–86, Kashipur witnessed a terrible drought, many people died due to starvation. It forced the then Prime Minister Rajiv Gandhi to visit the area. This ushered in a new era in the history of Kashipur block. Development plans were chalked out; International Fund for Agricultural Development (IFAD) came to enhance agriculture in the area. In the name of agricultural development, it introduced coffee plantation and sericulture. Earlier in their '*dangars*' (hills), they used to grow traditional crops, but now they were taught to grow coffee and mulberry for the benefit of traders and capitalists. IFAD also suggested development of road and communication to enable the people to participate in the national mainstream. So roads from Tikiri to Kashipur and railway line from Rayagada to Koraput were constructed. When in 1993 companies after companies made a queue to commercialise this area, the people of Kashipur realised the real motive behind this development.

The first main source of environmental destruction in the world is the demand for natural resources generated by the consumption of the nations or rich individuals and groups within nations. The second is that it is the poor who are affected the most by loses of livelihood and environmental destruction. Control over natural resources is an important reason for emergence of environmental movement in India. Some good examples of these kinds of movements are like Chipko and Narmada Bachao Andolan (NBA). In the first case, the reason for conflict was control over forest. The other angles by which we look upon the cause of emergence of environmental movements are the socio-economic reasons. Almost most of the environmental movements in India are somehow related with this aspect, also if we see the location where these movements have started then we would find that most of these areas are tribal dominated. These tribal people have strong beliefs regarding their forests, land and water. At the same time they are also totally dependent upon these resources for their survival. Therefore, when these forests or other sources of livelihood get disturbed by the outsiders, their socio-economic conditions get hampered and the ultimate resource is the movement against those people who are harnessing those resources. The women had generally played an important role in these movements, in tribal groups; women are accustomed to responsibility and leadership for community survival. Their work involves them directly and daily with forests and natural resources. So, whenever their survival comes into risk, they take the leading role for the protection of their community and its natural resources.

Table 6.4

Lands Required for Aditya Aluminum Project

Name of the Villages	*Forest Lands*	*Government Lands*	*Private Lands*	*Total*
Rayagada district				
Kansariguda	13.48	52.53	499.59	565.6
Puhundi	0.56	37.82	197.65	236.03
Phulajuba	—	22.09	170.77	192.86
Podapadi	—	4.79	36.10	40.89
Total	14.04	117.23	904.11	1,035.38
Koraput district				
Bariguda	66.02	—	134.93	200.95
Bhalujodi	—	60.17	75.50	135.67
Singaram	0.47	27.46	109.68	138.61
R.P. Guda	20.00	370.15	111.23	501.38
Total	100.53	576.01	1,335.45	2,011.99

Source: Tahasildar Office, Kashipur.

Several hundred million people have been increasingly forced to live far below the minimum levels required for a decent human existence, deprived of adequate water, food, clothing, shelter and education, health and sanitation. Development, which was supposed to alleviate such problems, has often increased them, especially by allowing the powerful sections of society to appropriate the natural resources of poor and resource dependent people. Their forests, water and lands are taken away for 'economic progress.' Biodiversity is part of their daily lives and livelihoods, constituting resources upon which families, communities, nations and future generations depend on. Biodiversity has numerous uses in agriculture, medicine, food and industry. It helps to maintain ecological balance and evolutionary processes, and has spiritual, cultural and recreational values.

A special mention must be made here of the indigenous and tribal people of Kashipur block virtually all of whom are faced with a serious crisis of survival. Their identity as dependent communities and peoples is threatened because the economic, social, cultural, and natural resource base which enabled them to thrive as distinct peoples is being trampled upon. This intrusion is very prominent in their economy. The traditional economy of the indigenous peoples rested on their concept and relationship with nature. For most such communities, land, water and forest belong to 'Mother Earth'; land, water and forest are an important ingredient of the indigenous people's identity not only for its economic usage but also for its spiritual and emotional quality.

The present crisis of the indigenous peoples of Odisha in general and Kashipur block in particular consists precisely in the weakening and damaging of the ultimate base of their sustenance, namely land and forest. Since independence the Odisha ruling class, effectively using the government machinery, has been alienating tribals, land and forest in the name of 'national interests'. The biggest threat to the tribals people in Odisha is the large-scale alienation of their land and forest through mega projects such as mines, industries, dams, wildlife reserves, townships, highways, military establishments, and other projects in the name of 'national development' and 'national interests'.

Peasants of Kashipur block have conventionally used a mix of livelihood strategies, involving cultivation, animal husbandry, and collection of resources like fuel, fodder and livelihood materials from forests and wetlands. Thus, 63 years after independence, the development plans for KBK districts and particularly of Kashipur block while the country has achieved great gains in industry and commercial agriculture, has generally failed in poverty eradication, livelihood security and environment protection fronts.

In the Kashipur block, the ecological degradation, erratic rainfall and a high risk of drought in the area have resulted in food insecurity, increasing out-migration and periodic deaths from starvation. Ecological imbalance is now seriously undermining the livelihood patterns and increasing vulnerability of tribal and dalit. A small land based, low agricultural productivity and low incomes, displacement due to big dams and industrial companies have led to rising indebtedness, trapping tribal into a vicious circle of exploitation. The life of the tribal is increasingly vulnerable due to a persistent lack of assured entitlements to their resource base. Land alienation has deprived them of their land; forest legislation has turned them into encroachers of land they have always used; and they have also been disproportionately affected by displacement due to mining operations, irrigation projects, wildlife sanctuaries etc. These have led to social discontent and unrest which provide fertile ground for extremist activities that only more meaningful development of the tribal areas can combat.

The movement has begun with two important questions: in what way such industrial activities benefit the people of the area and who are getting benefit from the company? Primarily tribal communities of that locality are going to lose their land. What could be the impact of the proposed investment and mining on the natural resource base, which is the prime source of sustenance for the most tribal people in this state?

Songs and Dances: The Localised Way of Mass Mobilisation

This ideology of *Maati Aamar Maa (our Mother Earth)* which formed the basis for the construction of identity of the actors of the movement was highlighted in the performance of the songs, dances and poems sung by women as they work and protect the gate during the years of struggle. It was a mythological interpretation of the local issue through musical drama. To have a novel understanding of its impact on people's thinking we can discuss the theme of such songs and dances.

The school building in a Kucheipadar village and the *haata pada* (weekly marketplace) in Tikiri village were the main centres for the performance of the songs and dances. And the other time when the rally was organised, the young men and women were in the front of the rally for dancing and singing. The performance started with the traditional ways like *sailodi nacha* (local dances). A small group of young men and women sung and danced. Some old people start music, with the local hand made kind of sitar, so the space has been cleared for the musicians who start the programme. The surrounding noise decreases and a full-throated voice starts ringing and through the song tells the following story.

This is the story of forests and the tribals people; how they live together since the beginning of creation. How they depend on each other for their survival? The forest is the god of the tribals, the forest gives food, shelter and water, they are dependent on the forest for their livelihood and the tribal are the watchmen of the forest, and they are the protector of the forest. When the story starts, the young men and women dance. The young men were role playing as the forest and the young women as the tribals. The young men asked the questions and the young women reply by singing a song and vice-versa.

'I am extremely upset because my people on earth, the tribals of Kashipur, are facing displacement. Oh god, how could you allow the Navin Patnaik government to take over this land? This land which you have blessed by making it the most fertile land of the region, this land whose people you blessed by giving the technology of raggi making, this land from whose people the rest of the world learnt how to make raggi, this land which gives its people the best that earth, and its soil can give, this land which is blessed with mother and sons who want to protect their *bheeta maati* (a place where forefathers were born). Oh god how can you allow the region that you have blessed to be misused?'.

Sometimes the songs and dance continue, entered the actor playing the role of the then Chief Minister Navin Patnaik. Navin Patnaik tries to convince god. These are the songs and the dance rendered by young men and women which gives a sense of identity to their action and their perception reflects that the fate of Baphalimali rested on their shoulders. Most of these songs and dance were weaved with local tribal language and Koraputias, *Desia Bhasa*. Further the peculiarities of rice production, cultivation of *raggi* and the nature of its environment cumulatively show that they were trying to protect the 'field', and the 'forest'. These are four examples of the songs used in the people's movement at Kashipur (translated from Oriya):

Song No. 1

Today I saw Baphalimali mountains and my eyes have become holy.

The mountains look so beautiful and the nightingale is singing.

Deers, antelopes and bears have been living there since ages.

We have used the forest leaves as medicines; we are staying here for generations.

Today I saw Baphalimali mountains, God please save these mountains.

The tribals and dalits are crushed by the demon UAIL.

Streams, Indravati and Badanadi river have dried up. God! please help us immediately. You have come to help us in any crisis.

Song No. 2 (Oriya)

He Jami chhadiba nahi, he gaan ru hatiba nahi ...

He jami chhadiba nahi re bhai jangala chhadiba nahi ...

Dazar madi aashichhi dhain gaan bhangiba pain ...

Jami badi nei kabal kariba, aamaku maariba pain ... (2)

Maatira manisa maatira poka maati chhadiba nahi,

Dangar jharana jangal paban chhadile banchiba nahi,

Maatira manisa maatira poka maati chhadiba nahi ... (2)

... he jami chhadiba nahi ... (2)

Mariba pachhe dariba nahi janama maati pain re bhai gaan ru hatiba nahi ... .

He jami chhadiba nahi ... (2)

English Translation

We will not leave our land and forest, we will not move from our village.

Land grabbers have come from all over to bulldoze our village,

Aditya Birla and Jindal have come here, we will prepare to resist.

We are the earthworms; we will not leave our land.

We can't live without hill, stream, forest, air,

We will die but we will not fear for our birthplace.

Song No. 3 (Oriya)

Paunda masar sambada katha, 16 tarikha December katha hetai dele re naanaa aakhiru luha jharuchhi … .

Bhabi dele re naanaa aakhiru paani baharuchhi …, (2)

English Translation

Thinking about the black Monday of December, the 16th, tears come to my eyes.

Song No. 4 (Oriya)

Hawa … . Hawa … he hawa, company hawa … (2)

Madu achhi bhaire odisha sara,

Nyaya pain ladiba, aasa sangram kariba,

Aame ladiba … (4)

Janma maati maa ku mukti kariba, aasa aasa maa bhauni aika hoiba … (2)

Kariba aame panare dariba nahi, company hate maati maa ku chhadiba nahi …

chhdiba nahi … (2)

Bela hua bhaire sabu gram basi … (2)

Dekha nahi nahire chupa chapa basi, bipada madi aasuchhi, jani paru naha kichhi … (2)

Dukh aasu chhi, dukha badu chhi … (2)… hawa … hawa … (2)

English Translation

Wind, wind, company wind … (2)

Blowing all over Odisha, let us all stand together for justice.

We will save our mother earth and redeem ourselves … let us … (2)

We will not hand over our land to these companies … (2)

… let us … (2)

Don't just watch us keep quite and sit, don't you see the danger, what we are facing today.

You will face tomorrow, you are not immune,

You are not paying enough attention, more suffering is coming … .

Role of Leadership in the Movement

Social movement is a deliberate collective endeavour to bring change in any direction by any means, it should have some degree of organisation and normative commitment and active participation on the part of its members (Shah, 1990: 16–17). The cohesiveness of the movement in integrating multiple objectives without losing track of the ground level (initial) protests are vital for its success.

In other movements, the committed leaders and their stature at local and national level belong to upper caste and middle class. But the leadership aspect of the Kashipur movement assumes the tribal dimension, for instance, the PSSP convener and the leader of the movement Mr Bhagaban Majhi is a tribal and 7th passed educated young leader from the Kucheipadar village. Before Mr Majhi, Mr Krushna Saunta and Mr Laxman Majhi were the leaders of the movement of the same village, who happen to be from the same category. So, it is not an exaggeration to mention here that the local tribals are leading the movement, the leadership is in the hands of the local tribals. On the other hand, other movements are led by the outsiders such as, people Baba Amte, Sunderlal Bahuguna and Medha Patkar etc. They are the middle class educated people, from outside the affected areas and are social activists. However, the study found that the backgrounds and leadership of Kashipur movement was initiated and organised by Krushna Saunta, Laxman Majhi, Bhagaban Majhi and the tribal women leaders like Sumani Jhodia and Mukta Jhodia. They all come from the tribal communities with poor family background. The two women leaders were awarded many times from the state government of Odisha and the Centre for their contribution in Kashipur block. They are not educated like the other leaders. The Kashipur movement's leaders and the people of that area have started addressing the problems of livelihoods of local tribal. To put it differently, assuming the dimension of the environment, the Kashipur movement is linked to immediate livelihoods and human rights issues which can invite mass popular support rather than environmental concerns. This reflects the present day priorities of the people of Kashipur. The evidence shows that livelihood issues gain prominence in Kashipur movement and the environmental issues have to be articulated by the academic intellectuals, social activists, and some NGOs to attract wider popularity and support from outside.

Photo 11

People gathered at the time of block gherao in Kashipur block office

Photo 12

Researcher's participation in front of Kashipur block

Photo 13

Researcher's participation in the people's protest in Kashipur block

Profile of Leadership

Bhagaban Majhi, age 33 years, has been one of the major leaders. He had no idea about the activities of the company. When company people came and did their survey and had a discussion in the village to open a market, at that time they did not oppose the company or the market. It was the weekly market that was held on Wednesday. The villagers of Kucheipadar needed some money to buy goods like, chicken skin, earthen pot, clothes, and some rice as offering for puja. They raised some funds by collection from villagers, but that was not sufficient, at that time someone was constructing a pillar for the company, they went to him and told that, 'We would carry the pillar for you for some money'. Thus, the puja for the market could be held. They thought that may be after a month *Disari* would die, but he did not die. They had asked for some money from the company and contractor for their work. So, they organised a village meeting which was attended by Anantram Majhi, Ex. Cabinet Minister of the Odisha state from Congress party. At that time Akhila Saunta was the M.L.A. of Laxmipur assembly constituency from Janata Dal and Biju Patnaik was the Chief Minister of Odisha. The decision took place in the meeting. Mr Majhi said, 'Brother, please think how much happy we all are with our traditional way of life. If the company is set up, we will lose our land, forest and our happiness forever. We won't be able to live without our lands, as we all are like earthworms'. He appealed to the people to oppose collectively the construction of the company. People were pleased with his words. The next morning all villagers, men, women, young and old alike, opposed the company with their sticks in hand. The way they protested against the company created fear among the company people. Some of them fled leaving their tools behind. They were beaten up, even A.R. Majhi was afraid to visit the village again. The protesters believed that they will do everything for those who help them in fighting for their rights. Within this perspective, they invited him in a meeting to follow his ideas but he did not attend that meeting. So, people thought that he was bribed by the company. At the first meeting, he promised that if they vote for him then he will help them. Evaluating the capacity of Akhila Saunta (M.L.A.), he promised to wipe out the company if he got elected. Abstracting the opportunities extended by the people in the form of electing him as M.L.A., nothing has changed in that area. He did not speak for them and started supporting the company. This provided the platform for the people to initiate the movement. When people started opposing the company in beginning, they filed false cases against them and took people to the jail. They presented their grievance to the Chief Minister by stating that they do not want the company to establish in their area. Then the Chief Minister assured them to shift the company elsewhere. Meanwhile, they conducted meetings around their villages and sought their opinion about the company. They discussed about the pros and cons of the company by citing the evidences of other industrial areas like NALCO at Damonjodi, Indravati hydropower project and upper Kolab hydropower project etc. as these cases are clearly reflecting the negative impacts on the local people. After seeing the dams and the industrial area's condition of the tribal people they thought that it is not going to be beneficial, if they give their land. During their rally they demanded to set up schools and hospitals in every village and not the company.

Bhagaban Majhi says, 'When we started meeting and discussion and we heard about the success of the protest against the BALCO, they came and explained the methods of protest against the BALCO and they won, so we learnt that, if we fight back, victory was certainly going to be ours'. How the Gandhamardan people had organised and mobilised? How the protest movement originated and developed? The protest movement won, people of Kashipur learned from them. People of the Baliapal and Chilika movements came in Kashipur and said that how they fought and won their rights. So, that the people of Kashipur again developed their hope to initiate the movement. Since origin of their protest movement has been in democratic, peaceful and Gandhian way of *Satyagraha,* they have obtained permission for holding meetings from the police and the government and also they have been supplying them with information about their activities. Earlier, they would not even let them hold a public meeting despite legal permission from higher authority. The company's hooligans would conspire with the police to disrupt their meeting. The police beat them, harassed them and behaved with them very violently. They were silent despite that. Mr Majhi says, 'Now we know how to fight for our right'. They held small meetings in every village and took decisions collectively for planning big meetings. Then, only after taking due permission, we used to undertake rallies. The companies have used force to prevent them from holding rallies. People have been attacked by police goons, police have implicated protest people with false cases and put in jails, but their resistance continues even after all these obstacles. Earlier when company people came; they would disguise themselves as veterinary doctors. And they would thus get the required data from the villagers, they would survey about their cattle, sheep and chickens. Again the company people came to the villages as Auxiliary Nurses and Midwives (ANM) and inquired about the statistics of the villages' population like, women, girls, boys, and their ages. Then this developed suspicion among the people. People thought that they are from the company people. After that people did not let them conduct further surveys. The company had to stop its activities because of people's protest. So, that the company formed an organisation called Utkal Rural Development Society (URDS), the idea was that people would not oppose this organisation as they did the company. They held free health check-up camps, free seed donation camps and started free adult education in this area. He says that 'We saw that these volunteers were in fact the stooges of the company, their real intention was to first win the confidence of the people and then divide us, that was the conspiracy so we opposed them'. Hence people even protested against this organisation. Some people of their villages understand the plan of company and other did not, so the URDS also failed. Then another organisation was established i.e. Business Partner for Development (BPD) and people opposed it too. The company now understands that people were not afraid of jails, false cases and lathi-charge but may be murder would scare them away.

Then there was an all party committee formed by the political parties like the BJD, BJP and Congress, their aim was to mediate between the pro-company and anti-company groups. All of them were financially supported by the company; the political parties were only carrying out the company's agenda. He says, 'All party committee is never neutral, they favour the company by welcoming the company so that the all party committee is also anti-people, they should not be allowed to operate in our areas, we oppose them'.

On 20 December 2000, people organised road blockade on the Rayagada-Koraput highway at Ruphakana chowk. People had demonstrated in front of the police station and the block office. They had intimated their grievance to the District Magistrate, the Chief Minister, the Prime Minister and the President of India but nothing had changed. So, they had held village level meetings in each and every village, later their programme was to block the road on a larger scale. People across the village know about their protest. Before road blockade they decided in village meeting. Their organisation was working in three blocks like, Kashipur, Laxmipur and Dasamantapur which in last 13 years has spread across those three blocks. Previously it was operating only in Kuchipadar village. Ruphakana is centre place for the three blocks so they decided that place for this roadblock. Before going to roadblock at Ruphakana, they organised some village meeting, such meetings were held at 4/5 different places and the one of the preparatory meeting was held on the 15 December 2000 at Maikanch village. The all party committee also had a meeting in the same day at Nuagaon village; they were pro-company people so they had to pass through the same way. People opposed any meeting that would welcome the company; people did not allow them to pass through the roads. The clash began between the all party committee people and the villagers. The political leaders of the all party committee are very renowned leaders of this area who have never met with such ill-treatment; being offended, they lodged false complaints against people in Kashipur police station. The next day, 16 December 2000, the all party committee returned to Maikanch village with magisterial power, shooting order and two platoons of police force. In the Maikanch village, the village meeting was held up to the evening of 15 December 2000, so people were still expecting the police to arrive and that was followed by the clash. The police came and asked for the village leaders so that the police and the political leaders could talk to the people. The police asked the women of the villagers about the village leaders. The women folk told them, that 'The village leaders are not here anymore, you can tell us what you want to tell them, they are off to the fields for work, we will tell them when they return'. The police got angry and began scolding the villagers, 'Rascal tribals you get them soon or we will get them finished'. The OIC of Kashipur police station knocked a woman down. All the women folk got scared, they began to run helter skelter so the near by working men also ran to the police and the police lathi-charged the crowd, the people were gathered again then they opened fire at the people, after that the police left soon. Their aim was to open fire to the crowd just to clear the road-blocks at Ruphakana. On 16 December 2000, three people were killed and many more injured by the police firing. The news spread across the village on the 17 December, everyone reached Kashipur block, and they cremated the dead bodies together in a heap in the night of the 17 December. The government of Odisha did not provide the injured even with preliminary treatment in the next 24 hours; people got them admitted in a hospital at Kashipur.

The company and the police had thought that the agitation would automatically lose its momentum with the firing. He says that 'we decided about our future plan of action, we would rather die but we will not leave our land'. So on 20 December 2000, about five thousands people arrived at Ruphakana chowk with traditional armed weapons in peaceful ways. The officers of the company were very frustrated because of their success of the road-block.

He says, 'We are not bothered if Superintendent, Collector or Chief Minister had come as we had obtained due permission, the election was coming, they had to beg for our votes and at that time Chief Minister also came with our due permission'. So this is how the people's agitation in Kashipur block is marshalled in a democratic, peaceful and Gandhian way of Satyagraha. He says, 'People have sought for explanation from the government about the people who had been displaced in the name of development. How many of them have been rehabilitated? You have not rehabilitated them at all. You have not provided them jobs. How can you again displace more people? Where will you relocate them and what jobs will you give them? You tell us first'. The government failed to answer these questions. So they colluded with the company, the police and leaders and lodged them in jails on false charges. He says, 'They have planned to scare us by caning us, by firing tear-gas and open firing at us but our agitation is for principles'. So people ideally ask a fundamental question, 'How can we survive if our lands are taken away from us? We have tribal farmers; we are earthworms, like fishes that die when taken out of water, the same thing is happening with the farmers when our land is taken away from us, so we won't leave our land'. People want sustainable development, they wanted irrigation facilities for their lands, established hospitals and schools in their villages, give them free medicine and they wanted right over forest and lands. People don't need the company, people have been repeatedly telling this since last 13 years but the government is not listening to people's voice. The parties like BJP, BJD and Congress, the party leaders are being elected from here since independence. All the BDOs, GPEOs and JEs who have served the block during their incumbency as MLAs, there has been rampant corruption. The crores of rupees which the government spends in Kashipur block for the people's development have been misappropriated; PC (Bribe) is root cause of corruption. Because all the leaders wanted to make money out of these government's programmes and projects. Because of their corruptions people have suffered like starvation, diarrhoea, death, malaria etc. The local leaders of the BJP, BJD and Congress are only responsible for these starvation deaths. But they don't take that in account. They only say that the huge amount of money has been spend for development in the Kashipur block for education, health and irrigation, but there has been no development. He says that 'When we want development like schools, hospitals and medicine in every village, they say that is only possible once the company is established'. 'The company is not developing for us; only development is for their own interest, the benefit is only temporary means for some people including some officials'. For the construction work, the company needs three thousand labours who will work for about four years. But where will people go after the construction work is over, is this the development? 'How many high schools, hospitals, colleges and engineering colleges can you set up in the twenty gram panchayats of Kashipur block', they asked those questions. The government has no answer, people do not oppose development; in fact, people want development but they need long term development. He says 'We won't allow our billions years old land and forest to go to ruins just to pander to the greed of some officials; we told them not to get engaged in these destructive works and stop this work, give us what we want if you really mean for development'. Tell this to their leaders, but the government has not even agreed to talk to them. Since generations the nature has created them, it is necessary for tribals' survival, the government should think that. Being a ruler, how can the government adopt those polices that would destroy their land and forest in the coming 30–35 years? Please stop the company, people asked these questions to their leaders. The government and the political leaders say that 'You are fools, you don't understand, if you would have been educated then you would not have opposed the company'. One day he asked question to S.P. of Rayagada, 'Sir what is development? What worth is development if it ends up in relocation of people?' According to Bhagaban Majhi the 'development' means that, 'the people for whom development is meant should reap benefits, and after that the succeeding generations should reap the benefits'. It should not be merely to cater to the greed of the few officers and politicians. To destroy the age old resources is not development. So, if the government has decided that, they need alumina and bauxite then the government has to oblige the people. 'As the tribals are farmers, thus won't be able to live without lands, if the alumina is very necessary then the government should give land in lieu of land, then there is some possibility'. 'If they need it so badly, they need to tell us why they need it', said Majhi. How much bauxite do the governments need? The government must give us complete account. The government could tell us that the resources will last for the next generation, but we know that the resources will get exhausted in another thirty years, then what next? They ask the question to the government and the company.

Again they say, 'The company will pollute our environment and export our resources to the foreign countries'. They say, 'please tell us what profit the governments get? How our country is benefited? How do the people get benefited? Then what benefit the company gets in contrast, we know of the loss; that is why we oppose the company'. 'They call us fools', the government officers and the company people say, 'You should learn from your leaders and officers'. 'You have become IAS, IPS and have earned more knowledge than us, your sheer knowledge has drowned your sense of reasoning, and hence you cannot see through this game plan, he became silent when I said this' says Majhi. 'The agitation is our birth right; through our agitation, we put these very fundamental questions', but the company and the officers have not given the question's answer. 'The government called our agitation as terrorism and naxalism; they are bringing in armed constables like the CRPF and IRPF from Odisha to repress our agitation'. 'They are threatening us to send to jail whosoever joins our agitation; they did not allow us to hold the weekly market'. They warned the villagers not to join the agitation, the government and the company people tell them that 'come and give in writing that, you would not oppose the company any more', the government officers promised that if the people did that, the cases against people would be withdrawn.

I asked him, why are you opposing company? He replied, 'We are tribals, these children who live on mangoes, raggi and pulses, our children are not educated, what will they do with money?'. 'The company is not going to give jobs in the company, we have been living on these mountains, we have sustained with children like this, so we don't want company's money'. 'We are protesting for our motherland, mountains, so we oppose company'. I asked again, you are opposing the company and the government, can you compete with them? He replied, 'it is not about wining or losing, we are protesting for our livelihood'. No grazing land for their cattle and also the dust after the blasting settles everywhere near their villages.

About Women Leaders of the Kashipur Movement

Mukta Jhodia: Mukta Jhodia, 45-year-old lady and resident of Sriguda village in Rayagada district, Odisha, is a tribal woman leader fighting against the Hindalco-led Utkal Alumina's bauxite mining and processing project in Kashipur. She has won the first 'Chingari Award' for women fighting against corporate crime. The 13-year-old struggle against mining in Odisha got after Goldman Award winners and leaders of the struggle for justice in Bhopal Rashida Bee and Champa Devi Shukla were handed over a trophy and citation, while writer Jyotsna Kamal presented ₹ 50,000 cheque to Mukta Jhodia (*Times of India*, 5 December 2007). Mukta has locked horns with a Birla-led mining consortium and has mobilised her community to successfully stave off plans to mine the bauxite rich plateaus in her motherland. The mother of a married son and a daughter, Mukta has been a key source of inspiration and awareness among Kashipur's tribal communities. She has tirelessly traveled to tribal villages around Rayagada, often on bicycle with her husband or son, informing them about Birla's plans to exploit their *bheeta mati* (motherland).

She says that there is a lot of talk on the unlimited powers of 'Gram sabha' in Scheduled Areas. The Gramsabhas of Kucheipadar and Maikanch panchayats had recommended scrapping of the treaty signed with the company. Again after Maikanch firing, government had organised on its own Gramsabha meeting on 29 December 2000 in six Gram Panchayats (Kucheipadar, Maikanch, Gorakhpur, Tikiri, Kodipari, Sunger) to seek the opinion of local people on the project. All the Gram Panchayats had given opinion against the project. We feel the slogan 'Power to people through Gramsabha' is nothing but eyewash.

She says, 'The collector, police, minister and the government have not created this land or this forest. They have not settled us. We have been living here form generations. We would never leave our land and forest. We cannot live without that. It gives us food and meets our other demands. Our land is based on perennial streams. With the help of the streams, we have been cultivating on our lands'.

She says, 'The government is forcing us to accept the Alumina project in Kashipur block. But we opposed the Alumina plants in our locality. On the course of struggle, three of our beloved brothers were gunned down by the police. But we are not afraid. We are determined not to forget supreme sacrifices of our beloved brothers to protect our lands. So we are opposing to all the big projects like, plant, mining, sanctuary, Big Dam etc. in the tribal dominated area of Koraput district'.

'We are concerned about our own development. We want agricultural development not industrial development. Small check dams of using stream of our area will be very helpful for agricultural development. We also want jungle based medical facilities and education system in harmony with our tradition, culture, in which we have been living'.

Sumani Jhodia: Sumani Jhodia is a 57 year-old lady and resident of Sriguda village in Rayagada district, Odisha. She says that, 'Baphalimali gives us food, shelter, culture and we live happily. This mountain is our god. We live in these mountains and so we survive .... We are tribal people. We are doing *dangar chasa* (shifting cultivation); that is our main occupation; we don't have land with which we can produce and meet our livelihood so we are dependent on the hills .... If we go somewhere else, we will die; we cannot leave our land, forest and the Baphalimali hills .... If the Baphalimali hills, the forests and the land are handed over to the company then the struggle is going to continue. Even they did not give any notice to take away the land and the hills'. The government officers say, 'This is not our land, it is Odisha's government land and hills'. The tribals say, 'Write and give it to us that these lands belong to the government and not the tribals and that the tribals have no right over it. The tribals' land cannot be transferred to non-tribals, not even to dalits. Then how the land was transferred to the company?'. As we know, the law says that the transfer of land has to be passed by the *gram sabha*. But when the gram sabha was called the people were not aware about the transfer of the land to the company. We were asked to sign and leave before the collector, we did it. It was done in the presence of collector and the police officers, later they said that, this was passed in the gram sabha but people never knew that the gram sabha was for the transfer of their land to UAIL. So the people refuse to give up their land even today.

The respondent says that the government forcefully took away the land and houses and evacuated. Then using bulldozers the administration leveled the land and houses. 'In some village, they took our farming land, they left some houses. They took the cremation ground, temple, well, pond etc. How will we survive?

The coal and bauxite powder comes into our food and water'. The S.P. of Rayagada came to our village and said, 'Either you agree for giving the land or you will be in the jail for 5 years'. So we got scared and agreed to give our land and the company gave some compensation money. We have a lot of problem with the sound from the company; we are not able to sleep at night. How would the animals live there? When we purchase land, we register it. But how did UAIL register our land in their name? Company gave one lakh per acre; for how long can we survive with that one lakh? Here we get mangoes, pineapple, turmeric, wood, leaves; we make ploughs; we make our livelihood from these things. There are elephants, medicines and many kinds of animals. Baphalimali is like our home, we cannot leave it. When the company start, the smoke, dust will go up and these areas of Kashipur block will not get rain; we poor people will die. Only outsiders are working in the company and our villagers are unable to find work. If we ask for jobs, they say, what do you know? Since the companies came to our areas, their *mafia* has grown, beating people has started in Kashipur block; and this was not here before. When we go to protest against the companies, we are arrested under various sections and put in the Rayagada jail. So many times people went to Tikiri police station. The ladies were in front and we were behind. The government ordered firing, lathi-charge and they killed our three brothers on 16 December 2000. How many can they kill?

Organisation of the Movement

Large number of people of the area gathered under the charismatic leadership of activist Bhagaban Majhi and local resistance organisations federated into a common platform known as the *Prakrutika Sampada Surakhya Parisad* (PSSP). Resistance strategies borrowed from Gandhian satyagraha included non-cooperation and civil disobedience, refusal to cooperate with project authorities, blocking of all project-related work, conducting rally and hunger strike in front of the project and refusal to leave their villages.

In the year 1993, when the employees of Utkal Alumina International came to Doraguda village of Kuchepadar panchayat to undertake survey work, the local people began to look upon them with suspicion and enquired from them about their purpose of work and the people came to know that an Alumina plant was to be established in their area. When the people came to know about the proposed alumina project on 11 November 1993, a group of 18 local representatives of the area met Biju Patnaik, the Chief Minister of Odisha. After discussion with the local representatives the Chief Minister assured that the site of the proposed project would be changed. Since the assembly elections were in the forefront the Chief Minister might have given such populist assurance without any sincere intention. After the assembly elections in 1995 a new government was formed. The same company again resumed its activity and the survey work had started. At this moment, the people of Kucheipadar and the nearby villages organised among themselves and decided to protest against the state and its proposed project company. In December 1994, people brought four employees of the company along with their machinery to Kucheipadar village and kept them under their custody. Then of course the police came and rescued these employees. After some days, a case was registered in the local police station against 12 persons of the villager. On 17 February 1995, more than five thousand tribals and dalits from the nearby 50 villages of Kashipur and Thumul Rampur blocks peacefully organised rallies from Sagabari village (the *Sijimali* mining village site) to the L&T company office at Sunger village to protest against the setting up of the plant. The next day, the Tahasildar of Kashipur visited the Sagabari village. However, to protect their land and resources, people from all the affected villages had organised themselves to form the *Anchalika Surahha Samiti* and they submitted a charter of demand to the Tahasildar. Their right to information made it clear that they would continue to obstruct the road till their demands were fulfilled. The sub-collector of Rayagada visited Sagabari village and asked the people to let the gate open for the vehicles of the company. The villagers repeated their demands before him but it did not yield any result.

On 16 March 1995, R.N. Jena, Collector of Rayagada district visited Sagabari village with a prior intimation. More than 2,000 people, mostly women handed over to him a note of appeal containing 19 points with regard to the proposed mining operation. Instead of commenting anything on the demands the Collector declared that the factory would be established by any cost since the decision has already been taken. Such a statement from the Collector infuriated the public and they started giving the slogan: 'Government must kill us first and then set up the factory' (PSSP Documents). Despite the protest of the people, the UAIL Company authorities installed some handpumps at the proposed plant site to fulfill the company requirements. The villagers destroyed the drilling machine and the handpumps and prevented the company officials from doing their work. On 20 April 1995, people from near about 20 villager organised a meeting and vowed to oppose the decision of setting up the plant in their locality (PSSP Documents, Kashipur). On 14 February 1996, a huge pubic rally was organised by the public at Kucheipadar village. This led to the emergence of *Prakrutika Sampada Surakshya Parisad* (Council for the protection of natural resources), a public organisation constituted to carry out all agitational programmes in order to protect the interest of the local area and the people. This rally was addressed by Medha Patkar, the great leader of Narmada Bachao Andolan, Manmohan Choudhry, the great Sarvodaya leader, Kisan Patnaik, the great socialist leader and many other leaders of people's movements all over the country. This rally was very significant in spreading the message of the local agitation to the outside world.

On 9 September 1996, about 10,000 people took out a rally from Kucheipadar to Tikiri and *gheraoed* the company office at Tikiri. In the meantime, people from the affected villages set up barricades in different villages and started resisting the movement of the employees and vehicles of the company. On 5 July 1997, the company started the construction of a rehabilitation colony near D. Koral village. On l0 July, the agitationists demolished some of the half constructed houses as a mark of organised protest. Again on 22 November 1997, on the occasion of the birth anniversary of Saheed Laxman Nayak, a tribal freedom fighter, a huge public rally was organised at Tikiri. More than five thousand people attended this rally where they had taken a promise 'we will die but not leave our homeland' (PSSP Pamphlet, Kashipur).

It was a matter of great surprise that when one company after another is rushing to this area to get established, no official information has been made available to the local people. Since the entire project work is carried out in a veil of secrecy, the suspicion about the project is also increasing everyday. This has upset the tribal people of that region, and they have taken to resistance and expressions of protests in various forms. People of that locality have protested to protect their land and natural resources from the state and the company. The right to information act is not just the means here; the governments also does not bother about the act and the people.

Supporters of the Movement

When any protests, revolutions, movements or political outfit is going to start, it is necessary to look into two things on social response: one is who are the supporters and who are the opponents. In Kashipur, some people have been opposing the movement, they wanted the establishment of the company and most of the people have been opposing the establishment of the company they have fear of losing their livelihoods. The under-mentioned table shows the social group wise, the supporters and the opponents of the movement.

Table 6.5

Social Group wise Supporters and Opponent of the Movement

Supporters of the Movements				*Opponents of the Movements*			
ST	*SC*	*Women*	*Total*	*ST*	*SC*	*Women*	*Total*
75	40	37	115	20	25	15	45
65.21%	34.78%	32.17%	71.87%	44.44%	55.55%	33.33%	28.12%

Total Respondents in My Field Work in Kashipur			
ST	*SC*	*Women*	*Total*
95	65	52	160
59.37%	40.62%	32.5%	100%

Source: My fieldwork in Kashipur and Thuamul Rampur blocks.

Note: Total 160 responded including 52 women responded.

Different Forces which Played Important Roles in the Movement

Local people: The majority of the population belong to tribal communities like Kandha, Paraja, Jhodia, Penga and the dalits (locally called 'Dombo'). Besides them, there are Gouda, Paikas and Sunddhis (the other castes). Participation of tribals in the movement is much more than any other community. As most of the dalits do not possess land and they also do not involve in *dangar* cultivation, their stake in the movement which is aimed at protecting land is definitely less. But there are some villages where dalits have lands; the participation in the movement is significant. On the other hand, landless tribals participate in the movement, because they are involved in the *dangar* cultivation. However, 65.21 per cent of the tribals people have participated actively in the protest movement and 34.78 per cent of dalits' population have participated in the movement. The 34.78 per cent of dalits, who have some cultivable lands have participated in the movement. As an overall, out of 160 respondents, 115 respondents means 71.87 per cent of the population, they are the supporters of the movement while 45 respondents means 28.12 per cent of the population, they are the opponents of the movement. Among the tribals, near about 34 per cent of the tribal people, those who did not participate in the protest movement include some educated young people, who are aspiring to get a job in the company, some local tribal political leaders and some tribal construction contractors. If they participate in the movement then the company does not give jobs in the company or other facilities, so they did not participated in the protest movement. I had interacted with local educated youth, who are employees of the company. They say 'Please don't tell to anyone, we know that the company is not good for our people, but we can't participate in the movement because we are employers of the company, if the company knows that then we will be out of jobs'. To put it differently, some people are really interested to participate in the movement but they could not due to some economic reasons. Few educated tribals and dalits are the contractors in the construction works like road, boundary wall, building and railway line construction works. So, they are the opponents of the movement.

Women: Although women participated in large numbers in the protest movements, they were hardly given due recognition. The women protesters are put up in the front to protect the men from police atrocities. They were rarely considered to participate in the decision-making. Mining operations have a serious impact on the lives and livelihood of women. It is highly gender discriminatory and abusive of their minds and bodies (The Hindu, 26–04–2003). Thus, the participation of women in the struggle has been remarkable. Their mobility is more here as compared to non-tribal women. Secondly, they are more attracted to *dangar* than the men. They want to protect it. So, 71.15 per cent of the women are supporters of the movement, they are more dependent on natural resources. They collect firewood, roots, leaves and other resources from nearby forests.

Political Parties and People's Representatives: Unlike the livelihood and anti-displacement struggle in Kashipur block of Odisha, no political party has so far directly participated in the movement. In the 1994 assembly election, Congress candidate won the election promising people that if voted to power he would drive out the company. Traditionally, Congress and BJD are two players in political scene. Recently, BJP is trying to make some inroads. All of them are openly supporting the project. During last 2004 and 2009 election, people asked all the political parties to clearly state their views on the project. Expectedly, no political party did that. Then the ex-Chief Minister, Giridhar Gomanga who was contesting election from that area tried to avoid it by saying the decision about project will be reconsidered. Keeping the next Lok Sabha and Assembly election in mind and his own political future, he stated if people don't want project it won't be. Most of the political parties are for the pro-project people because they get better compensation and proper rehabilitation and some share from the profit. Nothing to be surprised about it. It had happened when Nehru had set the tone for it to suffer for national interest. All are for the existing system, for the existing model of development. This has happened in Hirakud Hydro-electric project in Sambalpur district of Odisha. Late Prasanna Panda, the local MLA did not get support from his own Communist Party, neither of state nor at central level when he opposed the project. Political parties support or opposition to this sort of struggle depends on whether they are in or out of power. This has been proved in Anti-BALCO struggle in Odisha in 1980s. In Kashipur block the entire mainstream political parties Congress, BJP, BJD are hell bent on starting the project. These parties have formed an All Party Committee to support the project. The BSP as a political force is emerging in that area. They are supporting the movement not out of any political conviction but to spread their base to win the next election.

Table 6.6

Members of the Legislative Assembly, Name and their Constituencies, Years and the Political Parties

S.No.	Name of the MLAs	No. and name of the constituencies	Years	Political Parties
1	Jhajuru Jhodia	019 – Jaipatna-Kashipur	20.02.1952 to 04.03.1957	INC
2	Kishore Deo	027 – Kashipur	01.04.1957 to 25.02.1961	AIGP
3	Nabakumari Devi	035 – Kashipur	26.06.1961 to 01.03.1967	INC
4	A.R. Majhi	078 – Rayagada	01.03.1967 to 23.01.1971	INC
5	Raghunath Himirika	078 – Rayagada	23.03.1971 to 03.03.1973	Congress (R)
6	A.R. Majhi	083 – Laxmipur	06.03.1974 to 30.04.1977	INC
7	Akhila Saunta	083 – Laxmipur	26.06.1977 to 17.02.1980	Janata Party
8	A.R. Majhi	083 – Laxmipur	09.06.1980 to 09.03.1985	INC
9	A.R. Majhi	083 – Laxmipur	09.03.1985 to 03.03.1990	INC
10	Akhila Saunta	083 – Laxmipur	03.03.1990 to 15.03.1995	Janata Dal
11	A.R. Majhi	083 – Laxmipur	15.03.1995 to 1999	INC
12	Giridhar Gomanga (bye election)	083 – Laxmipur	1999 to 29.02.2000	INC
13	Bibhisana Majhi	083 – Laxmipur	29.02.2000 to 06.02.2004	BJD
14	A.R. Majhi	083 – Laxmipur	15.05.2004 to October 2008	INC
15	P.C. Majhi (bye election)	083 – Laxmipur	December 2008 to 19.05.2009	INC
16	Lal Bihari Himirika	140 – Rayagada	19.05.2009 to conti.	BJD

Source: Koraput and Rayagada districts public information offices 2009.

Thus, no political party has so far directly participated in the movement. And the people bypassed these political parties and remained apolitical. The following table reflects the political situation, who are the representatives of Kashipur block and from which political parties they belong to.

Before 1962, Kashipur block was a part of Kalahandi district. The Jaipatna block of Kalahandi district and the Kashipur block belong to the same assembly constituency. Then the assembly constituency also shifted to Kashipur and created a separate constituency from 1957 to 1967. Later on, the administrative power had shifted from Kalahandi to Koraput until 1992 and the Kashipur block belonged to the Rayagada assembly constituency up to 1973. In 1974 the Kashipur block, the Laxmipur, Narayanapatna and Bandhugaon blocks created a separate assembly constituency, called Laxmipur assembly constituency. Presently due to the delimitation of the state assembly and parliament constituencies in 2008, again the Kashipur block was shifted to Rayagada assembly constituency. It is surprising that, whenever the Kashipur block was shifted to other constituencies, I have seen the political domination of the Kashipur people since independence. In the above table, 13 MLAs out of 16 are belonging to Kashipur block, 2 Himirika and Gomanga are from outside the Kashipur block. Here I have found that the Indian National Congress has been the dominant political party, out of 16 MLAs, 11 MLAs are from the Congress party. Except two, all were from the tribal communities, because it has a tribal reserved constituency, so that the tribal and the dalit people get political representatives and political position but till now have not got the political power. The political power is in the hands of the upper caste people and state capital, Bhubaneswar. A.R. Majhi, six times MLA was from Kucheipadar village itself but he was the ideologue of the Kashipur movement. When he was defeated and his brother Akhila Saunta, from the same village won the 1990 election, in between the company started the survey work. One day the Kucheipadar people had organised a village meeting which was attended by Anantram Majhi, ex. Cabinet Minister of the Odisha from Congress party. At that time Akhila Saunta was the MLA of Laxmipur assembly constituency from Janata Dal and Biju Patnaik was the Chief Minister of Odisha. The decision took place in the meeting, Mr Majhi said, 'Brother, please think how much happy we all are without the company and leading the traditional way of life. If the company is set up, we will lose our land, forest and our happiness forever. We will not be able to live without our lands, as we all are like earthworms'. So, let us together oppose the company from tomorrow. People became very happy to hear him, speaking like this. Although he was given knowledge about their good future, he helped them. At the first meeting he promised that if they vote for him then he would help them in driving the company out of their area. He was elected in 1995 elections but did not speak for the people and took the companies' side. This is what Mr Majhi's position was about the company and to gain the political mileage, he was given this idea. In 1990 to 1995, Akhila Saunta was MLA and the Janata Dal was in power in the state, so they had taken initiative; and from 29.02.2000 to 06.02.2004, Bibhisana Majhi was the MLA from BJD, they were in power in the state, at that time the Maikanch police firing took place. In short, the Janata Dal and the BJD are responsible for the establishment of the company and the Maikanch police firing. On the other hand, the Congress party is responsible for the underdevelopment of Kashipur block because the congress party has been in power for a long time.

Role of NGOs in the Movement

Exploring the role and activities of NGOs in Kashipur, in the beginning the *Agragamee* has disseminated information relating to project and its possible impact on the life, livelihood and environment of the area. *Agragamee* was in a sense bound to do this because it has been working in Kashipur for the last two decades. In the absence of a collective process, *Agragamee* carved out a place for itself among the people in the area. Dependence on *Agragamee* can be seen from the initial steps taken and later from the sort of demands raised by the movement such as signature campaign, demand for information regarding the project, clarification regarding the benefits to be accrued to people from the project. The memorandum stating all these demands was presented on 22.2.1995. Before that spontaneously people had protested that resulted in the denial of the entry of survey team to the village, seize of the survey instruments etc. These activities and above-mentioned demands do not match really. This is because the NGO always wants to direct the movement in the constitutional framework and within the purview of law. This is a typical NGO tactic. As they have earned a pro-people image by doing certain reformist work, they cannot immediately withdraw from the people's problem at this magnitude. They worked to control and keep the movement within such a limit that their very existence will not be threatened and they will remain close to the people so that they will not be totally rejected. They sometimes even justify their own limitation by defining it as people's limitation.

Gradually, many more NGOs show interest in it. An NGO called *Norwatch* from Norway comes to know people's views. Local people strongly reject the question of compensation by saying 'We don't want compensation'. We will not leave our home and land for mining and industry. *Norwatch's* role to sensitise people in Norway to the problems of people in Kashipur may create a moral pressure on the company. But the same group is asking the people, after withdrawal of Hydro what next? Does *Norwatch* see a role after such withdrawal? In 1997, February–March with the involvement of some NGOs a public interest litigation was filed in the High Court of Odisha. The court gives its verdict in favour of the company. When people discuss the judgment they clearly state 'The Government which has given permission for the project, its court cannot give verdict in our favour. Government, court, police, company belongs to the same boat'. As the movement grows, NGOs see the opportunity to reap some benefits. And a tug of war between rival NGOs follows just to prove that they are closer to the people than the other ones. Each group tries to use the local activists.

During the first week of July 1999, Southern Revenue Divisional Commission convened a meeting of NGOs to discuss plant and mining issue. *Agragamee* did not participate in the meeting. But an NGO '*Ankuran*' said in the meeting that 'we will help the Government in installing the project if it withdraws its decision of de-registering our organisation'. Later *Ankuran* denies the statement by giving a rejoinder. A team headed by Muchukund Dubey visits the plant area. Everywhere people strongly protested against the projects and refused any proposal for rehabilitation package. But the Dubey Committee recommended for installation of plant after a sincere dialogue with people on the issue of rehabilitation. That has become the bottom line for the NGOs in Odisha. No NGO dares to go against it. But the fundamental question is, when people are struggling to save their land and home, who gave authority to NGO to discuss on the project? Again some leaders of the movement, with the support of Action Aid and Sanhati (NGO network in Odisha) went to Delhi and gave press statement protesting against the project. But the NGOs who were sponsoring the visit issued a different statement suitable to them to the press that in accordance with the Central Act full power be given to Gram Sabha and before the land acquisition; consent of the Gram Sabha must be taken. Under the banner of '*Odisha Adivasi Manch*' (an NGO outfit) a massive rally was organised in Rayagada with the impression that it is to discuss the Kashipur issue. Thousands and thousands of people from Kashipur area came to the rally to make it a success. But here the mantra of B.D. Sharma i.e. 'Gram Sabha' is chanted. Not a single line against the project came out in the press release, people were surprised about it. This shows the beautiful marriage of worldviews of Dr B.D. Sharma and NGOs. Both complement each other. Both think change is possible within the boundary of constitution and law. The whole approach is to create some new laws, to modify old laws and to establish rights within the scope of law (read Gram Sabha). This suits well to the NGOs. On the one hand, a progressive label can be earned by giving slogan 'power to Gram Sabha', on the other, wrath of the state power can be avoided by demanding changes through constitution. Director of an NGO 'Viswash' of Kalahandi/Nuapada who shared the platform of Odisha Adivasi Mancha as an advisor of the forum makes an agreement with the company to formulate a compensation package but pretends to be the supporter of the movement. In the beginning *Agragammee* (NGO) has disseminated information relating to the project and its possible impact on the life, livelihood and environment of the area; gradually, many more NGOs showed interest in it.

Let us examine the role of the *Agragamee* (NGO), the first NGO to reach Kashipur in 1980s. The primary work of the NGO was to help to implement the schemes and projects of the Government and familiarise the people with the state and to inform them about its welfare measures, such as non-formal education, watershed projects, Indira Awas Yojana, Rural Sanitary Programme etc. Secondly, to implement certain projects with the help of the foreign fund which the Government is not doing. The state has made itself indispensable both through its coercive power and welfare measures. The NGOs have also created a sense of their indispensability in the mind of the people. Before 1980s, people had primarily seen the state in terms of exploitation due to oppression of police, block officials, revenue and forest officials. But the presence of NGO gave a different image of the state which is very much concerned about people's betterment. Because of some of the dishonest politicians and officers or legal drawbacks the benefits are not reaching them. Otherwise, their fate would have changed. This approach of NGO not only makes the people more loyal to the state/existing order but also helps them rediscover their faith in the system. On the one hand, continuous famine, starvation death and resultant of food crisis in 1980s have invited the increasing intervention of state and NGOs and on the other hand people have become more and more dependent on them. NGO intervention has made a dent on certain aspects. For example, people began to fear less. This fear was very strong earlier. As a result, all sorts of betti (in terms of hen and food grains) which the government servants used to collect from people by force started stopping. Manipulation in implementing minimum wage also comes down. PDS rice gets distributed more fairly. Community fund is created in the village. This helps villagers to come out of the clutches of the money lenders (*sahukars*). Some government works are executed through village committee or women committee. This shows that within the boundary of the existing order, NGO has done something to give spoon-feeding justice to the people. This prompts one to ask: What is the role of people? In answer, another question can be asked – Will these initiatives continue in the absence of the NGO? Can the people do own; NGOs do not try to create an environment to question the existing social order. Their approach to seek solution has always been within the spoon-feeding schemes and projects (to identify beneficiaries, pension, housing, reservation, and distribution of loan). But can there be any solution through these schemes and projects? What is the root of the problem? Is it just bribe, corruption and dishonesty of some government functionaries and local leaders or something else? NGOs do not try to help people think deep into these questions. For their own safety and security they take a policy of non-confrontation. Otherwise, they will draw the wrath of state power. In fact, even when they try to faithfully implement the schemes sponsored by the state, sometime they become victims of wrath of bureaucrats and leaders. This shows the intolerance of the people who are at the helm. They do not tolerate even NGOs who indirectly help to strengthen the existing order.

Role of Media

In the early phase of the movement through the sponsorship of the NGOs, some of the activists have addressed press conferences in Bhubaneswar and Delhi. This is partly responsible for the ill-reputation of the movement that it is an NGO inspired/led movement. At the behest of the company or administration, media has always projected this as an NGO movement. Thus, local people's struggle does not get any credibility. The whole movement is nothing but provocation of the NGO people. This sort of falsification distracts other people's mind from the real issue. And all the local regional prints media and electronics media are supporters of the company, because, local media is getting money from the company. How can they go against the company? On the other hand, the national and international media are not reaching to them. Without the media, how can the issues be nationalised or internationalised? People of the country have no ideas about the protest movement. However, only through the contributions of the academicians, some social activists and independent researchers, the issues are spreading in most parts of India and outside India.

Response of the State and Administration

From the beginning, the democratic state has maintained a stony silence on the exact nature of the project – how many villages will be displaced or affected, how many people will lose their land, what will be the nature of compensation. On the other hand, it has been continuously harassing people on one pretext or the other. People have been beaten up, fired upon, jailed, lathi-charged and implicated in false cases. Sometimes, local administration and police have tried to weaken the movement by setting one community against the other. As fallout, when violence erupts, it becomes easier for the police to fulfill its nefarious designs. All the administrators from block level to district level, even state administrators and political leaders of the state are '*chamchas*' of the company. They are getting money from the companies; they don't bother about the local people. In 1994/1995 Odisha general Assembly election, the Indian National Congress candidate Mr Ananta Ram Majhi won the election from the Laxmipur constituency, because he was supporter of the movement. After winning the election he was the supporter of the company. Then in 1999/2000 assembly election, Ananta Ram Majhi was defeated and the youth candidate from the BJD Party Bibhison Majhi won the election, because earlier he was associated with the movement. And we know Dr Giridhar Gomango, he has been elected M.P. from Koraput parliamentary constituency since 1972 to till today. He was a Chief Minister of Odisha for nine months and several times minister at the centre. What he did for the people of Koraput? Now in undivided Koraput district, the Below Poverty Line is 82 per cent and literacy rate is 34 per cent, he has a black spot for the people of Koraput district. He has been winning elections because he gets ticket from Congress party and the people of Koraput have loyalty towards Gandhi family.

On 5 January 1998, a significant incident took place at Kucheipadar village. The agitationists had setup a barricade near the village as mark of protest against the company. Since then no vehicle of the company passed through the road. But on this day, the sub-collector of Rayagada, Tahasildar of Kashipur, DSP of Rayagada, OIC of Tikiri came to this place with a platoon of police force and demolished the barricade and lathi-charged the protestors. In this incident, 46 people along with 12 women sustained injuries. On 29 March 1998, on the occasion of the martyr day of Saheed Laxman Nayak, a tribal freedom fighter, a huge public rally was organised at Kashipur with necessary intimation to the police. But this rally was foiled by anti-social elements hired by the company who assaulted the people in the presence of police and forced them to shift the place of the meeting.

Muchkund Dubey Committee report confirms the repression of the tribals of region, adding a new lead in the chapter of repression on 16 December 2000 in Maikanch village. Police in an unprovoked firing killed three tribals and others suffered major and minor bullet injuries (*Samaj*, Oriya Daily, 17–12–2000). Going one step further, the state appointed P.K. Mishra commission on Maikanch firing, which in its report held that 'Maikanch firing is justified' and 'Mining project should not be stopped for the sake of environment' (*Dharitri*, Oriya Daily, 10–10–2003). But the firing episode on 16 December 2000 instead of demoralising the agitating tribals, has further added to their determination to fight against the state and its decision to impose the Alumina project over the people of Kashipur. Four days after the killing, they organised a successful *Rasta Roko* (road-block) programme at Ruphkona chowk as per their earlier decision. They have taken a pledge to fight unto the last till the MOUs signed by the Odisha government with the companies for mining and setting up of the plant are cancelled.

They have further stated that their struggle so far has been peaceful and will continue to be peaceful despite provocation (Watch Report, 14–01–2001).

Maikanch Police Firing: The Example of State's Response

Very little is known about the ensuing struggle and irrevocable resistance of Kashipur tribals against the setting up of an aluminium plant (UAIL, a joint venture with Hindalco of India, Alcan of Canada and Hydro of Norwegian company) over 13 years. If this project takes place, then more than 25,000 indigenous people will be affected. The resistance is on the grounds of displacement, encroachment upon their life patterns and livelihood. Over these years, the district administration has clubbed hands with the pro-company goons implicating hundreds in false cases, putting many more behind bars; while company goons run freely in some of the villages, terrorising occasionally even beating up the tribals. Muchukund Dubey committee report confirms the repression of the tribals in the Kashipur region.

Adding a new leaf to the chapter of repression, on 16 December, police in an unprovoked firing killed three tribals while 30 others suffered major and minor bullet injuries. The course of events can be presented in this manner. On 15 December, some ruling state BJD party members like, Mr N. Bhaskar Rao, Krushna Chandra Mohapatra with pro-company people loaded in two jeeps and tried to reach the Nuagaon village near Maikanch village – a key village of pro-company people – to stage a meeting in favour of UAIL. Earlier they had distributed leaflet inviting people to come on 15th to Nuagaon for the discussion in favour of company.

On the eve of 20 December, road blocked at Rupkana on Koraput-Rayagada road, was called by PSSP for pressurising government for cancellation of Memorandum of Understanding (MOU). Knowing the fact that the Nuagaon meeting is meant to disturb the road blocked programmes by tribals prevented those political leaders from reaching Nuagaon village on 15 December, in a manner in which some of these outsiders were beaten up. After such incident those political people came to Rayagada town and ransacked the OPDSC office (a sister NGO of *Agragamee* operating in Rayagada). Some of its employees and local indigenous people attempted to murder them (which is a wisely woven wily made up story). On the next day that is on 16 December, two platoons of

Odisha state i.e. armed police force and other police officials including a magistrate-in-power in three jeeps reached the Maikanch village at noon time, while most of the frightened male members had fled at the sight. The police wrangled the women folk who attended to them and started lathi-charging. In the course of the unfortunate incident of the last fifty-five-years old tribal woman Mrs Danai Jhodia fell on the ground and lost her consciousness. Amidst the hue and cry of the women folk misconcluding her for dead, the men folk rushed to the spot from all directions and suddenly seeing the stream of men police began its shooting spree in which three tribals, Abhilash Jhodia of Maikanch, Raghunath Jhodia and Damodar Jhodia of Baghrijhola died. More than thirty people had suffered major or minor bullet injuries and six among them, seriously wounded were admitted in the Rayagada district hospital. The police torched its own jeep for apparent reasons, later reporting that the tribals did so. Probably, this masquerading was done by police only to consolidate the made up story of aggression of tribals in defense of which the police resorted to lathi-charge and firing. It is suggested from the callous misinterpretation provided by past experiences especially in Majhiguda on 30 December 1999.

In the aftermath, such inhuman killings needed to be condemned by all quarters, the travesty lies in the fact that the following day that is 17 December was observed as a 'victory day' in Rayagada by ruling BJD people in full presence of all its high ranking police and administrative officers who watched the celebration. State's repression over tribals is not a matter of surprise. It is needed to be understood in the wake of the 20 December 2000 Rupkana road-block that the Kashipur tribals had planned much before. From the very beginning the district administration had resumed an unfavourable approach toward the people's movement against the proposed UAIL. The unprovoked firing, therefore, seems to be a premeditated contriving of psychologically victimising people in Kashipur region so that the movement suffers setback and finally ceases to continue. The immediate achievement for the state was in the foiling of Rupkana road blockage, which otherwise could have registered itself as a potential threat to the pro-company quarters and as unified democratic voices of people against the proposed setup UAIL. Despite the December 16th episode, it was aspiratory to see that the 20 December Rupkana road blockage was successful with assemble of more than 8,000 tribal adorned with their traditional drums, bows and arrows and other traditional weapons.

Photo 14

The memory of police firing at Maikanch village

Photo 15

The cremated place of Saheed Raghunath, Abhilash and Damodhar at Maikanch village

Summary

It may be mentioned here that the researcher has tried to understand and analyse these movements in diverse ways. The Kashipur movement is grouped under tribal and dalit people and comes under the 'New Social Movements.' This is so because livelihood and dignity of life aspects are particularly associated with tribals and dalits whose livelihood is associated with the natural resources like land, forests and water. The Kashipur movement's primary concern is livelihood rather than environment but generally some academicians, social activists and intellectuals articulated it as an environmental movement and highlighted it in the national and international levels.

Environmental and livelihood movements are among the important examples of the collective mobilisation of several social groups in Kashipur block. Protection of constitutional and democratic rights, which are the most important part of the day-to-day living of the rural poor people like the control over their resources, the right of indigenous people to preserve their culture, protection of livelihood, environment and maintenance of ecological balance are significant concerns of these movements.

This chapter seeks to discuss various perspectives on people's protest movement in Kashipur block. It also analyses people's views on the movement and focuses on origin and development, difficulties, police repression, the leadership of the movement, supporters of the movement and participation of people and gender dimension. This chapter deals with the background of the movement, nature of the movement, contextualising the movement, songs and dances; the localised way of mass mobilisation, organisation of the movement, demand for right to information, role of NGOs in the movement, role of media, response of the state and administration, the constitutional and environmental issue, some facts about the companies and some of the important events of the movement in Kashipur block.

7

Conclusion

The basic framework of the study was to bring out the emerging issues of the livelihood and environmental movement at Kashipur block of Koraput, Odisha. The basic objective of the study was to identify the reasons for people's opposition to the establishment of alumina plants in Kashipur. The study also made an attempt to understand the socio-economic and cultural aspect of Kashipur people due to the industrial establishment. It was also guided by the understanding of evaluating the role of NGOs in mobilising the tribals of Kashipur against the industrial set up. It also aimed to explore the role of women and analysed the role of the state apparatus. Within this perspective, the thesis examined the following important issues.

We have also critically analysed the process of developmental model at Kashipur block of the tribals and dalit people who have lost their rights to the minor forest productions, their home, land and livelihood which led to the violation of human rights. It also analysed the establishment of aluminum companies which has created major negative socio-economic changes among the tribal peoples of Kashipur and apathy of the government and the bureaucracy towards the people of Kashipur block to understand the core issues of the people's right to livelihood. We have also analysed the role of the NGOs to mobilising the tribals against the aluminum plants in Kashipur block.

II

A number of social scientists argue that there is no difference between social and political movements; both are used synonymously. The study of social movement seeks to focus on political sociology, that is, the study of politics of the masses, their aspirations and demands, articulation of their problems, the technique in asserting their demands outside the institutional framework and their occasional efforts at overthrowing the existing state power. Political scientists had largely ignored this area of study for greater understanding of political processes. The components of a social movement are the ideology, programmes, strategy, objectives of social change, leadership and patterns of mobilisation. The idea of 'social transformation' or 'change' is at the core of social movement and, therefore, challenges the fixed notions of values, norms, power and hierarchy in the society. The state perceives the protest or social movements as a challenge to its legitimacy of governance. So the immediate response of the State is negative and suppressive. Rajni Kothari (1988) maintains that the transformation of the state is to be achieved through the transformation of the civil society through grassroots model of mass politics as against the parliamentary or presidential or party model of mass politics.

Ghanshyam Shah (1990) classifies movements into revolt, rebellion, reform and revolution to bring about changes in the political system. Reform seeks to change the part of the system and does not challenge the political system *per se*; revolt poses a challenge to political authority, aiming at overthrowing the government; rebellion aims at attacking the existing authority without any intention to seize state power and in revolution, a section or sections of the society launch an organised struggle to overthrow not only the established government and regime but also socio-economic structure which sustains it, and replace the structure by an alternative social order. T.K. Oommen (1990) believes that social movements provide the stage for confluence between the old and new values and structures. M.S.A. Rao (1978) also offers a typology of those movements as reformist, transformatory and revolutionary. However, each category is sub-divided into violent and non-violent protests on the basis of issues around which participants get mobilised. Rajendra Singh (2001) has also broadly divided the theoretical tradition of social movements into (a) classical (b) neo-classical and (c) contemporary or new social movements. He claims, human right movement and environmental movement are new phases within the new social movement. The emergence of 'New Social Movement' in India that forms and styles of their mobilisation, their issues and the mass participation of across the caste and class including the justification of the 'newness' in contemporary system of the Indian society. However, to comprehend the social movement in a more lucid manner, researchers have explained different approaches in this regard: Marxist approach, structural-functional approach, Johnson's value consensus approach, Smelser's strain theory and Eisentadt's modernisation theory.

The Indian sociologists and the political scientists including Ramachandra Guha (1989), Gail Omvedt (1993), B.S. Baviskar (1995), Rajendra Singh (2001), Ghanshyam Shah (2002), Poona Wignaraja (1993), Manoranjan Mohanty (1998), T.K. Oommen (1990) etc. have contributed through analysing the women, environmental, farmer, and dalit (ex-untouchables) movements as the NSMs.

III

It has explored the theoretical explanation on origin and development of social movement and how social movement transmitted into new social movement. Though the concept of social movement is western in origin, the concept and nature, its use and nature bear the similar features in India. Social movement in India emerged as a crusade against imperialism and colonialism. The post-independence dimension of new social movement emerged within the background of social movement as a mechanism to nip exploitable nature of the state in the bud. Unlike social movement, new social movement is universal, overarching, non-class and non-materialistic in nature. Nevertheless, environmental movement is the pre-eminent of new social movement because it is the matter of livelihood security and sustainability.

Here we have analysed the nature and emergence of social movements in Odisha. The similarity between all these movements is that these movements are revolving around a wide range of resistance and protest. However, most of these protest movements have been undertaken by the tribes of Odisha having the core idea of livelihood and right to natural resources which they have been using for centuries. This is arguing that there is a mismatch between the nationalistic perspective of development and tribal development and these projects are marginalising the already marginalised section of our society.

It has also explored the demographic profile of Kashipur with special emphasis on male-female ratio, tribal-non-tribal population and that they depend on natural resources for their livelihood.

This study also found that the livelihood and people's movement in Kashipur which deal with Non-Timber Forest Products (NTFPs) form an important source of subsistence and livelihood in the tribal life. The cultural and the religious significance of the place are also defined and how people deal with their everyday life. It has land based approach i.e. it aims at increasing the agricultural production and income generation activities centring around agriculture.

This study also explored to discuss various perspectives on people's protest movement at Kashipur block. It also analysed people's views on the movement and focuses on origin and development, difficulties, police repression, the leadership of the movement, supporters of the movement and participation of people and gender dimension. This is so because livelihood and dignity of life aspects are particularly associated with tribals and dalits who have a harmonious relation with the natural resources like land, forests and water. The Kashipur movement's primary concern is livelihood rather than environment but some academicians, social activists and intellectuals articulate it as environmental movement due to which this movement is being highlighted in the national and international levels within environmental framework. This people's agitation in Kashipur where the people gathered and lockeded the main gate of the plant side of the company and started rally hunger strike in front of company, has a democratic, peaceful and non-violent Gandhian way of satyagraha.

IV

The study has found the considerable violation of basic rights and varying socio-economic situation of the people due to exploitative nature of the companies which are in consonance with the first and the second hypotheses of the research. The underlined narration gives a broader understanding about the socio-economic situations of the Kashipur block. The significant finding of environmental movement in Kashipur block is that they have mainly involved the tribals, women, the dalits, and the poor people who have been directly affected by or the victims of Utkal Aluminum International Limited (company) which led to loses of their livelihood. Thus, the study has shown that the main reasons for opposing the establishment of the company is in relation to the issues of livelihood and the dignity of the indigenous people of the Kashipur block. They fear to lose their land, forest and water which they depend on, and the imminent threat to their traditional culture. After the establishment of the industries and big dams such as, NALCO at Damonjodi and HAL at Sunabeda and dams areas like upper Kolab, Indravati and Balimela in Koraput district, the condition and the situation of the people have never improved. On the other hand, they have been marginalised and their state is getting worsened. They are opposing the establishment of the companies. Therefore, the Kashipur people's movement is an environmental in general and livelihood movement in particular. On the contrary, at the national or at international level, the academicians, social activists and intellectuals are articulating this movement as the environmental movement. This is because livelihood and dignity of life aspects are particularly associated with tribals and dalits. Livelihood is associated with the natural resources like land, forests and water. The Kashipur movement's primary concern is about their livelihood rather than environment. Kashipur believes that the forest is the storehouse of their needs, so the exploitation of resources is on daily use basis. They do not exploit the forest for greedy purposes.

A huge number of people of the area gathered under the charismatic leadership of activist Bhagaban Majhi and local resistance organisations converged into a common platform known as the *Prakrutika Sampada Surakhya Parisad* (PSSP). Resistance strategies were borrowed from Gandhian satyagraha including non-cooperation and civil disobedience and refusal to cooperate with project authorities, blocking of all project-related work, rally, hunger strike at the project site and refusal to leave their villages.

This study has tried to understand and analyse these movements in diverse ways. The participation of tribals in the movement is much more than any other community due to the issue of livelihood security. To sum up, livelihood movement became prominent in Kashipur block since the 1993s along with environmental movement. The concerns of this movement are not confined to any particular groups. They are encompassing the entire village and rural communities, women, tribals, peasants, poor and different classes for whom the issue of livelihood plays an important role as demonstrated by Rajendra Singh and T.K. Oommen. So, this kind of movements can be considered as 'New Social Movement'. Thus, Kashipur people's movement is a glaring example of NSM.

The rights of people over their resources, livelihoods and democratic ways of life are threatened. Government is making a big effort to sell tribal lands to the investors in the form of guarantees, tax concessions and investment subsidies. In the last 50 years because of various developmental efforts, tribal system has come under the domain of market economy. Their main sources of livelihood are cultivation, shifting cultivation and collection of minor forest product. Besides, practising paddy cultivation, raggi cultivation and collection of minor forest product, they have depended on hunting and food gathering mode of economy as the source of their livelihood. Some of the tribals work as agriculture wage labourers and some work as labourers in construction work like National Rural Employment Guarantee Act Programme.

It is found that despite economic backwardness the development gap of the literacy rate of population in Odisha is not so low when it is compared with the average literacy rate of population at the national level. However, in the inter-district level it is noticed that the backward tribal and highland districts like Rayagada, Koraput, Malkangiri and Nabarangpur have comparatively lower level of literacy rate i.e. 36.15 per cent, 35.72 per cent, 30.53 per cent and 33.93 per cent respectively.

Issues of livelihood and environmental movements are among the important examples of the collective mobilisation of several social groups in Kashipur block. Protection of constitutional and democratic rights, the control over their resources, the right of indigenous people to preserve their culture, protection of livelihood, environment and maintenance of ecological balance are significant concerns of these movements.

Environmental protest movements are within the fold of 'New Social Movement' in India. However, strictly speaking environment movements are more organised form of social movements for saving environment and survival of people. It emerged as a critique of the dominant development paradigms. The environmental movement reflects people's significant protest against the western model of development. The struggles of the people on the issues of their livelihood and access to forest and other natural resources are coined as environmental movements. The poor people of Kashipur as well as the tribal communities under the pressure of 'national interest' or development projects in the Koraput districts are reeling under duress and impoverishment. For e.g. industries, dams and mining have physically displaced these unprivileged communities. Similarly million of forest dwellers, tribals, dalits and peasants since independence of India have been thrown out from their habitat making them not only powerless but insecure in food and occupation.

People have experienced in the NALCO area of Damanjodi, Sunabeda, upper Kolab and Indravati that the episodic environmental incidents such as flooding, drought, industrial accidents, and outbreaks of water borne disease produce environmental vulnerability. These incidents especially in their most severe manifestations affect everyone, but the poorest and most resource-dependent people are typically the most vulnerable. So, the condition and the situation of the people of that area are very gruesome. In short, this is the clear violation of human rights in Kashipur block.

The environmental movement is a broad term which is generally used to describe and understand different types of local struggles and conflicts concerned with livelihood issues in consonance with environmental degradation within the larger context of the development debate. The post-independent state failed to build up a development agenda based on the needs of the destitute and continued to advocate the modern capitalist agenda which led to loses of livelihood, destruction of environment, increased poverty and further led to marginalisation of rural indigenous communities particularly in Kashipur block.

These movements also reflect an enlarged vision of socio-political and economic issues. These movements sought a larger vision like enhancement in the quality of life through recognition of people's right over their natural resources, their right to live with dignity. These movements focus not only on basic survival and livelihood issues but also on larger ecological concerns. These are different from earlier social movements and there is need to understand them in terms of their nature and strategies.

The third hypothesis pins down on the disinclination of the government and bureaucrats to take care of the demands of the local people. This is what the study has found while looking into the process of industrialisation in Koraput district. Industrialisation has been accompanied by rapid urbanisation. On the other side, modernisation, urbanisation and industrialisation have also disrupted the traditional relationship that prevailed among the various sections of the communities bringing them into increasing conflict with one another. The process of rapid industrialisation and urbanisation has led the development experts to undertake mega projects of growth without acknowledging the livelihood of the local people and animals. State and society have distanced since this decade and as a reaction the society has started consolidating itself against the injustices of the state. The last two/three decades witnessed the spread of a large number of mega projects for power generation and mining. Thus, there have been several people's movements to prevent deforestation like the Chipko in the Himalayas and Apikko in the Western Ghats, Silent Valley Movement against the Kudremukh power project, Tehri Movement against the Tehri power project in Garhwal region and Narmada Movements and Sardar Sarovar Project over the Narmada river adjoining Madhya Pradesh, Maharashtra and Gujarat.

This study has provided a picture of the nature and emergence of environmental movements in general and livelihood movement in particular. A common thread which covers each of these movements is that these are protest movements which revolve around livelihood rights and are often projected against either government or the industrial capitalists. However, many of the protest movements have been undertaken by people particularly the tribes of Odisha having the core idea of livelihood security and right to use natural resources which they have been using for their survival since time immemorial. The emergence of Kashipur movement really makes it clear that development projects are antithetical to tribal's rural life and livelihood security. In the process of undertaking development projects the government is in a way marginalising the already marginalised section of tribal and dalit people in Kashipur block. The analysis of movement at Kashipur block of Odisha also makes it clear as to people's agency or mass participation which can bring change in society, which has experience with the movements like Baliapal, Chilika Bachao Andolan and Gandhamardan Movement of Odisha.

Examining the hypothesis on the role of NGOs is important. The hypothesis has given prominence to the effective role of NGOs in mobilising the people, but the study has shown a different dimension. At the beginning, more specifically *Agragamee,* a preeminent NGO, had disseminated information relating to project and its possible impact on the life, livelihood and environment of the area. *Agragamee* was in a sense bound to do this because it has been working at Kashipur for the last three decades. In the absence of a collective process, *Agragamee* carved out a place for itself among the people in the area. Dependence on *Agragamee* can be seen from the initial steps undertaken by it and later from the sort of demands raised by the movement such as signature campaign, demand for information regarding project and clarification regarding the benefits to be accrued to people from the project. In short, NGOs had initially mobilised the people against the industries but presently these NGOs are also sidelining the livelihood issue of the local people owing to their vested interest.

This may go under the garb of development, but the destruction of people's livelihoods and the degradation of the environment causing the breakdown of fragile ecosystems should make one pause to ponder over the development strategy of the company and government. In spite of this, the Odisha Government pretends that there is no problem for the tribals of the area and behaves almost like a business company. To put it differently, the state is not responding positively to the issue of livelihood of the local people.

The above-mentioned observation gives a comprehensive understanding on the development projects at Koraput district where company rules along with the forthright support of the Government of Odisha. The buzz of development has hijacked the issue of livelihood security in particular and environmental protection in general. Development is only for the sake of company, not for the people. So, people's protest movement at Kashipur holds out good hope in the coming future to secure livelihood security concomitant with environmental security.

Appendix

The Constitutional and Environmental Issue

Part IV

Directive Principles of State Policy (Article, 48A): Protection and improvement and safeguarding of forests and wildlife – The State shall endeavour to protect and improve the environment and to safeguard the forests and wildlife of the country.

Part IV-A

Fundamental Duties (Article, 51 A): It shall be the duty of every citizen of India to protect and improve the natural environment including forests, lakes, rivers and wildlife, and to have compassion for living creatures.

Seventh Schedule (Article, 246)

List III – Concurrent List
Item no. 17 Prevention of cruelty to animals
Item no. 17A Forests
Item no. 17B Protection of wild animals and birds

Incorporation, within the Fundamental Duties, the responsibility of panchayats and municipalities to give due regard to ecological aspects and to protect the environment, including life supporting natural ecosystems such as forests, rivers, lakes, and wildlife, in the preparation of plans for economic development and social justice.

Environment and Related Laws and Policies in India

(Note: This is not a comprehensive list, but contains most of the key laws and policies. It is arranged in chronological order of year of enactment or passing.)

The Indian Forest Act, 1927: An Act to consolidate the law relating to forests, the transit of forest produce and the duty leviable on timber and other forest produce. Created the various categories of forests for different management and regulatory regimes.

The Prevention of Cruelty to Animals Act, 1960: An Act to prevent the infliction of unnecessary pain or suffering on animals.

The Water (Prevention and Control of Pollution) Act, 1974, amended 1988: An Act to provide for the prevention and control of water pollution and the maintaining or restoring of wholesomeness of water.

Forest (Conservation) Act, 1980, amended 1988: An Act to provide for the conservation of forests and for matters connected therewith or ancillary or incidental thereto.

The Air (Prevention and Control of Pollution) Act, 1981, amended 1987: An Act to provide for the prevention, control and abatement of air pollution.

The Environment (Protection) Act, 1986, amended 1991: An Act to provide for the protection and improvement of environment and for matters connected therewith the following key rules/notifications:

- Declaration of Coastal Stretches as Coastal Regulation Zone (CRZ), 1991, amended 2001
- The Scheme on Labeling of Environment Friendly Products (ECOMARK), 1991
- Eco-sensitive Zone (a series of notifications declaring specific sites)
- Environment Impact Assessment Notification, 1994, amended 2002
- The Rules for the Manufacture, Use, Import, Export and Storage of Hazardous Micro-organisms, Genetically Engineered Organisms or Cells, 1989
- Hazardous Substances Management (a series of rules dealing with municipal solid wastes, batteries, recycled plastics, chemical accidents, 20 hazardous micro-organisms and

genetically engineered organisms/cells, hazardous chemicals, biomedical wastes, and other hazardous wastes)

- Noise Pollution (Regulation and Control) Rules, 2000

The Forest Policy, 1988: A policy that emphasises the twin objectives of ecological stability and social justice. Highlighting the need for stronger conservation measures, it points to symbiotic relationship between tribals and other poor people and forests. It recommends treating local needs as 'the first charge' on forest produce, and creates space for the participation of forest-dependent communities in the management of forests.

The Public Liability Insurance Act, 1991, amended 1992: An Act to provide for public liability-insurance for the purpose of providing immediate relief to the persons affected by accident occurring while handling any hazardous substance and for matters connected therewith or incidental thereto.

Constitution (73rd Amendment) Act, 1992: An Act to empower the panchayat bodies to manage local affairs, including environmental resources such as water, land, agriculture, animal husbandry, social/farm forestry, minor forest produce, and fisheries.

National Conservation Strategy and Policy Statement on Environment and Development, 1992, with guidelines for integrating environmental considerations into development.

The National Environment Tribunal Act, 1995: An Act to provide for strict liability for damages arising out of any accident occurring while handling any hazardous substance and for the establishment of a National Environment Tribunal for effective and expeditious disposal of cases arising from such accident, with a view to giving relief and compensation for damages to persons, property and the environment and for matters connected therewith or incidental thereto.

Panchayat (Extension to Scheduled Areas) Act, 1996: An Act to extend the 73rd Constitutional Amendment to Scheduled (predominantly tribal) areas, providing ownership or control over some natural resources such as minor (non-timber) forest produce.

The National Environment Appellate Authority Act, 1997: An Act to provide for the establishment of a National Environment Appellate Authority to hear appeals with respect to restriction of areas in which any industries, operations or processes or class of industries, operations or processes shall not be carried out or shall be carried out subject to certain safeguards under the Environment (Protection) Act, 1986 and for matters connected therewith or incidental thereto.

The Wildlife (Protection) Amendment Act, 2002: An Act to provide for the protection of wild animals, birds and plants and for matters connected therewith or ancillary or incidental thereto with a view to ensuring the ecological and environmental security of the country.

The Biological Diversity Act, 2002: An Act to provide for conservation of biological diversity, sustainable use of its components and fair and equitable sharing of the benefits arising out of the use of biological resources, knowledge and for matters connected therewith or incidental thereto.

The Right to Information Act, 2005: An Act to provide the right to information to all citizens (useful in accessing information regarding environmental matters, including projects/processes that affect the environment).

Scheduled Tribes (Recognition of Forest Rights) Bill, 2005: A bill to recognise and vest the forest rights and occupation in forest land in forest dwelling Scheduled Tribes who have been residing in such forests for generations but whose rights could not be recorded; to provide for a framework for recording the forest rights so vested and the nature of evidence required for such recognition and vesting in respect of forest land.

Bibliography

Books

Acselbrad, Henri (ed.). 1992. *Environment and Democracy*. Botafago: IBASE.

Agarwal, Anil and Sunita Narain. 1989. *Towards Green Village*. New Delhi: Centre for Science and Environment.

Agarwal, Anil, et al. (ed.). 1987. *The Fight for Survival: People's Action for Environment*. New Delhi: Centre for Science and Environment.

Archana Prasad. 2004. *Environmentalism and the Left: Contemporary Debates and Future Agendas in Tribal Areas.* New Delhi: Leftword Books.

Bandyopadhyay, J. (ed.). 1985. *India's Environment: Crises and Responses.* Dehradun: Natraj Publication.

Baruah, Bipasha. 1999. 'The Narmada Valley Project: displacement of local populations and impact on women', Natural Resources Forum 23. pp. 81–84.

Baviskar, Amita. 1995. *In the Belly of the River: Tribal Conflicts Over Development in the Narmada Valley*. New Delhi: Oxford University Press.

Bogaeart, M.V.D. 1992. *Saving Chilika Lake: Saving the People of Chilika.* Bhubaneswar: Xavier Institute of Management.

Brinton, C. 1965. *The Anatomy of Revolution*. New York: Norton.

Chakraborty, Somen. 1999. *A Critique of Social Movements in India*, New Delhi, Indian Social Institute.

Chandhoke, Neera. 1995. *State and Civil Society: Exploration in Political Theory*. New Delhi: Sage Publications.

Colin Barker, et al. 2001. *Leadership and Social Movements.* United Kingdom, Manchester University Press.

D'Souza, Rohan. 2006. *Drowned and Dammed: Colonial Capitalism and Flood Control in Eastern India.* New Delhi: Oxford University Press.

Das, B.B. 1996. *Chilika: The Natures Treasure, Will it be Allowed to Die*? Bhubaneswar: Orissa Krushakmahasangha.

Das, Veena. 1995. *Critical Events: An Anthropological Perspective on Contemporary India.* New Delhi: Oxford University Press.

Daspatnaik, P.S. 1984. 'Ownership Pattern, Land Survey and Settlement and its Imact on the Dongaria Kondh of Odisha', *Adivasi Journal*, January, vol. xxiii, No. 4, pp. 26.

Dhanagare, D.N. 1983. *Peasant Movements in India*. New Delhi: Oxford University Press.

Dixon, Homer and F. Thomas. 1995. 'The Ingenuity Gap: Can Poor Countries Adopt to Resource Scarcity?', *Population and Development Review*, 21 (3), 587–612.

Dogra, B. 1992. *Chilika Lake Controversy: Dollars Versus Livelihood,* New Delhi: Prativa.

Doyle, Timothy and Doug McEachern. 1998. *Environment and Politics.* London and New York: Routledge.

Dreze, Jean and Amartya Sen. 2002. *India: Development and Participation.* New Delhi: Oxford University Press.

Eisenstadt, S.N. 1966. *Modernization: Protest and Change*. Englewood Cliffs, N.J: Prentice-Hall Publication.

Fernandes, W. and S. Anthony Raj. 1992. *Development, Displacement and Rehabilitation in the Tribal Areas of Orissa*. New Delhi: Indian Social Institute.

Gadgil, Madhav and Ramachandra Guha. 1992. *This Fissured Land: An Ecological History of India*. New Delhi: Oxford University Press.

Gadgil, Madhav and Ramachandra Guha. 1995. *Ecology and Equity: The Uses and Abuses of Nature in Contemporary India.* New Delhi: Penguin.

Gasper, Des. 2004. *The Ethics of Development*. New Delhi: Vistar Publication.

Guha, Ramachandra and Juan Martinez-Alier. 1997. *Varieties of Environmentalism: Essays North and South.* New York: Earthscan.

Guha, Ramachandra. 1989. *The Unquiet Woods: Ecological Change and Peasant Resistance in the Himalaya*. New Delhi: Oxford University Press.

Guha, Ramachandra. 2000. *Environmentalism: A Global History*, New Delhi, Oxford University Press.

Guha, Ranjit. 1983. *Elementary Aspects of Peasant Insurgency in Colonial India*. New Delhi: Oxford University Press.

Gurr, Ted R. 1970. *Why Men Rebel?* New Jersey: Princeton University Press.

Gusfield, J.R. 1971. *The Study of Social Movements in Social Sciences.* New York: McMillan.

Habermas, Jurgen. 1985. *The Theory of Communicative Action*. vol.1. Boston: Beacon Press.

Habermas, Jurgen.1976. *Legitimation Crisis*. London: Heinemann.

Heberle, Rudolf. 1951. *Social Movements: An Introduction to Political Sociology*. New York: Appleton-Century-Crofts Inc.

Heberle, Rudolf. 1960. 'Types and Functions of Social Movement' in David Shills (Ed.) *International Encyclopedia of Social Sciences.* New York: McMillan.

Heberle, Rudolf. 1968. 'Types and Functions of Social Movements' in David Shills (ed.) *International Encyclopedia of Social Science*. New York: Mc Millan.

Jayal, Niraja Gopal (ed.). 2001. *Democracy in India*. New Delhi: Oxford University Press.

Jayal, Niraja Gopal. 1999. *Democracy and the State: Welfare, Secularism and Development in Contemporary India*. New Delhi: Oxford University Press.

Kalland, Arne and Gerard Persoon (ed.). 1998. *Environmental Movements in Asia*. Richard Curzon. Nordic Institute of Asian Studies: Man and Nature in Asia Series. IV.

Karana, M.N. (ed.). 2002. *Social Movements in North-East India*. New Delhi: Indus Publishing Company.

Klingensmith, Daniel. 2007. *One Valley and a Thousand: Dams, Nationalism and Development*. New Delhi: Oxford University Press.

Kohli, Atul (ed.). 2001. *The Success of India's Democracy*. New York: Cambridge University Press.

Kothari, Rajani. 1988. *State against Democracy: In Search of Human Governance*. New Delhi: Ajanta Publishers.

Kothari, Rajni. 1988. *Rethinking Development: In Search of Human Alternatives*. New Delhi: Ajanta Publishers.

Krishna, Sumi. 1996. *Environmental Politics: People's Lives and Development Choices*. New Delhi: Sage Publications.

Kumar, Anand. 1989. *State and Society in India: Making of the States Agenda*. New Delhi: Radiant Publication.

Kumar, Anand.1999. *Nation Building in India*. New Delhi: Radiant Publication.

Larana, Enrique, et. al. (ed.). 1995. *New Social Movements: From Ideology to Identity*. Philadelphia: Temple University Press.

Lele, Jayant and Fahimul Quadir. 2002. *Democracy and Civil Society in Asia: Democratic Transitions and Social Movements in Asia*. Vol.2. Houndmills: Palgrave Macmillan.

Marion, Irish Young. 2000. *Inclusion and Democracy*. Oxford: Oxford University Press.

Martinez-Alier, Joan. 2005. *The Environmentalism of the Poor: A Study of Ecological Conflicts and Valuation*. New Delhi: Oxford University Press.

Mc Adam, D., Mc Carthy, J.D and Zald, M.N. 1996. *Comparative Perspectives on Social Movement*. Cambridge: Cambridge University Press.

McLaughlin, B. (ed.). 1969. *Studies in Social Movements: A Socio-psychological Perspective*. New York: The Free Press.

Meadows, D.H. et. al., 1974. *The Limits to Growth: A Report of the Club of Rome's Project on the Predicament of Mankind*. London and Sydney: Pan Books.

Mohanty, Manoranjan (ed.). 1998. *People's Right: Social Movements and the State in the Third World*. New Delhi: Sage Publications.

Omvedt, Gail. 1993. *Reinventing Revolution: New Social Movements and the Socialist Tradition in India.* London: East Gate Book.

Oommen, T.K. 1990. *Protest and Change: Studies in Social Movements.* New Delhi: Sage Publications.

Pandey, B. 2000. *Displacement: A Case Study from Orissa.* New Delhi: Organising Strategies, Friedrich Ebert Stiftung.

Pandey, B.1998. *Displaced Development: Impact of Open Cast Mining on Women.* New Delhi: Friedrich Ebert Stiftung.

Pandey, B.1998a. *Depriving the Underprivileged for Development.* Institute for Socio-Economic Development: Bhubaneswar.

Pawar, S.N., R.B. Patil and S.A. Salunkhe (ed.). 2005. *Environmental Movements in India: Strategies and Practices.* Jaipur: Rawat Publications.

Pearce, David.1990. *Sustainable Development: Economics and Environment in the Third World.* Hants: Edward Elger.

Peet, Richard and Elaine Hartwick. 2005. *Theories of Development.* Jaipur and New Delhi: Rawat Publications.

Peet, Richard and M. Watts.1996. *Liberation Ecologies: Environment, Development, Social movements.* London and New York: Routledge.

Peritore, N. Patrick. 1989. *Third World Environmentalism: Case Studies from the Global South.* Gainesville: University Press of Florida.

Pieterse, Jan Nederveen. 2001. *Development Theory: Deconstruction/Reconstructions.* New Delhi: Vistar Publications.

Porta, Dontella Della and Diani, Mario. 1991. *Social Movements: An Introduction.* Global South University of Florida: Blackwell Publishers.

Puri, H. et al. (ed.). 2000. *Social and Political Movement.* Jaipur: Rawat Publications.

Raj, Sebasti L. and Arundhati Roy Choudhury (eds.). 1998. *Contemporary Social Movements in India: Achievements and Hurdles.* New Delhi: Indian Social Institute.

Rangarajan, Mahesh (ed.). 2007. *Environmental Issues in India: A Reader.* New Delhi: Dorling Kindersley (India).

Rangarajan, Mahesh and V. Saberwal (eds.). 2003. *Battles over Nature: Science and the Politics of Conservation.* New Delhi: Permanent Black.

Rangarajan, Mahesh. 1997. *Beyond State and Market: The Indian Environmental Debate.* Centre for Contemporary Studies, New Delhi: Nehru Memorial Museum and Library, Teen Murti House.

Rangarajan, Mahesh. 1999. *Fencing the Forest: Conservation and Ecological Change in India's Central Provinces, 1860–1914.* New Delhi: Oxford University Press.

Rao, D.V. and P. Lakshki. 2008. *Dalits and Environment: A Critical Analysis.* New Delhi: Sunrise Publication.

Rao, M.S.A. 1978. *Social Movements in India.* Vol-I. New Delhi: Manohar Publishers and Distributors.

Rao, M.S.A. 1948. (ed.). *Conceptual Problems in the study of social movements in India*, New Delhi: Manohar Publication.

Redcliff, M. 1984. *Development and the Environment: Red or Green Alternatives*. London: Methuen.

Redcliff, Micheal. 1984. *Development and the Environmental Crises*. London; Methuen.

Rootes, Christopher (ed.). 1999. *Environmental Movements: Local, National and Global*, London: Frank Cass.

Rostow, W.W. 1969. *The Stages of Economic Growth*, London: Cambridge University Press.

Rout, B. 1999. *Development-Induced Displacement: Analysis of the Rengali Irrigation Project in Orissa, India, thesis No. AC. 99. 33* (unpublished masters thesis). Bangkok, Thailand: Asian Institute of Technology.

Roy, Kartik. C. et al. (ed.). 1992. *Economic Development and Environment: A Case Study of India*. New Delhi: Oxford University Press.

Samantara, Prafulla. 2000. *People's Struggle for Right to Livelihood, Gopalpur Coast Environment Protection Forum (Orissa)*. New Delhi: Lok Shakti Abhiyan.

Sarkar, S. 1993. *The New Social Movements: The Greens* (Vol. 1). New Delhi: Promila and Co. Publishing.

Satpapathy, et al. 2002. *Women's Role and Participation in Struggles Against Development-Induced Displacement in Orissa and Jharkhand*. Bhubaneswar: Institute for Socio-Economic Development (ISED).

Scott, Allan. 1990. *Ideology and New Social Movements*. London: Unwin Hyman.

Sen, Amartya (1999), *Development as Freedom*, Oxford, Oxford University Press.

Shah, Ghanshyam (2001), *Environmental Movement in India*, New Delhi, Sage Publications.

Shah, Ghanshyam (ed.). 2002. *Social Movements and the State*. New Delhi: Sage Publications.

Shah, Ghanshyam. 1990. *Social Movements in India: A Review of Literature*. New Delhi: Sage Publications.

Shah, Ghanshyam. 2004. *Social Movements in India: A Review of literature*. New Delhi: Sage Publications.

Sharma, S.L. 1986. *Development: Socio-Cultural Dimensions*. Jaipur: Rawat Publications.

Sheth, Pravin. 1997. *Environmentalism: Politics, Ecology and Development*. Jaipur: Rawat Publications.

Shiva, Vandana. 1991. *Ecology and the Politics of Survival: Conflicts over Natural Resources in India*. New Delhi: Sage Publication.

Singh, Rajendra. 2001. *Social Movements, Old and New: A Post Modernists Critique*. New Delhi: Sage Publications.

Singh, Suresh (ed.). 1972. *Social Movements Among the Tribals of India*. Indian Institute of Advanced Studies, Shimla and Motilal Banarasidass, Delhi.

Singh, Upjit. 1988. *Jharkhand Movement in Bihar*. New Delhi: Nines Publication.

Sinha, B.N. 1999. *Geography of Orissa*. New Delhi: National Book Trust.

Smelser, Neil. 1959. *Social Change in the Industrial Revolution: An Application of Theory to the British Cotton Industry. Chicago*, Chicago: University of Chicago Press.

Tarnow, Sidney. 1994. *Power in Movement: Social Movements, Collective Action and Politics*. Cambridge: Cambridge University Press.

Vora, Rajendra and Suhas Palshikar (eds.). 2004. *Indian Democracy: Meanings and Practices*. New Delhi: Sage Publications.

Wignaraja, Ponna. (ed). 1993. *New Social Movements in the South: Empowering the People*. New Delhi: Vistar Publications.

Wilkinson, Paul. 1971. *Social Movements*. London: Pall Mall.

Wilson, John. 1973. *Introduction to Social Movements*. New York: Basic Books.

Wolfe, Marshall and Matthias Stiefel. 1994. *A Voice for the Excluded: Popular Participation in Development*. London: Zed Books.

Wolfe, Marshall. 1996. *Elusive Development*. New Delhi: Vistar Publication.

Articles

Agarwal, Anil. 1988. 'Ecological Destruction and the Emerging Patterns of Poverty and People's Protests in India', *Social Action*, 35: pp. 55 80.

Agarwal, Anil. 1996. 'Rough ride ahead' in *Directors Report*. Centre for Science and Environment, Delhi. pp. 4–6.

Agnihotri, A. 1996. 'The Orissa Resettlement and Rehabilitation of Projects Affected Persons Policy, 1994: An Analysis of its Robustness with Reference to the Impoverishment Risk Model', in A.B. Ota and Anita Agnihotri (eds.). *Involuntary Displacement in Dam Projects*. New Delhi: Prachi Prakashan.

Ajaya G. and G. Vijay. 2000. 'Civil Society, State and Social Movement' (Review Article), *Economic and Political Weekly*, 18: pp. 1035–36.

Amin, Samir. 1993. 'Social Movements at the Periphery' in Poona, Wignaraja (ed.). *New Social Movements in the South: Empowering the People*. New Delhi: Vistar Publications, pp. 76–100.

Andharia, Janki and Chandan Sengupta. 1998. 'The Environmental Movement: Global Issues and the Indian Reality', *The Indian Journal of Social Work*, TISS, 59(I): pp. 422–449.

Anieri, Paul D. et.al. 1990. 'New Social Movements in Historical Perspective', *Comparative Politics*, 22(4): pp. 445–458.

Arora, Vibha. 2001. 'Politics of Class (ness) in the Farmer's Movement in India: Validity of the New Social Movement Paradigm', *Sociological Bulletin*, 50(I): pp. 84–121.

Baboo, Balgovind. 1991. 'State Policies and People's Response: Lessons from Hirakud Dam', *Economic and Political Weekly*, 26(41): pp. 2373–379.

Bahuguna, Vimala. 1990. 'The Chipko Movement' in I. Lina Sen (ed.). *A Space Within the Struggle: Women's Participation in Peoples Movements*, New Delhi: Kali for Women (Women Unlimited).

Bakshi, Rajni. 1996. 'Development not Destruction: Alternative Politics in the Making', *Economic and Political Weekly*, 31(5): pp. 255–57.

BALCO. 1983. 'A Birds Eye View of Gandhamardan Bauxite Project' Pamphlet Distributed by Balco on the day of Foundation Stone Laying Ceremony of the Project, May 15.

Baxi, U. 1986. 'Activism at Crossroads with Signposts', *Social Action*, 36(5): pp. 378–79.

Bhaskaran, S.T. 1990. 'The Rise of the Environmental Movement in India', *Media Journal*, 37(2): pp. 22–29.

Blumer, Herbert. 1969. 'Social Movements' in B. McLaughlin (ed.). *Studies in Social Movements: A Social Psychological Perspective*. New York: Free Press, pp. 8–29.

Bowman, J.S. 1976. 'The Environmental Movement: An Assessment of Ecological Politics', *Environmental Affairs,* 5(4): pp. 649–667.

Brass, Tom. 1991. 'Moral Economists, Subalterns, New Social Movements, and the (Re) Emergence of a (Post) Modernised (Middle) Peasant', *Journal of Peasant Studies*, 18(2): pp. 173–205.

Buechler, Steven M. 1993. 'Beyond Resource Mobilization? Emerging Trends in Social Movement Theory', *The Sociological Quarterly*, 34(2): pp. 217–235.

Buechler, Steven M. 1995. 'New Social Movement Theories', *The Sociological Quarterly,* 36(3): pp. 441–464.

Centre for Science and Environment. 'Chronicle of People's Struggle at Kucheipadar and its Neighbouring Villages to Protect their Homeland and Environment from the Clutches of UAIPL – A Joint Venture of INDAL, HYDRO and TATA' undated paper, New Delhi.

Centre for Science and Environment. 'Chronicle of Peoples Struggle to Protect their Homeland and Environment from the Clutches of L&T Company Bent upon Undertaking Mining Work at Sijimali of Sagabari Village of Kashipur and Kutrumali of Thuamul Rampur Block' undated paper, New Delhi, pp. 1–4.

Centre for Science and Environment. 'Development or Destruction: The Travails of Marginalized Minority Groups', undated paper, New Delhi.

Chandoke, Neera. 1998. 'The Assertion of Civil Society against the State: The Case of the Post-Colonial World' in Manoranjan Mohanty, et. al., *Peoples Rights: Social Movements and the State in the Third World.* New Delhi: Sage Publications, pp. 29–43.

Cohen, Gary. 1998. 'Environmental Movements', *Social Policy,* 28(3): pp. 79–82.

Cohen, Jean L. 1985. 'Strategy or Identity: New Theoretical Paradigms and Contemporary Social Movements', *Social Research,* 52(4): pp. 663–716.

Cohen, Jean L.1983. 'Rethinking Social Movements', *Berkeley Journal of Sociology,* 28: 97–113.

D'Monte, Darryl. 1989. 'Green at the Grassroots'(Special Issue on New Social Movements), *Seminar* 355: pp. 16–21.

Dasgupta, Biplab. 1978. 'The Environment Debate: Some Issues and Trend', *Economic and Political Weekly,* 13 (6 and 7): pp. 385–400.

Deshpande, Rajeswari. 2004. 'Social Movements in Crisis?' in Rajendra Vora and Suhas Palshikar (ed.). *Indian Democracy: Meanings and Practices.* New Delhi: Sage Publications, pp. 379–407.

Dhanagare, D.N. 1988. 'Two Approaches to Social Movements in India', *Social Change,* 20(1): pp. 51–61.

Dhanagare, D.N. and J. John. 2002. 'Cyclical Movement Towards the 'Eternal' – 'Nine Thesis of Social Movement: A Critique' in Ghanshyam Shah (ed.). *Social Movements and the State.* New Delhi: Sage Publications, pp. 56–67.

Dwivedi, Ranjit. 2001. 'Environmental Movements in the Global South: Issues of Livelihood and Beyond', *International Sociology,* 16(1): pp. 11–29.

Eder, C. 1995. 'Does Social Class Matter in the Study of Social Movements?: A Theory of Middle-class Radicalism', in L. Maheu (ed.). *Social Movements and Social Classes: The Future of Collective Action.* London: Sage Publications, pp. 21–54.

Eder, Klaus. 1985. 'The 'New Social Movements': Moral Crusades, Political Pressure Groups, or Social Movements?', *Social Research,* 52(4): pp. 869–900.

Fernandes, W. 1996. 'Development-Induced Displacements and Marginalization in Orissa', in A.B. Ota and Anita Agnihotri (eds.). *Involuntary Displacement in Dam Projects,* New Delhi: Prachi Prakashan.

Frank, A.G. and Marta Fuentes. 2002. 'Nine Theses on Social Movements' in Ghanshyam Shah (ed.). *Social Movements and the State.* New Delhi: Sage Publications, pp. 32–55.

Frechet, Guy and Barbara Worhdl. 1993. 'The Ecological Movements in the Light of Social Movements, Development', *International Journal of Comparative Sociology,* 34(1–2): pp. 56–74.

Gadgil, Madhav and Ramachandra Guha. 1994. 'Ecological Conflicts and Environmental Movement in India', *Development and Change,* 25(1): pp. 101–136.

Gadgil, Madhav and Ramchandra Guha. 1998. 'Towards a Perspective on Environmental Movements in India', *The Indian Journal of Social Work,* TISS, 59(1): pp. 450–471.

Gasper, Des. 2004 'The Meaning of Development' in *The Ethics of Development.* New Delhi: Vistar Publication.

Gore, M.S. 1987. 'Social Movements and the Paradigm of Functional Analysis with Reference to the ...', *Economic and Political Weekly,*. XXXV(34): pp. 1503–1510.

Gore, M.S. 1989. 'The Concept of Social Movements', I.P. Desai Memorial Lecture, Centre for Social Studies, Surat Part-1, 9 January, Reproduced in Gore. 1993. *The Social Context of an Ideology.* New Delhi: Sage Publications.

Guha, Ramachandra. 1982. 'Ecological Crisis and Ecological Movements: A Bourgeois Deviation?' (Review Article), *Economic and Political Weekly*, 17(52): pp. 2093–95.

Guha, Ramachandra. 1988. 'Ideological Trends in Indian Environmentalism', *Economic and Political Weekly*, 23(49): pp. 2578–81.

Guha, Ramachandra. 1989. 'The Problem', *Seminar* (Special issue on New Social Movement), 355: pp. 12–15.

Habermas, Jurgen. 1981. 'New Social Movements', *Telos*, 49: 33–37.

Harris, J. and M. Todaro. 1970. 'Migration, Unemployment and Development: A Two-Sector Analysis', *American Economic Review*, 40: 126–42.

Haynes, Jeff. 1999. 'Power, Politics and Environmental Movements in the Third World' in Christopher Rootes (ed.). *Environmental Movements: Local, National and Global*. London: Frank Cass, pp. 223–250.

Hebert, Rudolf. 1968. 'Types and Functions of Social Movements' in *International Encyclopedia of Social Sciences*, Vol. 14, USA: Macmillan Co. and the Free Press.

Hensman, Rohini. 1994. 'Social Movements: What's 'New'?', *Economic and Political Weekly*, 39(21): pp. 1270–1272.

Jayal, Niraja Gopal. 1999. 'The Developmental State' in her own book *Democracy and the State: Welfare, Secularism and Development in Contemporary India*. New Delhi: Oxford University Press, pp. 151–236.

Karan, P.P. 1994. 'Environmental Movements in India' *Geographical Review*, 84(1): pp. 32–41.

Katzenstein, Marry, Smitu Kothari and Uday Mehta. 2001. 'Social Movement Politics in India: Institutions, Interests and Identities' in Atul Kohli (ed.). *The Success of India's Democracy*. New York: Cambridge University Press.

Kothari, Rajni 1990. 'The Rise of Peoples Movements', *Social Action*, 40: pp. 230–240.

Kothari, Rajni. 1984. 'The Non-Party Political Process', *Economic and Political Weekly*, 19(5): pp. 216–224.

Kothari, Rajni. 1986. 'Need for a New National Movement', *Hindustan Times*, Sunday Magazine, 14: p. 9.

Kothari, Rajni. 2002. 'Masses, Classes and the State' in Ghanshyam Shah (ed.). *Social Movements and the State*. New Delhi: Sage Publications, pp. 68–90.

Kothari, S. 1995. 'Development, Displacement and Official Policies: Critical Review', *Lokayan Bulletin*, March–April, No. 11.5.

Kothari, Smitu. 1996. 'Whose Nation? The Displaced as Victims of Development', *Economic and Political Weekly*, Vol.31, No.24, Mumbai, June 15.

Kumar, Anand. 2003. *'Political Sociology of Poverty in India: Between politics of poverty and poverty of politics'* in A.K. Mehta (ed). *Poverty in India*. New Delhi: IIPA Publication, pp. 144–196.

Kumar, Anand and et. al. 2004. 'Global Quest for Participatory Democracy' Paper presented at International Seminar, February 20–22, CSSS/SSS/JNU, New Delhi.

Kumar, Lalit. 'Do We Have a Theoretical Framework to Explain Social Movements? Third System, Third Sector, Third Way – No Way', undated and unpublished paper (Deputy Adviser, Planning Commission, Yojna Bhavan).

Kumar, Ravinder. 1993 'Social Movements in a Broader Historical Perspective', *Economic and Political Weekly,* XXII (10): pp. 332–335.

Kurien, J. 1978. 'Entry of Big Business into Fishing', *Economic and Political Weekly*, XL(36): pp. 1213–1215.

Kyong-Dong, Kim. 1973. 'Towards a Sociological Theory of Development: A Structural Perspective' *Rural Sociology*, 38(4): pp. 462–476.

Lindberg, S. 1990. 'Civil Society against the State? Farmers Agitation and New Social Movements in India', Papers presented to XII World Congress of Sociology, Madrid, July.

Mahapatra, L.K. 1996. 'Involuntary Displacement in Dam Projects in Orissa', in A.B. Otta and Anita Agnihotri (eds.). *Involuntary Displacement in Dam Projects*. New Delhi: Prachi Prakashan.

Mehar, Shibalal. 2003. 'Environment and Natural Resources in Orissa' *Journal of Social and Economic Development*, 5(1): pp. 225–240.

Melucci, Alberto. 1980. 'The New Social Movements: A Theoretical Approach', *Social Science Information*, 19: pp. 453–468.

Melucci, Alberto. 1984. 'An End to Social Movements', Introductory Paper to Sessions on 'New' Movements and Change in Organizational Forms, *Social Science Information,* 23: pp. 819–835.

Melucci, Alberto. 1985. 'The Symbolic Challenge of Contemporary Movements, *Social Research,* 52(4): pp. 789–816.

Mishra, A.B. 1987. 'Mining a Hill and Undermining a Society: The Case of Gandhamardan' in Anil Agarwall, Darryl D' Monte and Ujwala Somarth (ed.). *The Fight for Survival: People's Action for Environment*. New Delhi: Centre for Science and Environment, pp. 124–144.

Mishra, C.G. 1992. 'Forest Problems in Orissa', *The Samaj*, 5 July 1992.

Mohanty, Manoranjan. 1998. 'Social Movements in Creative Society: Of Autonomy and Interconnection' in Manoranjan Mohanty et. al., *People's Right: Social Movements and the State in the Third World.* New Delhi: Sage Publications, pp. 63–81.

Mohanty, Ranjita. 2003. 'Save the Chilika Movement: Interrogating the State and the Market', in Rajesh Tandon and Ranjita Mohanty (eds.), *Does Civil Society Matter? Governance in Contemporary India*. New Delhi: Sage Publications, pp. 167–197.

Monterio, Anjali and Laxmi Lingam. 1998. 'Towards a Common Voice?: An Introduction to Movements and Campaigns in India', *The Indian Journal of Social Work*, (TISS), 59(1): pp. 3–34.

Mukherjee, Partha Nath. 1977. 'Social Movement and Social Change: Towards a Conceptual Clarification and Theoretical Framework', *Sociological Bulletin,* 26 (1). pp. 38–59.

Offe, Claus. 1985. 'New Social Movements: Challenging the Boundaries of Institutional Politics', *Social Research,* 52(4): pp. 815–868.

Omvedt, Gail. 1988. 'New Movements', *Seminar*, 352: pp. 39–44.

Omvedt, Gail. 1989. 'India's Movements for Democracy: Peasants, Greens, Women and People's Power', (Unpublished Manuscript).

Omvedt, Gail. 1998. 'Peasants, Dalits and Women: Democracy and India's New Social Movements' in Manoranjan Mohanty et. al., *Peoples Right: Social Movements and the State in the Third World*. New Delhi: Saga Publications, pp. 223–240.

Omvedt, Gail. 2004. 'Struggle against Dams or Struggle for Water? Environmental Movements and the State' in Rajendra Vora et. al., *Indian Democracy: Meanings and Practices*. New Delhi: Sage Publications, pp. 410–431.

Oommen, T.K. 1977. 'Sociological Issues in the Analysis of Social Movements in Independent India', *Sociological Bulletin,* 26(1): pp. 14–37.

Oommen, T.K. 1982. 'Theoretical Framework and Empirical Research: Their Interaction in the Analysis of Two Social Movements', *Sociological Bulletin,* 36(2): pp. 346–360.

Oommen, T.K. 1985. 'Social Movements', *Survey of Research in Sociology and Social Anthropology 1969–1979*, Prepared by ICSSR, New Delhi, Satvahan, 2: pp. 125–136.

Panda, Abhash C. and A.K. Sharma. 1998. 'Reconstructing the Theory of Social Movements' in Sebasti. L. Raj and Arundhati Roy Choudhury (eds.). *Contemporary Social Movements in India: Achievements and Hurdles*. New Delhi: Indian Social Institute, pp. 12–29.

Panda, Hrushikesh. 1986. 'Threat to Ecosystem: Case of Gandhamardan Hills', *Mainstream*, 17: pp. 9–10.

Parajuli, Pramod. 2001. 'Power and Knowledge in Development Discourse: New Social Movements and the State in India' in Niraja Gopal Jayal (ed.), *Democracy in India*. New Delhi: Oxford University Press, pp. 258–285.

Patel, Sujata. 1989a. 'Agni, Cyclone and Baliapal Agitation', *Economic and Political Weekly*, XXIV (25): pp. 1381–82.

Patel, Sujata. 1989b. 'Baliapal Agitation: Socio-Economic Background', *Economic and Political Weekly*, XXIV (17): pp. 604–605.

Patel, Sujata. 1989c. 'Baliapal Crisis', *Economic and Political Weekly*, XXIV (25): p. 40.

Patel, Sujata. 1990. 'Baliapal Agitation: Leadership Crisis', *Economic and Political Weekly*, XXXV (23): pp. 1238–41.

Patel, Sujata. 2001. 'Community, Identity and Politics: The Balliapal Movement' in Surinder S. Jodka (ed.). *Community and Identities: Contemporary Discourses on Culture and Politics in India*. New Delhi: Sage Publications, pp. 140–159.

Patkar, M. 1992. 'The Strength of a People's Movement' interviewed by G. Sen and A.K. Roy in G. Sen (ed.). *Indigenous Vision, People's of India, Attitudes to the Environment.* Inside, Sanctuary. XII (4): p. 29.

Patkar, Medha. 1992. 'The Strength of a Peoples' Movement (Interview with Medha Patkar)', *India International Centre Quarterly*, Spring-Summer.

Patnaik, Sarmistha. 2003. 'Development, Globalization and the Rise of a Grassroots Environmental Movement: The Case of Chilika Bachao Andolan (CBA) in Eastern India', *Indian Journal of Public Administration*, XLIX (1): pp. 55–65.

Peritore, N. Patrick. 1993. 'Environmental Attitudes of Indian Elites: Challenging Western Post-Modernist Models', *Asian Survey*, 33(8): pp. 804–818.

Ramdas, N. 1998. 'A Range of Protest', *Frontline*, July 25 August 5, p. 81.

Ravi, K. 1988a. 'A Fortress of the People', *The Statesman*, 23 January.

Ravi, K. 1988b. 'Resistance Ignored, Order to Acquire Land' *The Statesman*, 22 January.

Reddy, V. Ratna. 1998. 'Environmental Movements in India: Some Reflections', *Journal of Indian School of Political Economy*, X: pp. 685–695.

Rootes, Christopher. 1999. 'Environmental Movements: From the Local to the Global' in Rootes, Christopher. (ed.). *Environmental Movements: Local, National and Global*. London: Frank Cass, pp. 1–11.

Roy, D. 1996. 'People's Politics: The Third Force', *Lokayan Bulletin*, 12(6): pp. 11–16.

Roy, S.M. 1995. 'Voluntary Action: Where do we go from Here?' *Lokayan Bulletin*, 12(3): pp. 31–39.

Samal, Kishor C. and Shibalal Meher. 1999. 'Socio-Economic Survey of Villages in and Around Chilika' (Mimeo), NCDS, Bhubaneswar.

Samal, Kishor C. and Shibalal Meher. 2003. 'Fishing Communities on Chilika Lake: Comparative Socio-Economic Study', *Economic and Political Weekly*, 38(31): pp. 3319–3325.

Sankar, Uday. 1992. 'Chilika: A Lake in Limbo', *Down to Earth*, I (7): pp. 25–27.

Sarangi, Deba Ranjan (undated), 'Kashipur's Account', Paper presented by the author on behalf of *Prakritika Sampad Suraksha Parisad* (PSSP), Kuchipadar, Kashipur, Rayagada, Orissa.

Sarangi, Deba Ranjan. 2001. 'India, Orissa, Tribals War Against Industrialisation and Corporatisation. Paper presented – 31 March.

Seers, Duley. 1969. 'The Meaning of Development, *International Development Review*, December, pp. 2–6.

Sen, Raj Kumar. 1992. 'Environment Versus Development: The Indian Experiences of Narmada and Balipal' in Kartik C. Roy, Clement A. Tisdell and Raj Kumar Sen (eds.). *Economic Development and Environment: A Case Study of India*. New Delhi: Oxford University Press, pp. 113–133.

Sethi, H. 1993. 'Action Groups in the New Politics' in P. Wigharaja (ed.). *New Social Movement in South: Empowering the People*. New Delhi: Vistar Publication, pp. 230–235.

Sethi, H. 1998. 'Micro Struggles, NGOs and the State' in Manoranjan, Mohanty and et. al., *Peoples Right: Social Movements and the State in the Third World*. New Delhi: Sage Publications, pp. 405–420.

Sethi, H. 1985. 'The Immoral 'other' Debate between Party and Non-party Groups', *Economic and Political Weekly*, 20(8): pp. 378–380.

Sethi, H. 1993. 'Survival and Democracy: Ecological Struggles in India' in Poona Wignaraja (ed.). *New Social Movements in the South: Empowering the People*. New Delhi: Vistaar, pp. 122–147.

Sharma, S.L. 1980. 'Criteria of Social Development', *Social Action*, 30: pp. 62–82.

Shiva, Vandana and J. Bandopadhya. 1988. 'Political Economy of Ecology Movements' *Economic and Political Weekly*, 33(34).

Shiva, Vandana. 1986. 'Ecology Movements in India', *Alternatives*, 9(2): pp. 255–73.

Singh, Dalip. 1991. 'Protest Movements in India', *The Indian Journal of Political Science*, 52(4): pp. 448–57.

Singh, K. 1990. 'Baliapal Test Range: People's Struggle for Survival', *Unnayan*, Baliapal.

Singh, Kavaljit. 1998. 'New Challenges for People's Movement', *Mainstream*, 36(51): pp. 15-19.

Swain, Ashok. 1997. 'Democratic Consolidation? Environmental Movements in India', *Asian Survey*, XXXVII (9): pp. 818–832.

Swain, Ashok. 2000. 'Social Capital and Popular Mobilisation: Studying Environmental Protests in an Indian State', *Asian Journal of Political Science*, 8(1): pp. 33–46.

Swain, Ashok. 2002. 'Social Networks and Social Movements: Are Northern Tools Useful to Evaluate Southern Protests?' *Uppsala Peace Research Paper No. 4*, Department of Peace and Conflict Research, Sweden, Uppsala University.

Tarrow, Sideny. 1996. 'Social Movements in Contentious Politics: A Review Article', *American Political Science Review*, 90(4): pp. 567–588.

Tilly, Charles. 1985. 'Models and Realities of Popular Collective Action', *Social Research*, 52(4): pp. 717–748.

Touraine, Alain. 1985. 'An Introduction to the Study of Social Movements', in *Social Research*, 52(4): pp. 749–788.

Wagle, Subodh. 1999. 'Environmental Movements in India: A Critique and A Note', *Journal of Indian School of Political Economy*, XI (1): pp. 111–121.

Reports

Centre for Science and Environment. 1991. *The State of India's Environment. Third Citizens Report*, New Delhi.

Centre for Science and Environment. 2003. *The State of India's Environment. Fourth Citizens Report*, New Delhi.

Centre for Science and Environment. 2004. *The State of India's Environment. Fifth Citizens Report*, New Delhi.

Government of India. 1986. *Environmental Aspects of Gandhamardan Bauxite Project*. Views of Department of Environment, dated 11 June.

Government of India. 1990. *Twenty-ninth Report of the Commissioner of Scheduled Castes and Tribes*, New Delhi.

Government of India. 1993. *Working Group on Development and Welfare of Scheduled Tribes during the Eighth Five-Year Plan (1990–1995)*, New Delhi.

Government of India. 2004. *Economic Survey 2004*. Ministry of Finance, New Delhi.

Government of India. 2005. *India 2005: A Reference Annual.* Published by Director Publications Division, Ministry of Information and Broadcasting, New Delhi.

Government of India. *Orissa Development Report* (2002). Planning Commission, New Delhi.

Government of Orissa. 1993. *Circulars and Orders on Rehabilitation Policy for Major and Medium Irrigation Projects of the State.* Department of Irrigation, WALMI, Pratapnagari.

Government of Orissa. 1994. *The Orissa Resettlement and Rehabilitation of Projects Affected Persons Policy*. Department of Water Resources, Bhubaneswar.

Government of Orissa. 1994a. *The Orissa Resettlement and Rehabilitation of Projects Affected Persons Policy.* Department of Water Resources, Bhubaneswar.

Government of Orissa. 2001. *Orissa Watch Report,* which was meant for private circulation on 14 January.

Government of Orissa. *Human Development Report 2004.*

Our Common Future. 1987. World Commission of Environment and Development.

People's Union for Civil Liberties (1986), *Gandhamardhan Mines: A Report on Environment and People*, PUDR, New Delhi.

Peoples' Union for Democratic Rights. 1988. *Bheeta Maati, Our Soil, Our Earth, Our Home' A Report on Baliapal Missile Base and Peoples Struggle,* PUDR, New Delhi.

Report of the Fact-Finding Committee on Chilika Fisheries, submitted to the High Court of Orissa, Cuttack on 16 August 1993.

Report of the High Level Committee on Environmental and Ecological Aspects of the Gandhamardan Bauxite Project Orissa, Government of India, Department of Mines.

The Hindu *Survey of the Environment*. 2004.

Newspapers

Business Standard, 9 April 1988.

Dharitri (Oriya Daily), 10 October 2003.

Economic Times, 23 January 1988.

Economic Times, 26 December 1987.

Financial Express, 29 January 1988.

Hindustan Times, 22 December 1987.

Indian Express, 25 January 1988.

Indian Express, 31 January 1988.

Indian Express, 8 December 1987.

Jansatta, April, 1988.

Manisara Bartabaha Swabhimaan (Oriya Fortnightly), Vol. 6, Issue 21, 16 August 2004, p. 8.

Manisara Bartabaha Swabhiman (Oriya Fortnightly), Vol. 2, Issue 18, 16 December 2008.

Manisara Bartabaha Swabhiman (Oriya Fortnightly), Vol. 3, Issue 23, 16 January 2006.

Manisara Bartabaha Swabhiman (Oriya Fortnightly), Vol. 6, Issue 21, 16 August 2004.

Manisara Bartabaha Swabhiman (Oriya Fortnightly), Vol. 7, Issue 25, 17 December 2005.

Manisara Bartabaha Swabhiman (Oriya Fortnightly), Vol.4, Issue 13, 12 August 2009.

Manisara Bartabaha Swabhimann (Oriya Fortnightly), Vol. 6, Issue 22, 1 September 2004, p. 5.

Navbharat Times, 30 November 1987.

News Time, 27 December 1987.

Patriot, 27 April 1988.

Patriot, 5 January 1988.

Samaj (Oriya Daily), 17 December 2000.

Samaj (Oriya Daily), 1 December 1996.

Sambad (Oriya Daily), May, 2001.

Sun Times, 4 June 1990.

Telegraph, 31 January 1988.

Telegraph, 3 April 1988.

The Dharitri (Oriya Daily), 12 May 1986, p. 3.

The Hindu, 26 April 2003.

The Samaj (Oriya Daily), 16 December 2000.

The Samaj (Oriya Daily), 21 December 2000.

The Samaj (Oriya Daily), 3 January 2006.

The Samaj, (Oriya Daily), 25 May 1986, p. 5.

The Sentinel, December, 1987.

The Times of India, 27 January 1988.

Index

Actor Network Theory, 34
Agragamee (NGO), 224
Agrawal, Arun, 32
anti-Balco movement, 109
anti-POSCO movement, 113
Auxiliary Nurses and Midwives (ANM), 206

Baliapal movement, 85
Banerjee, Sumanta, 37
Baviskar, Amita, 27, 28, 32, 75
Beck, U., 34
Bhatt, S., 25

Carson, Rachel, 29
Chipko movement, 74, 76
collective behaviour, 55
collective mobilisation, 54, 58, 60
Correa, Mariette, 33

Dalit Panther movement, 37
Dhanagare, D.N., 36, 37
displaced persons (DPs), 163
Dubey Committee, 223

ecological modernisation theory, 34
Eisentadt, S.N., 62
emergence, 35
environmental movements (EMs), 22, 73
  in India, 73
  role of civil society in, 77
environmental movements in Odisha, 83
environmental problems in India
  causes, 181
ethno-botany, 166

forcefully displaced persons (FDPs), 163
Frank, A.G., 36, 69
Fuentes, M., 69

Gadgil, M., 75
Gandhamardan movement, 104

Gandhi, Rajiv, 91, 139
Gole, Prakash, 26
Gomango, Giridhar, 227
grassroots environmental movements (GEM), 173
Green Kalahandi, 121
green politics, 73
Green Revolution, 28
Guha, Amalendu, 38
Guha, Ramachandra, 29, 31, 69, 75
Gupta, Dipankar, 37
Gurr, T., 53, 63

Hannigan, John, 34, 35
Harris, J., 82
Hauser, Korn, 61
Hindu Liberation Movement, 38
Hoon, Vineeta, 27
Horopathy, 167

insurgencies, 55

Jeffery, Roger, 31–32
John, J., 36
Joint Forest Management (JFM), 32

Kalinga Nagar Movement, 111
Kashipur Environmental Movements (KEMs), 39
Kashipur movement
  background, 178
  contextualising, 185
  important events, 183
  nature, 183
  organisation, 214
  role of leadership, 202
  role of media, 226
  role of NGOs, 222
  role of state, 226
  sites, 193
  women leaders of, 212
Kashipur
  awareness of citizens, 141
  education, 138
  festivals, 168
  food pattern, 169
  healthcare systems in, 136
  history, 135
  language and religion, 168
  market, 169
  PDS in, 140
  resources, 146
  social composition, 146
  source of livelihood, 155
  topography, 134
Kerala Sastra Sahitya Parishat (KSSP), 76
Khedut Mazdoor Chetna Sangathan (KMCS), 28
Koraput-Bolangir-Kalahandi (KBK) region, 132
Kothari, Rajni, 36, 45, 233
Krishna, Sumi, 24
Kumari, Punam, 166

Lingam, Lakshmi, 37
Livelihood movement, 173
Locke, Catherine, 33

Maikanch Police Firing, 228
Majhi, Bhagaban, 205, 210, 211
mass mobilisation, 198
McLaughlin, B., 52
Melucci, Alberto, 66
Merton, R., 53
minor forest produce, 161
Mishra, Vasavada, 33
Mol, 34
Movement Against Vedanta in Lanjigarh, 118
movement, 43
  components of, 54
Muchkund Dubey Committee, 227
Mukherjee, Partha, 48
multiple displacements, 177

Narmada Bachao Andolan (NBA), 28, 77–78
National Test Range (NTR), 85
New Social Movement (NSM), 21, 50, 66, 71, 68, 231, 234, 237
New Social Movement in India, 70
NGOs in Kashipur, 222
Non-Timber Forest Products (NTFPs), 151, 161, 235
Norwatch, 223
Odisha Adivasi Manch, 224
Omvedt, Gail, 37, 69
Oommen, T.K., 46, 233, 237

Panchayat (Extension to the Scheduled Area) Act (PESA), 1996, 180
Patkar, Medha, 77
Patnaik, Navin, 117, 199
Prakrutika Sampad Surakshya Parishad (PSSP), 39, 236
project affected persons (PAPs), 163

quasi-movements, 58

Rao, M.S.A., 47, 48, 233
Redclift, Michael, 25
revolutionary movements, 49
risk society, 34
Roy Burman Committee, 156
Roy, Madhumita, 115

Sarin, Madhu, 33
Savyasaachi, 33
Saxena, N.C., 33
Shah, Ghanshyam, 36, 38, 47–48, 233
Sharma, B.D., 224
Silent Spring, 29
Silent Valley movement, 78
Singh, Rajendra, 51, 233, 237
Sivaramakrishnan, 32
Smelser, Neil, 53, 61
social change, 59
social conflict, 50
social mobilisation
  theoretical paradigm, 64
social movement, 43, 45
  approaches, 59
  causes of, 60
  classified, 46

conceptualising, 53
conceptual problems, 53
defining, 51
Indian context, 46
origin and development, 43–46
theoretical tradition of, 233
typology of, 57
various stages, 68
social movements in Odisha
chronology, 84
social transformation, 233
Spaargaren, 34
spontaneous rebellions, 55
Sten, Lonez Von, 56
Strain theory, 53
Sundar, Nandini, 31–32

Todaro, N., 82
Touraine, Alain, 66
transformative movements, 48, 49

Utkal Rural Development Society (URDS), 206

Van der veer, Peter, 38
Vira, Bhaskar, 33

Wignaraja, Poona, 69
Wilkinson, Pal, 47, 52
Woodgate, Graham, 25